Soul, Self, and Society

Soul, Self, and Society

A Postmodern Anthropology for Mission in a Postcolonial World

~

Michael A. Rynkiewich

CASCADE Books · Eugene, Oregon

SOUL, SELF, AND SOCIETY
A Postmodern Anthropology for Mission in a Postcolonial World

Cascade Books
An Imprint of Wipf and Stock Publishers
199 W. 8th Ave., Suite 3
Eugene, OR 97401

www.wipfandstock.com

ISBN 13: 978-1-60608-773-2

Cataloging-in-Publication data:

Rynkiewich, Michael A.

    Soul, self, and society : a postmodern anthropology for mission in a postcolonial world / Michael A. Rynkiewich

    xvi + 280 p. ; 23 cm. Includes bibliographical references and index.

    ISBN 13: 978-1-60608-773-2

    1. Anthropology of religion. 2. Missions—Anthropological aspects. I. Title.

BV2063 R95 2011

Manufactured in the U.S.A.

Dedicated to my wife, Teresa, who has shared the missionary calling;

to my daughter Katie and her generation of anthropologists;

and to my sons Jacob and Michael,

who always self-identified as missionaries even when they were young.

Contents

Tables and Figures

Preface

The Book

THE FORMAL APPLICATION OF THE PERSPECTIVE OF ANTHRO-
pology to the practice of mission began in the late 1950s with the
publication of *Customs and Cultures* by Eugene Nida (1914–2011).
Through the 1960s and 1970s, great strides were taken by people like
Alan R. Tippett (1911–1988), Jacob Loewen (1922–2006), Kenneth
L. Pike (1912-2000), Charles Taber (1929–2007), Charles Kraft
(1932–), and others to work through anthropological concepts
such as culture, culture shock, ethnocentrism, communication,
language, social structure, values, worldview, and other anthropological concerns. In those decades, missiology developed as an academic discipline, journals like *Practical Anthropology* (later renamed
Missiology) were founded, and the use of anthropological concepts
greatly enriched our understanding of mission and evangelism. The
expansion of the work in the 1980s and 1990s by anthropologists
like Louis Luzbetak (1919–2005) and Paul Hiebert (1932–2007)
pushed the paradigm even further, but something else was happening in those decades as well.

While missiologists were looking the other way, anthropology walked off in a different direction, and the world itself took
some strange turns. In particular, anthropology, along with literary
criticism, led the way to, and itself was changed by, the postmodern
movement and postcolonial critique. The world was urbanizing and
globalizing such that diversity and multiculturalism became an everyday, and sometimes in-your-face, phenomenon.

The result is that missiology, as it is taught in colleges and seminaries now, tends to be based on an outdated anthropology that is recommended to potential missionaries for a world that no longer exists. In the missiological imaginary, a Western missionary sits across the table from a local person who embodies one identity, one culture, one language. The missiological problem, on this reading, is to communicate the gospel from one culture to another in a village setting. In the 2010s this is rarely the case, and in the 2020s this context will no longer exist.

The turn that anthropology has taken is toward a postmodern understanding of identity, culture, and society. The turn that the world has taken is toward a postcolonial, urbanizing, and globalizing dynamic that casts a critical gaze on all the old understandings, deconstructs and discards them, and then moves on toward a different social order based on multiple identities (deftly displayed by the same person for different others), multilingualism (changing with the setting and the agenda), the rise of networks and the demise of groups, the move to decentralization and away from hierarchy, and a political economy based on global channels and flows and not on nation-states.

The world of the missionary today involves partnerships with people who are migrating, fleeing as refugees, urbanizing, living in diaspora and/or are transnationals (moving back and forth from home to host country, from periphery to center). These are people on the move—Indonesian laborers working in Kuala Lumpur, Filipina wives contracted by South Korean farmers, Indian teachers living in Dubai, Lithuanian factory workers in Ireland, Maminde Indians who no longer want to live in the Brazilian jungle or speak their own language but desire to live in Rio, speak Portuguese, and sing popular songs.

In *The Postmodern Condition: A Report on Knowledge* (1979), Jean-François Lyotard famously defined postmodernism as an "incredulity toward meta-narratives."[1] Meta-narratives or "grand narratives" are philosophies that encompass the totality of life providing ultimate meanings to things, people, and events. Modern science is such a meta-narrative, and so are the modern religions, including Christianity. In postmodernity (postmodernity is the *era* that represents postmodernism, the way of *thinking*), people are no longer willing to buy the whole story. The meta-narrative does not include everyone's story;

---

1. Lyotard, *The Postmodern Condition,* xxiv.

the meta-narrative does not favor everyone; the meta-narrative does not represent everyone's desires. In postmodernism, meta-narratives always represent power, so in order to recognize difference and diversity postmodern thinkers work to expose and subvert meta-narratives. Modernity itself is such a meta-narrative, with its roots in the European Enlightenment, and its faith in science and progress, which led to, among other things, colonialism and two world wars.

When anthropologists made a 90-degree turn, missiology barely noticed. Teaching what is essentially a 1960s modernist model of culture, missiologists tend to be out of touch with anthropology in the beginning of the twenty-first century. This is serious enough, because it was the advances in anthropology that occurred after World War II that helped transform our understanding of the dynamics of mission. However, the change has not just been a shift in theories, discarding some for others. The truth is that the world has also changed. The speed and ease with which people, ideas, and goods travel around the world, and the frequency of movement of migrants, refugees, and transnationals that creates diasporas, ethnicities, and hybridity has increased dramatically at the end of the twentieth century and continues to increase now into the twenty-first century.

Anthropology still involves doing fieldwork, writing ethnographies, and presenting at least glimpses of this world, but missiologists trained in a 1960s "jungle anthropology" are ill-equipped to understand this new world, and have trouble engaging in dialogue with postmodern anthropologists. This book is structured to appreciate the best of the old paradigm for mission studies and then show how we need to incorporate newer paradigms in order to understand and engage the world as it is.

The Author

It may be that my absence and then reentry into anthropology served to focus my attention on the differences between theories of the 1960s and theories of the 2000s. I was trained well in anthropology by Claude Stipe and Tom Correll at Bethel College between 1962 and 1966. My training at the University of Minnesota began with my first advisor, E. Adamson Hoebel, himself a student of Franz Boas, the father of American anthropology. He was "old school," immersed in the lore of the anthropological project. I learned to appreciate basic

descriptive ethnography. My research methods were honed under the tutelage of Pertti Pelto and Frank Miller through my participation in the Upper Mississippi Research Project. Based on two summers' field-work in northern Minnesota, I wrote a master's thesis on "Chippewa Powwows" (1968). That first year, a professor with a new PhD arrived who had worked with Homer Barnett on a study of the displaced Bikini Marshallese. The Bikini people had been relocated from their coral atoll to a small coral islet, where they were not faring well. The reason for the move? So that the United States could test atomic and hydrogen bombs on a distant atoll instead of in its own back yard.

Bob Kiste suggested that I go to the Marshall Islands and study a stable population on Arno Atoll, and so I did. Eugene Ogan also worked in the Pacific, but on Bougainville in Papua New Guinea, and from him I learned about social anthropology and the colonial cri-tique because there a massive copper mine was disrupting the lives of the people.

Thus, in 1969 my wife Linda and I settled on Ine Island of Arno Atoll in the southern Marshall Islands. I studied land tenure and how the use and transmission of rights in land had changed under three colonial regimes: the Germans, the Japanese, and the Americans. I spent 18 months in the Pacific doing this research, and defended my dissertation in 1972. I taught anthropology at Macalester College with colleagues James Spradley and David McCurdy in a three-man depart-ment from 1971 to 1981. There I published two books with Spradley: *The Nacirema: Readings in American Culture* (1975) and *Ethics and Anthropology: Dilemmas in Fieldwork* (1976), as well as a book about *Traders, Teachers and Soldiers: An Anthropological Survey of Colonial Era Sites on Majuro Atoll, Marshall Islands* (1981).

In the 1980s I quit my job, moved to southwestern Indiana, and worked as a grain merchandiser at an elevator on the Ohio River. During that decade my wife Linda died of cancer. Soon afterward, I took a part-time appointment as pastor of a rural United Methodist church. I remarried, then several years later quit my job, took a second church, and attended Asbury Theological Seminary. I was a pastor until 1997, when my wife, three young children, and I went to Papua New Guinea as missionaries.

I tried to get back into the ethnography of the Pacific Islanders, but something had changed in anthropology while I was gone. The

discipline was questioning its own metanarrative of the possibility of objectivity, of being able to understand the "other," and the place of the anthropologist in the power structure of the world as it is. This was both necessary and good for the discipline, but when I turned back to the missiology literature I did not find the same self-reflexiveness, nor even much awareness that anthropology had changed.

I was seconded to the United Church in Papua New Guinea, who assigned me to be on the faculty of the Melanesian Institute for Socio-Economic and Pastoral Care in Goroka. The ecumenical institute provided culture courses for new missionaries and conducted research projects on issues of interest to the church. While there I edited three more books: *Politics in Papua New Guinea*; *Land and Churches in Melanesia: Issues and Contexts*; and *Land and Churches in Melanesia: Cases and Procedures*. I also wrote a small book on *Cultures and Languages of Papua New Guinea*.

We returned to the States in 2002, and I taught anthropology for Christian mission in the E. Stanley Jones School of World Mission and Evangelism at Asbury, with anthropologists Darrell Whiteman and Steve Ybarrola as well as missiologists John Hong, George Hunter III, Eunice Irwin, Art McPhee, Terry Muck, Kima Pachuau, Howard Snyder, and Russell West. I benefitted greatly from the experience and knowledge of these colleagues. In 2010, I retired to the farm. What follows here is a culmination of my life's work.

1

Introduction

Anthropology, Theology, and Missiology

> He answered them, "When it is evening, you say, 'It will be
> fair weather, for the sky is red.' And in the morning, 'It will
> be stormy today, for the sky is red and threatening.' You know
> how to interpret the appearance of the sky, but you cannot in-
> terpret the signs of the times." Matthew 16:2–3

The Missionary Context

LAKAN IS CONSIDERING LEAVING HIS VILLAGE AGAIN BECAUSE
he is unable to support his family there, he tells himself, not read-
ily admitting his additional desire to have enough money to buy a
vehicle.[1] Not that the roads are that numerous or in good condition,
but his desire is more for the prestige of owning a car and being able
to obligate others to himself by giving rides and transporting cargo.
Lakan lives in Kup, a village in the Southern Highlands, a province
of Papua New Guinea. Kup is a four-hour drive to Mt. Hagen in the
Western Highlands Province. In the village, he is associated with the
Tree Kangaroo Clan, he is the nephew of a recently deceased Big Man,[2]
and he is considered as one of several political rising stars. He speaks
with convincing rhetoric on issues that concern the village.

---

1. This is a fictional story, but it carries a realistic message relevant to the world
we live in today.

2. More on this style of leadership in chapter 7.

Missionaries had come to the Kup area in the 1970s, and now there is a church, a Bible in the vernacular language, and a local pastor. That vocational route looked attractive when there was support from the denomination in Australia but, since they have withdrawn their missionaries and much of their support, a pastor has respect but not much influence on daily life.

Lakan left Rita behind, found a ride in the back of a ute[3] to Mt. Hagen, then rode a PMV[4] from Mt. Hagen to Goroka in the Eastern Highlands. Goroka is a town of over 20 thousand people built up after World War II by coffee and other commercial interests. Lakan has relatives in Goroka, so he calls on them for a place to sleep and have his meals. Townspeople have long suffered in silence, as a custom of sharing everything—a practice appropriate for an economy based on gardening, hunting, and fishing—seems like a hangover for people in a working, buying, and consuming economy. A paycheck only goes so far and there are no forest resources in town to fall back on.

In town, Lakan is not identified as a man from a particular clan, but as a migrant from the Southern Highlands. He does not speak his village language in Goroka since there are many people in town from other language areas, but rather he speaks the lingua franca, which is Pidgin English, also known as *Tokpisin* ("talk pidgin").[5] Other, younger men from his area, having despaired of ever finding work in the town, have joined a gang that robs houses and businesses at night. Lakan benefits indirectly because he lives in the community, but Lakan is not a *rascol* (member of an urban gang).

With the money from intermittent day labor, Lakan buys a ticket and boards a plane for the capital city, Port Moresby. There is only one road in and out of the Highlands of Papua New Guinea, and it goes down to Lae, on the north coast of the island, not to Port Moresby on the southeast coast. The infrastructure left by the Australian colonial

3. Australian for "utility vehicle," or what Americans would call a "pickup truck."

4. A small bus the size of a 15-passenger van, called a "people moving vehicle" or PMV.

5. A language developed on plantations in Queensland and New Guinea in the late 1800s. Here is John 3:16: "God i gat wanpela Pikinini tasol i stap. Tasol God i laikim tumas olgeta manmeri bilong graun, olsem na em i givim dispela wanpela Pikinini long ol. Em i makim olsem bilong olgeta manmeri i bilip long em ol i no ken lus. Nogat. Bai ol i kisim laip i stap gut oltaim oltaim." Bible Society of Papua New Guinea, *Nupela Testamen*, 352.

administration does not always work to the advantage of the independent nation of Papua New Guinea. The Air Niugini flight takes less than an hour, but flies over some of the most rugged terrain in the world. That is what kept the Highlands people isolated from each other in mountain valleys, unknown to the world until the 1930s, and mostly unexplored until after World War II.

In Port Moresby, a city of over a quarter of a million people, Lakan makes his way to the settlements on the edge of the city, specifically the one closest to the Baruni dump. Here he finds *wantoks* (one-talks), or people who speak the same language as him. Yet, for most in the city, he is no longer identified by his association with the Tree Kangaroo Clan or the recently deceased Big Man, both unknown to most here, and is not even identified as a Southern Highlands man, but rather just as a Highlander. The operative division at this level of society is the distinction between *Nambis* (people from the islands and coastal areas) and *Hilands* (Highlands people). This distinction has historical precedent.

First, most island and coastal people speak languages in the Austronesian language family, a language family that represents more recent (about four thousand years ago) immigrants than the more ancient peoples in the Highlands and elsewhere who speak non-Austronesian languages. Second, cultural differences come along with language differences. Third, the coastal people have 150 years of contact history with the outside world, particularly the English, German, Australian, and American people. The Highlands people have a short history of contact, for some going back only forty years, a time within memory of the oldest residents. All of these differences contributed to their differential treatment by the Australian administration up to 1975, and by the central government, seated in Port Moresby, after 1975. Insofar as there is economic development, it is meager in the Highlands, where widely scattered gold mines and coffee plantations dominate the economy.

What Lakan's *wantoks* mean to him, though, is that he can expect them to fulfill the obligations of a kinsman to supply the needs of other kinsmen. Complaints about this traditional system now operating in an urban setting—old wine put into new wineskins—are more

vocal, even finding their way into a popular song played on the radio, "There Goes My Pay."[6]

Lakan attends a familiar church on Sunday morning. The coastal people in the United Church of Papua New Guinea, the daughter church of the old Australian Methodist Mission and the London Missionary Society churches, are fourth-generation Christians, and some of their ancestors were actually missionaries to the Southern Highlands province, which was opened up to missionary activity in the 1950s. Yet, when he approaches the pastor, a *Nambis* man, for some help with food, the pastor asks where he is from, and then suggests that he go back home and make a garden so that he will have food. He is an outsider in this church.

Through some occasional work and contributions from relatives, Lakan puts together enough money for a plane ticket to Brisbane, Australia. He has heard that there might be work there. When he arrives, none of his established identities make much difference. He is a citizen of the nation-state of Papua New Guinea when he goes through customs. He has to throw out some food and a reed basket that he had brought along because the latter harbored a couple of small beetles that were exposed when the basket was rapped hard on the table. Neither his village language nor the city language, *Tokpisin*, help him in Australia. He now must practice his limited English. In each case, his identity is defined as much by what he is not as by what he is. In the village it was significant that he was not a member of the Regiana "Bird of Paradise" clan, then in Goroka it was significant that he was not from the Eastern Highlands. In Port Moresby it was significant that he was not from the *Nambis* area of PNG, and now he is not an Australian but a Pacific Islander. When he is not looking, he is sometimes called a *Kanaka* (bush native) or, worse yet, a *Wog*, a more derogatory term. However, he did find a job—one that a number of migrants from PNG hold—as a night watchman at a hotel in Brisbane. Now he is able to send money back home—remittances that, in addition to supporting his family, help maintain his position in the clan, his promise as a rising political leader, and help secure his rights in clan land. He spends his days making plans for his return to his wife and children, but the days keep rolling away, one like the other, and he is still in Brisbane.

6. Goddard, *Unseen City*, 13.

Here is the problem. How can a missionary in today's world, not the modern world that is rapidly passing away, but a missionary in an urbanizing, globalizing world, be in mission to Lakan? Where will a missionary catch him along the way? Where will the missionary settle down? What community will the missionary get to know in order to be in mission to Lakan? What language must the missionary learn in order to minister to Lakan? On any given day, who is Lakan? What are Lakan's needs, and how will his needs be addressed by the missionary, mission agency, and/or church? Is Lakan an individual in the Western sense of the term, or is he more properly seen as a part of various groups along the way? How can Lakan meet Jesus Christ and experience salvation? The same questions need to be asked about Rita as well since, in Lakan's absence, she has left one child with her mother, taken another child with her, and has moved to Mt. Hagen to work as a maid for an American missionary family.

Missiology

In the initial exchange between anthropology and missions theology that produced the subdiscipline of missiology in the 1950s and 1960s, theorists imagined the missionary problem as the communication of a message across cultures. How could a missionary learn language and culture in a setting, usually a village, and then shape the gospel in a way that an individual from that language and culture who was sitting across the table would understand it? In those decades, missionaries learned a lot from anthropology and extended what they learned in practical ways.[7]

Eugene Nida initiated the postwar challenge to missionaries to pay attention to culture and language with the much read and still readable *Customs and Cultures: Anthropology for Christian Mission.* He staked his claim in the preface.

> Good missionaries have always been good "anthropologists." Not only have they been aware of human needs, whether stemming from the local way of life or from man's universal need of salvation, but they have recognized that the various ways of life of different peoples are the channels by which their

---

7. The first missionary anthropologist journal was *Practical Anthropology,* published 1953–72, and then merged into the journal *Missiology: An International Review,* whose first editor was the missionary anthropologist Alan R. Tippett.

needs take form and through which the solutions to such must pass. Effective missionaries have always sought to immerse themselves in a profound knowledge of the ways of life of the people to whom they have sought to minister, since only by such understanding of the indigenous culture could they possibly communicate a new way of life.[8]

In the 1950s, there were a great number of new missionaries heading to the field, especially evangelical and Pentecostal missionaries, who were rushing out in response to the reports brought back by American servicemen and women about conditions overseas. However, not all missionaries were prepared, and Nida was concerned about them in particular.

On the other hand, some missionaries have been only "children of their generation" and have carried to the field a distorted view of race and progress, culture and civilization, Christian and non-Christian ways of life. During some ten years as Secretary for Translations of the American Bible Society, I have become increasingly conscious of the tragic mistakes in cultural orientation which not only express themselves directly and indirectly in translations of Scriptures but in the general pattern of missionary work.[9]

The solution, Nida claimed, lay in teaching missionaries about language and culture as anthropologists had come to understand them.

Accordingly, this treatment of *Anthropology for Christian Mission* is directed to those who may have been unaware of the invaluable assistance which the science of anthropology can provide or who have become desirous of knowing more of its implications in various parts of the world.[10]

It was not only Nida, and other pioneers in missionary anthropology such as Jacob Loewen, William Reyburn, William A. Smalley, Charles Taber, Robert B. Taylor, and William H. Wonderly, who were finding anthropology useful. There was a student at Wheaton who was majoring in anthropology so that he could enter a ministry of mission and evangelism. Years later, when asked if he had any regrets about

8. Nida, *Customs and Cultures*, xi.

9. Ibid., xi.

10. Ibid., xi.

his career, he did not hesitate, but declared that his one regret was that had not gone on to earn a PhD in anthropology. The young student was Billy Graham.[11]

Graham found that the anthropology that he had taken in case he became a missionary also helped him in his first church.

> Harder to take than that, though, was the superior attitude some of them had toward the new believers and people from other denominations who were coming our way. It was a judgmental attitude based on different lifestyles and associations.[12]

Graham told the church in no uncertain terms that they needed to repent of the sin of troublemaking, and that their opposition to people who were different would only isolate them from the work of God happening around them.

The anthropological consensus that developed in the 1950s and 1960s was founded on Boasian historical particularism, built up by British (Malinowski and Radcliffe-Brown) structural functionalism, and being enticed in different directions by French structuralism (Levi Strauss) and cultural materialism (Leslie White, Julian Steward, Marvin Harris). It had links to sociologists Max Weber and Talcott Parsons, the latter of which was developing a grand vision of the social sciences.[13] The model of anthropology appropriated by early missiologists featured the concept of and informed missionaries about the organic unity of *society*, the functions of various institutions, the deeper meaning of different customs, the links between language and culture, and the detailed work that would be required to learn a language, do Bible translation, and preach the gospel.

As missionary anthropologists developed this model in order to orient prospective field missionaries, they expanded on the concepts of *culture shock, ethnocentrism, cultural relativity*, and the need for *contextualization*[14] of the gospel. These developments provided the foundation for teaching classes on Anthropology for Christian Mission.

11. See lecture by Robert Priest at Wheaton Chapel in Fall 2008. Online: http://www.wheaton.edu/wetn/chapel.htm.

12. Graham, *Just as I Am*, 65, 89.

13. Parsons, *Social System*.

14. Known earlier as "indigenization" among Protestants and "inculturation" among Catholics.

However, that is not the end of the story. Sometime in the 1980s, the academic discipline of anthropology took a major turn in a new direction. The works of Michel Foucault, Jacques Derrida, and Jean Baudrillard, and the analysis of the impact of those works by Jean-François Lyotard[15] signaled a shift toward postmodernism, deconstruction, and the loss of certainty in the social sciences as well as philosophy. For example, Derrida's concept of *différance* not only reveals how slippery terms can be, but also implies that we can never get a complete definition of a term because it's meaning is constantly being *deferred*.[16]

Although anthropology is one of the causes of the postmodern shift,[17] the impact of the movement on the discipline has been revolutionary.[18] Even the concept of culture has been found lacking,[19] while the work of the field researcher has been problematized and the writings of the ethnographer subject to deconstruction. The 1960s model of culture was a modernist construct that imagined that there could be an objective observer, tended to reify the concept of culture as a causative agent, and tended to depersonalize people as subjects of study.

Anthropology changed in the 1980s and 1990s, but missiology did not get the news. Anthropology gained some new insights, but missiology seemed satisfied with what it had already learned.

The approach that we will take here is to begin by accessing the initial insights gained from anthropology and show why they were revolutionary in their time for missiology. Then, we will follow the lead of anthropology into postmodern times and try to learn some new lessons.

It is not just that the discipline of anthropology has changed over time. The world itself, the world of the third millennium AD, has also changed. The situation of the missionary is no longer to settle into village or *barrio* life in a place where people stay put, speak one language,

15. Lyotard, *Postmodern Condition*.

16. The French term here, in spoken form, sounds like "difference" as well as "defer-ance," implying the continual deferral of meaning.

17. "If any single occupational group deserves the credit—or the blame—for bringing us into the postmodern era, it is the anthropologists." Anderson, *Truth about the Truth*, 53.

18. In the sense of Thomas Kuhn's notion of scientific revolutions. Kuhn, *The Structure of Scientific Revolutions*.

19. Rynkiewich, "World in My Parish," 301–21.

live by one culture, and have little contact with the outside world. That world, if it ever existed, no longer does. In the past, there might have been regional flows, primarily through trading routes, that included a few people who moved from place to place.[20] But now there are global flows of people, goods, and ideas that go from nearly everywhere to everywhere, albeit in a rather uneven fashion. Now people have connections with the outside world, people use communication links to reach nearly everywhere, people travel through certain pathways to almost any destination, and people settle, less permanently than before, in new landscapes alongside other migrants.

Now, people mix and mingle, culture is marked by *hybridity*, food is marked by *fusion*, and language has become *languages* as most people in the world are at least bilingual if not multilingual. Once people have arrived in a new place, they still do not stay put, but travel again back and forth to home (transnationalism*)* or move on to other worldwide destinations and never go home. It is not just people, but goods—particularly technology—and ideas, like neoliberalism, that loose their bonds, no longer tethered to a particular geographical site or cultural setting, and move with lightning speed to create an "ethnoscape,"[21] a people rooted in several different places on the globe with ties of kinship and friendship linked through unprecedented new lines of communication and transportation.

No longer is there an illusion that the creator or purveyor of an idea, philosophy, or theology is able to retain control over how that idea is interpreted and used once it escapes its owner. For example, one time a visitor to a Japanese shopping mall during the Christmas season turned a corner and saw this strange juxtaposition: Santa Claus nailed to a cross.[22]

Is there a reason to be concerned about culture any more? Yes, more than ever. Is there a reason yet to learn a language? Yes. However, what these things mean has also changed. Neither the person (self), nor language, culture, society, nor ecology are the same as they were in the modern world or, more accurately, are understood the same way

---

20. The "Mediterraneanization" of southern Europe, the Middle East, and northern Africa in the first centuries BC and AD is an example of regionalization.

21. This concept is Appundurai's attempt to get a non-geographical hold on where people live. Appadurai, *Modernity at Large*.

22. Shweder, "Santa Claus," 73.

they were under the standard anthropological model of the 1960s. Now, the postmodern missionary, as the postmodern anthropologist, will have to be as mobile, flexible, and clever as the postcolonial people she is trying to identify and be in mission with.[23]

What are the differences between what a previous generation of missionaries learned from anthropology and what they might learn now? This is what we will explore throughout this book, but an initial characterization of the differences can be presented in a chart.

Table 1. Paradigm Shifts in Anthropology

Assumptions regarding:	Standard (Modern) Anthropological Model	Emerging (Postmodern) Anthropological Model
Nature of culture	Essentialist	Constructivist
Position of the observer	Objective	Relative
Position of the observed	Subject	Observer
Ethnography	Totalist	Pastiche
Representation	Observer's Voice	Many Voices
Explanation	Structure and function	Hegemony and irony
Colonized people	Victim	Agent
Anthropologist	Neutral	Activist
Religion	An Institution	A Cultural Construct
Christian mission	Skeptical	Postcritical

23. Suggested reading for understanding this shift in anthropological thinking: Knauft, *Genealogies for the Present in Cultural Anthropology*. There has been a lively relationship between anthropology and mission studies since before the 1950s. For further reading, see Whiteman "Anthropology and Mission: The Incarnational Connection" and Rynkiewich "Do We Need a Postmodern Anthropology?"

2

Culture, Ethnocentrism, and Contextualization

O LORD, our Sovereign, how majestic is your name in all the earth! . . . When I look at your heavens, the work of your fingers, the moon and the stars that you have established; what are human beings that you are mindful of them, mortals that you care for them? (Psalm 8)

Soul, Self, and Perception

THE PSALMIST ASKS THE QUESTION, BUT DOES NOT ANSWER IT. The writer's focus is on God, what God has done for humans, and why God should care at all about these rather insignificant and troublesome creatures. The historical quest to understand who humans are, how they are constructed and interrelated, and what their existence means has taken various paths. Some philosophies and religions have suggested that human existence is an illusion, like smoke scattering in the wind, or, at the other extreme, that the physical reality is all that there is to life; that there is no spiritual dimension.

An imagined dualism between the body and the soul has deep roots in Western thought and has influenced Christian theology and mission. Western thought, especially as revealed in the social sciences, has imagined that the basic unit of society is an individual. This model of society leads to questions about how individuals create society by developing relationships and joining groups, and how individuals deal with society as agents of change. Each of these assumptions about

11

social reality has an influence on how people in the West conceive of mission and how they carry out that mission. There are other places to begin spinning social theories than with an imagined individual naked of privileges and obligations to others, but this is where the social sciences, and thus missiology, usually begin. It is not where people in other cultures would begin.

The concerns addressed in this chapter are the issues of *perception* or sensing reality, *cognition* or thinking about reality, and *emotion* or feeling about reality. Work in the neurosciences in the last decade suggests that there is little support for the idea that people perceive the world *as it is*. Rather, the links between parts of the brain and the senses are not direct, but require interpretation at every step along the way. In fact, considering recent neuroscience research, Reyna has suggested that our understanding of the world is based on layers of interpretative schema, beginning with neural networks and rising up to the symbolic networks that we call "culture."[1]

At the neural level, information travels along several pathways, through networks linked with various emotions and memories. For example, LeDoux[2] has demonstrated that there are two pathways for fear responses. One is a short path through the thalamus to the amygdala and the other is a longer path through the visual cortex to the amygdala. The first route carries less information, but stimulates a response within a few thousandths of a second; something absolutely necessary to get us out of danger quickly. The second route carries more information, but takes twice as long to get to the amygdala. Emotion heightens the first pathway so that an alarm goes off. Fortunately for us, in times of real danger, we have little control over this pathway. The second pathway offers us more choice after the immediate danger is over or turns out to be a false alarm.

The danger may be something that we hear or see, a noise or a flash of light. Other work shows, however, that it is not a given that we will sense an anomaly even when it is directly in front of us. In fact, our brain is constantly smoothing out the picture for us, matching what we see with patterns that we have already constructed. One test of this interpretative activity of the brain is simple. Look out a window and watch someone walking by. The person does not walk

1. Reyna, *Connections*.
2. LeDoux, *Emotional Brain*.

a few seconds, disappear for a split second, and then reappear a step ahead of where you last saw him or her. The motion seems continuous, but you are blinking your eyes and thus you lose the picture at regular intervals. Why is your record of the experience not disjointed? Because your brain fills in the missing pieces and you experience reality as continuous rather than fragmented.

This function of the brain, coupled with our ability to focus on one thing and pay less attention to other things, accounts for our difficulty in seeing anomalies. We experience this when we have difficulty seeing the rabbit in the optical illusion below if we see the duck first, and vice versa.

Figure 1.[3] One Way It's a Rabbit, Another It's a Duck

In this process of relating to the world around us, the actions of perception, cognition, and emotion contribute to our humanity. Damazio[4] argues that all animals work through stimulus and response, but the ability to step back and watch ourselves during the process is the first step in developing a sense of self. The second step is to realize that there are other selves like us and that we can interact with them. With that interaction comes a shared sense of the world around us, an agreement about certain precepts that become concepts with which to think, concepts that become charged with emotion with which to value the reality we experience, concepts that, in turn, shape how we experience the world the next time. As Berger and Luckmann say, the irony is that once we have created a world according to our concepts we forget that it is imagined, and begin to think of that imagined world as reality.[5]

3. Adapted from Romano, "Divider Line."
4. Damazio, *Feeling of What Happens.*
5. Berger and Luckmann, *Social Construction of Reality.*

We see ourselves but, of course, we do not see ourselves perfectly. As the poet Robert Burns said in these lines from his poem "To a Louse":

> O Jeany, dinna toss your head,
> An' set your beauties a' abread!
> Ye little ken what cursed speed
> The blastie's makin:
> Thae winks an' finger-ends, I dread,
> Are notice takin.
>
> O wad some Power the giftie gie us
> To see oursels as ithers see us!
> It wad frae monie a blunder free us[6]

It would seem that the Apostle Paul knew what he was talking about when he said, "Now we see through a glass darkly."[7] Our very perception of the world is partial and limited, so our brains construct plausible pictures of reality according to neural pathways that have been developed through experience and repetition. That is, we make sense out of a reality that comes to us in fragments. And, with this experience, we construct a sense of ourselves, allowing us to step back and see ourselves involved in stimulus and response with the environment. From this we can imagine others like ourselves, from which understanding comes our sense of ethics.

Anthropology

Anthropology[8] is the study of "the ways of mankind,"[9] the different ways in which humans perceive, evaluate, and respond to the world around them. As an academic discipline, anthropology is barely over one hundred years old. Edward B. Tylor (1832–1917) took the first chair in anthropology at Oxford in 1885 and Franz Boas (1858–1942) began to teach in America in 1888 at Clark University (and in 1896 founded the first Department of Anthropology, at Columbia

---

6. http://www.robertburns.org/works/97.shtml.

7. 1 Cor 13:12.

8. *Anthropos* = humanity; *logos* = word or reason and thus an area of study.

9. "The ways of mankind" is a theme developed by Walter Goldschmidt, first in a series of radio broadcasts (the early 1950s) that were then made into records to be played in the classroom, followed by a textbook titled *Exploring the Ways of Mankind*, which went through three editions (1960, 1971, 1977).

University). Before that time, anthropology was an amateur endeavor pursued by people who were either wealthy or positioned well enough to be able to spend time reading, exploring, and writing. For example, anthropological-type accounts were written by missionaries (e.g., Fr. Joseph-François Lafitau[10]), colonial administrators (e.g., Sir Henry Maine[11]), and lawyers (e.g., Lewis Henry Morgan[12]). Many of the earliest academic anthropologists depended on accounts written by missionaries, traders, and administrators. For example, James Frazier produced his famous 12-volume work, *The Golden Bough: A Study in Magic and Religion* (completed in 1941), without ever leaving England himself. The job of the amateur anthropologist was to sift the accounts because many of them were unreliable or second-hand observations, or included prejudicial evaluations of other people's customs and modes of reasoning. The problem was that amateur anthropologists also had their prejudices.[13]

From the beginning, particularly in the United States, academic anthropology was a four-field discipline. Interest in human origins and the reasons for particular biological adaptations (such as sickle-cell anemia) gave rise to *physical anthropology*. Interest in cultural origins and the rise of agricultural and urban life gave rise to archaeology. Interest in the origin of language, the distribution of languages, and the nature of speech and communication gave rise to *anthropological linguistics*. Finally, interest in people's customs, the origin and distributions of institutions, and explanations for cultural diversity across the globe gave rise to *cultural anthropology* in America and its sister discipline, *social anthropology*, in Britain and France. This last field is sometimes designated as "sociocultural anthropology."

10. Fr. Lafitau (1681–1746) was a Jesuit missionary among the Iroquois and Huron in western New York. He wrote *Moeurs des sauvages amériquains comparées aux moeurs des premiers temps* (1724).

11. Maine (1822–1888) was a judge assigned to the British colonial administration in India. He wrote *Ancient Law* (1861).

12. Morgan (1818–1881) was a lawyer who studied the Iroquois and published *The League of the Ho-dé-no-sau-nee or Iroquois* (1851).

13. The distinction that I am making between anthropology as an academic discipline and amateur anthropologists is an important one. Students continually bring something written about another culture and too easily assume that it is an "ethnography" written by an "anthropologist." Most often it is not and falls far below the standards that the discipline has set for itself.

While one or another of these might be found in a biology department, a classics department, or a sociology department, only anthropology brings these fields together in an attempt to explain human behavior. Many of the questions that anthropologists ask are best approached from more than one field or subfield.

A classic example of the need for anthropologists and, in fact, a team of researchers, in order to understand complex human situations is seen in a long-term research project dedicated to solving the mystery of *kuru*, the "shaking sickness." Australian patrol officers in colonial New Guinea (later to become part of the independent nation of Papua New Guinea) in the 1950s noted a sickness that involved uncontrollable shaking, unsteady gait, and slurring of speech that progressively worsened until death came within a few months or years of onset. The disease seemed to be confined mostly to the Fore census division around Okapa in the Eastern Highlands district.

At first, some suggested that it was a psychosomatic disease caused by the fear of sorcery. The colonial administration had a history of explaining social movements, later called "cargo cults," by reference to the "stress" of rapid social and cultural change. Thus, an early cargo cult movement was called "the Vailala Madness."[14] Medical doctors Vincent Zigas and Carleton Gajdusek quickly ruled out this guess by noting "the evidence for direct central nervous system damage is far too great . . ."[15]

Gajdusek initially theorized that the disease was a hereditary disorder passed along within families by the females. The team had noted that the disease occurred primarily among females, with some cases among children and old men, but not adult men. The disease seemed to run in families and the incidence dropped off quickly outside of Fore country.

A doctor in England, W. J. Hadlow, recognized the similarities between *kuru* and *scrapie*, a disease involving degeneration of the nervous system in sheep. At the time, the origin and diffusion of this disease was linked to a "slow virus," although no virus had yet appeared in the microscope. Here "slow" represents the long incubation period

14. See the study by a government anthropologist of an earlier time, Williams, *Vailala Madness*.

15. Gadjusek, in a letter to Australian anthropologist Ronald Berndt, quoted in Lindenbaum, *Kuru Sorcery*, 15.

before the infection actually showed pathological results. Gajdusek began to experiment with material from the damaged brains of *kuru* victims and soon demonstrated that something was being passed along to primates inoculated with this material. The disease was looking more like a virus, although the disparity in the gender and age of the victims still raised questions.

Cultural anthropologists Shirley Lindenbaum and Robert Glasse lived in the Fore area and conducted anthropological fieldwork for all but three months of the time between July 1961 and May 1963.[16] Lindenbaum's study of Fore kinship ruled out one of the theories, noting that

> any of the supposedly related kuru victims were not closely related biologically, but were kin in an improvised, non-biological sense. An analysis of the Fore kinship system does not support a purely genetic interpretation of the disease.[17]

Lindenbaum collected oral histories about the arrival and spread of *kuru*, an event that happened within the old people's experience and was preserved in their memories. These confirmed that the initial and continued impact of the disease was on women. Lindenbaum collected stories of the local diagnosis, which was that sorcerers were at work, and this account persisted among a people who believed that physical disease is linked to social disorder.

After collecting accounts of *kuru* victims from them and their families, a new link emerged. Though not a long-standing tradition, the stories told that cannibalism had begun among the Fore in the 1920s, and *kuru* appeared about ten years after the adoption of this new cultural practice. The turn to cannibalism did not fit the usual accounts of eating the bodies of enemies (exo-cannibalism) or eating the bodies of powerful persons in order to access their characteristics (ritual cannibalism), but rather, from the stories, it seemed to be a case of diffusion of a custom from neighboring groups that was adopted because of the protein that it provided. Ecologically, the Fore were in the process of adopting more widespread gardening and pig herding, and thus were transforming their landscape from forest to grasslands. As less wild game was available, and since adult men claimed the pigs,

16. Lindenbaum, *Kuru Sorcery*, vii.
17. Ibid.

women and their young children (older boys transfer to the men's house) tended to be the consumers of those who had died among them (endo-cannibalism). The brain was reserved for the female relatives of the victim.

It took the study of medical doctors and anthropologists on the kinship system, the local economy, the political system, the exchange system, oral history, and case studies to complete the picture of disease etiology for the Fore.

At the time of the publication of Lindenbaum's classic study, the assumption was that a slow virus similar to what causes *scrapie* and Kreutzfeld-Jakobson Disease was the culprit, and it was passed along when women ate the brains of those who had died of *kuru*.[18] However, more recent studies have identified not a virus but *prions* that are ingested with the brain as the cause of these neurological disorders, the most famous of which now is Mad Cow Disease. In the Fore area, the incidence of *kuru* has rapidly declined due to the influence of the colonial administration and missionaries in the 1950s and 1960s.[19]

Fieldwork in Sociocultural Anthropology

It took some time for social and cultural anthropologists to realize the importance of *fieldwork*, that is, research conducted in the local language over a long period of residence with a single group of people. Beliefs and behaviors that were earlier described as "strange customs" began to make sense within a system of thought that anthropologists called "culture."

The concept of culture (or the German *Kultur*) itself, in the early nineteenth century, served initially as a synonym for civilization, at a time when missionary work, the colonial project, and academia tended to go hand in hand. Thus, those in contact with the colonized "other" in the nineteenth century could speak of people as more or less "civilized" or more or less "cultured." A similar evaluation was made of the "lower classes" in Western societies, i.e., that they were less cultured and thus less civilized.

18. Lindenbaum and Lock, eds., *Knowledge, Power, and Practice*. See also Lindenbaum, "Kuru, Prions."

19. The discovery of the link between the sickle-cell mutation and resistance to malaria is another fascinating story of the need for a multidisciplinary approach to research.

As anthropology grew through extended fieldwork, the writing of descriptive accounts (*ethnography*), and the comparison of various ethnographic accounts (*ethnology*), the grand theories of amateur anthropologists and some early professionals were found to be based too much on Western philosophy and too little on what people actually do. Most anthropologists rejected this kind of thinking early in the twentieth century, but this perspective has persisted to this day in popular culture.

The Concept of Culture

By the mid-1900s, anthropologists tended to define culture as the beliefs, behavior, and artifacts of a particular society.[20] Many of these definitions have their origin in Tylor's idea of culture.

> Culture or civilization, taken in its wide ethnographic sense, is that complex whole which includes knowledge, belief, art, morals, law, custom, and any other capabilities and habits acquired by man as a member of society.[21]

There are three good objections to this kind of omnibus definition. First, it includes everything and thus defines nothing in particular. Second, this kind of definition leaves little room the dynamics that produce change. Finally, it dismisses other powerful ways of explaining why people do what they do, specifically the concept of society (with subsets of economy, politics and religion) as well as the concepts of personality, history, and ecology.

Culture is a more or less integrated system of knowledge, values and feelings that people use to define their reality (worldview), interpret their experiences, and generate appropriate strategies for living; a system that people learn from other people around them and share with other people in a social setting; a system that people use to adapt to their spiritual, social, and physical environments; and a system that people use to innovate in order to change themselves as their environments change.

Behavior is not culture, but it is a product of culture, or rather a product of the interaction between culture and people's physical, social, and spiritual environment. Culture is not tradition, but rather culture includes the reasoning behind selecting and deploying certain

20. Kroeber and Kluckhohn, *Culture.*

21. Tylor, *Origins of Culture*, 1.

stories, beliefs, and rituals in a social setting. Culture is not artifacts, but culture includes the knowledge behind the production, distribution, and consumption of goods. Culture is not society, but it is what makes sense out of actions, events, relationships, and groups within a particular society.

Culture has systemic properties, but it is not a totalizing system. That is to say, culture is influential but not determinative. While the parts of culture fit together and make sense, there is never a perfect fit and culture does not always make perfect sense. Some ideas grate against each other, some values contradict each other, some feelings present people with paradoxes or just seem to be mysterious, and this sometimes as much to insiders as outsiders. Of course, the differences seem obvious when generations change as fast as they do today, or when two cultures come into contact and ideas are exchanged. However, variation is also a feature of culture in and of itself.

In *Political Systems of Highland Burma* (1954), Edmund Leach (1910–1989) first presented a local political system not as an ideal type (e.g., democratic or authoritarian) but as a product of conflict between two ideals. That is, over time, the government in power is an expression of commitment to one of two ideal types (*gumsa* and *gumlao*). This reflected a long-standing disagreement within Kachin society concerning the kind of government they should have, and the result was that, over time, they oscillated back and forth between two ideals. In fact, most societies are like this. In the case of the United States, the tensions are perceived to cycle between elitist and populist, federalism and states' rights, conservative and liberal, right and left, and capitalist and socialist interests.

Culture, particularly as it is entangled in language, gives shape to objects and events in the world, leads us to recognize and value some of these objects and events but not others, and helps us develop specialized knowledge about the part of the world that is important to us. It is becoming more obvious to some of those working for economic development that indigenous people have a great deal of knowledge about their own environment. The classic case that is often quoted is that the Inuit[22] have many more words for different kinds of snow than people who live indoors in winter. In the same way, Pacific

---

22. The people once known as "Eskimos" now are called by the name they prefer for themselves, *Inuit*, meaning "The People."

Islanders who are trained in navigation are able to read stars, waves, clouds, and even flights of birds in order to sail from one island to another. Grain traders know how to read the CBOT,[23] the variations in barge and rail traffic, and the seasonal cycles of the basis at the Gulf. When something is important for survival, people make more and more distinctions in order to "see" what may be helpful under certain circumstances.

Culture, through remembered stories, acquired models, and shared public symbols, helps us make sense out of the people and places that we encounter each day. Clifford Geertz (1926–2006), in "Notes on a Balinese Cock-Fight," argues that an event that pits roosters against one another is more than a sport.[24] He examines the event at a variety of levels, something he calls "thick description," and finds different meanings at personal (sexual), family, village, and national political levels. The Muslim veil in French society also begs for a thick description and multilayered analysis.[25]

Culture is a toolkit for cobbling together responses to what other people do, for dealing with the challenges and opportunities that the environment presents to us, and for managing the forces that we perceive to be in the world. Bronislaw Malinowski (1884–1942), writing about the "Kula Ring" in the Massim[26] area off the eastern coast of Papua New Guinea, noted that the trading voyages made to exchange armbands for necklaces were dangerous and challenging in more ways than one. Storms could blow canoes off course, or worse, sink them. Spirits could attack the traders along the way. Warriors could decide to break the "peace of the Kula."[27] Malinowski noted that, in preparation for the annual expeditions,[28] traders not only readied their shells and canoes, but also prepared spiritually through rituals and formulas for safety and success in voyaging and trading.

Culture is learned and shared. What is peculiar to the individual, that is, neither learned from others nor shared with others, is not cul-

23. Chicago Board of Trade.

24. I recognize that some readers may think that it is less than a sport.

25. See Gudorf, Case # 7, "Matter of Veils."

26. I worked for a year on Misima, an island whose misspelling gives rise to the regional name, the Massim.

27. Uberoi, *Politics of the Kula Ring*.

28. Malinowski, *Argonauts of the Western Pacific*.

ture. It is idiosyncratic. Culture, society, and the environment already exist when people are born, so knowledge, relationships, and adaptations have to be learned. Various cultures have more or less formal ways of transmitting knowledge and lore from one generation to the next. Among the Lmaa[29] of Kenya and Tanzania, gathering around the fire with the elders in the evening provides a teaching moment when values and perceptions embedded in oral narratives are passed from elder to younger. Children in many cultures learn by doing the same things that adults do. But, in some cultures, parents work away from home. These cultures tend toward educational forms like schools. Although these cultures, such as Chinese culture, tended in the past to provide education only for the elite, most places in the world are working toward universal education.

Culture is peculiar. Although culture is a human construction of a particular understanding of the world, once children learn a culture they sense the world through that culture as if it were the only reality, and, as adults, they forget that their reality is a social construct. For example, in America it is a given that there is a secular side of society and a sacred side, as well as secular and sacred approaches to social problems. Thus, Americans separate prayer and education and can only cobble together the secular and the sacred with difficulty, as seen in the concept of "faith-based organizations." However, this separation was not characteristic of Middle Ages Europe. Only after the Reformation and Enlightenment did such an idea come into existence. There was a time when "secular" did not exist, and only when some writers imagined the secular did it come into being as something distinct from "sacred," at least for Westerners. Now, to the Western mind, it does seem as if reality is, in fact, divided and further subdivided into family, state, religion, economy, and polity. A recent debate in the Society of Biblical Literature about whether it is possible for a scholar to also be a person of faith working in the service of the church reveals this division.[30] Some scholars imagine that biblical studies can only be done from an "objective" perspective, as if there were such a thing as a neutral pose. Thus, the majority seem to support the notion that a person of faith cannot be a biblical scholar.

29. A nomadic, cattle-herding people known in the literature and popular imagination as Maasai but properly called the Lmaa. See Lolwerikoi, *Orality and Land.*

30. Hays, "Reading the Bible."

Another concept that seems self-evident is the modern nation-state. To those with little sense of history, contemporary nation-states, represented in the list of nations that belong to the United Nations, seem normal and natural. In fact, when some people read about "the nations" in the Bible they think that modern nation-states are in view. However, as Benedict Anderson has argued, modern nation-states are not natural but are constructed realities.[31] Nations, as we know them, are of recent origin, usually have been constructed by force, have arbitrary boundaries, and often do not hold together in the long run. Many states formed after the collapse of three empires at the end of World War I, for example: Yugoslavia, Czechoslovakia, Austria, Hungary, Syria, Lebanon, Iraq, Palestine, Saudi Arabia, and Yemen. Some ethnic minorities that had been absorbed into the Russian Empire re-emerged as states: Lithuania, Latvia, Estonia, and Poland. Some of these disappeared, only to re-emerge again, and some of the states that were constructed after World War I no longer exist.

Culture helps people adapt to challenges that are presented to them each day. For example, in many isolated societies, the task of getting enough food and water takes up most of the day. Culture provides a people with a detailed knowledge of the ecology, especially knowledge of when fish, animals, and plants are available in numbers, knowledge of how to build a fishing boat, knowledge of how to work the ground and plant seed, or knowledge of which relative controls which body of knowledge about the environment and has the technology available to exploit it.

Culture provides the resources for mixing and matching ideas and goods into new configurations that can lead to change in society. Innovation, according to Homer Barnett (1906–1985), usually involves putting together two existing items or ideas into a form that is new. An innovation such as the machine that "combines" the tasks of cutting and threshing wheat, though not available on the farm before World War II, spread quickly because it reduced the amount of time and manpower required during harvest. Other innovations, such as using citrus fruit to ward off scurvy, are not as easy to adopt because there is a delay between the preventative treatment and the result. Sometimes the diffusion of innovation is agonizingly slow. Consider the following timeline of adoption.

31. Anderson, *Imagined Communities.*

Table 2. How Long Does Change Take?[32]

1497: Vasco de Gama sailed from Portugal to the Cape of Good Hope in South Africa with a crew of 160 men; 100 died of scurvy.
1601: Capt. James Lancaster conducted an experiment to evaluate the effectiveness of lemon juice in preventing scurvy while commanding four ships sailing from England to India. On one ship, he gave sailors lemon juice. Nearly half the sailors on the other three ships died of scurvy, but not one on the test ship.
1747: Dr. Lind, on the HMS Salisbury, gave each scurvy patient on the ship a variety of supposed cures, including citrus fruit. The scurvy patients who received the oranges and lemons recovered in a few days, the rest did not.
1775: Captain Cook reported from his voyages in the Pacific that citrus fruit did not help cure scurvy.
1795: The British Navy finally adopted this innovation, and, when they did, scurvy was eliminated as a threat to sailors (194 years after the discovery).
1865: The British Board of Trade adopted the innovation and eradicated scurvy from the merchant marine (264 years after discovery).

There are many cultures in the world, and when people from two different cultures come together there is an opportunity for understanding, and even sharing and learning. However, there are also other forces at work.

Ethnocentrism

Ethnocentrism is the all-too-human tendency to respond to other people's ways by using one's own culture, especially values and feelings, to prejudge people's behavior and explain differences as if they were the result of perceived physical and mental differences (racism) or spiritual and moral differences (elitism). Ethnocentrism may have its origin in the justifying myths that parents tell their children to build social identity. Children often hear, "We are the people of XXX, we do good things, and we do not do those terrible things like the people of YYY." At another level, larger political entities, up to and including the nation-state, often use the same kind of rhetoric to enhance group solidarity and legitimize the dominant culture. The rhetoric tends to demonize others, whether it is people of another skin color living in the land (racism) or people in another cultural tradition (jingoism).

32. Adapted from Rogers, *Diffusion of Innovations*, 7–8.

These prejudices and misunderstandings can lead to miscommunication and intergroup conflict in the hands of political manipulators.

For example, we no longer call the people of the northernmost latitudes "Eskimo." The word "Eskimo" means "eaters of raw flesh," an Algonkian term for the people who actually call themselves the "Inuit," meaning "the people" or "human beings." While the British were busy naming the tribes of West Africa, the Yoruba of western Nigeria named the white Europeans "Oinbo," which means "he who has been peeled." Both were ethnocentric, but there is a crucial difference: Who had the power to enforce their worldview on the other?

Greeks called all other people "barbarians" because, to the Greeks, their language sounded like someone babbling "bar-bar-bar." It is ironic that the "barbarians" who speak American English have now returned the favor. When they are unable to read or interpret some text, they tend to say, "It's all Greek to me." The Greeks thought that culture was built into character. The Southern Barbarians (in Mesopotamia and Egypt) were thought to be capable of building and living in great civilizations, but incapable of living as free men. They were susceptible to despots: pharaohs, kings, emperors. On the other hand, the Northern Barbarians (Scythians and other early Europeans) were seen as hard-fighting, free warriors, but far too savage to be able ever to develop a civilized way of life. Only the Greeks combined the best qualities of both: civilized, free, and democratic. According to the Greeks, only they themselves were able to live out the "golden mean."

Table 3. Who Are These People?

I saw how the (people) had arrived with their wares, and pitched their camp beside the Volga. Never did I see people so gigantic; they are tall as palm trees and florid and ruddy of complexion. They wear neither camisoles nor *chaftans*, but the men among them wear a garment of rough cloth, which is thrown over one side, so that one hand remains free. Every one carries an axe, a dagger, and a sword, and without these weapons they are never seen. Their swords are broad, with wavy lines, and of Frankish make. From the tip of the fingernails to the neck, each man of them is tattooed with pictures of trees, living beings, and other things. The women carry, fastened to their breast, a little case of iron, copper, silver, or gold, according to the wealth and resources of their husbands. . . . They are the filthiest race that God ever created. They do not wipe themselves after going to stool, nor wash themselves after a nocturnal pollution, any more than if they were wild asses. They come from their own country, anchor their ships in the Volga, which a great river, and build large wooden houses on its banks. In every such house there live ten or twenty, more or fewer. Each man has a couch, where he sits with the beautiful girls he has for sale. Here he is as likely as not to enjoy one of them while a friend looks on. At times several of them will be thus engaged at the same moment, each in full view of the others. . . . Every morning a girl comes and brings a tub of water, and places it before her master. In this he proceeds to wash his face and hands, and then his hair, combing it out over the vessel. Thereupon he blows his nose, and spits into the tub, and, leaving no dirt behind, conveys it all into this water. When he has finished, the girl carries the tub to the man next to him, who does the same. Thus she continues carrying the tub from one to another, till each of those who are in the house has blown his nose and spit into the tub, and washed his face and hair.[A]

A. From an account titled "Scandinavians on the Volga in 922," by Ahmed ib n Fadlān, reprinted in Dundes *Every Man His Way*, 17–18.

Who are these people? They are Vikings, ancestors of today's Swedes and Danes. The chronicler, Ahmed ibn Fadlān, encountered these Scandanavians encamped along the Volga River in AD 922, and then wrote about them in his report. These are the ancestors of the infamous "Nordic Race" of Madison Grant,[33] the finest example of the "Ayrans" imagined by Adolph Hitler. Every question about human beings requires multiple disciplines to answer. Here is an economics question: What were the Vikings doing along the Volga River in AD 922?

Of course, Americans, Germans, and Arabs are not the only people who are ethnocentric and who exhibit prejudices toward people of different cultures or even different looks. In a recent travel memoir, Peter Hessler reports the results of an English assignment for his Chinese students. He asked them to imagine that they were American settlers moving west when they discover American Indians in the way.

33. Grant, *Passing of the Great Race*.

What would they do if they were in this situation? Hessler says "nearly all responded like the following":

> The Indians should become a part of American society like everyone else. Even though they are poor and savage, we can help them found reservations to make them civilized, and give them advanced knowledges and experiences to change their lifestyle and develop their economy. By this way, we can make them become rich and be suited for modern life. At last, the Indians can get along well with us and advance together.[34]

That gave Hessler insight into the way that the Han Chinese treat the Uighur, and the Tibetans, and the other officially recognized minorities. There are no people on earth who are able to step completely outside their own culture in their evaluation of other people's ways—not even anthropologists, even though we try.

Cultural Relativism

Cultural relativism is the assumption that each culture is unique, has an inherent logic to its structure, and has parts that are functionally interrelated. Thus, each culture can be understood and appreciated only in its own context.

---

34. Hessler, *River Town*, 213.

Table 4. Racism and the Origins of Academic Anthropology
in America

Historically, the notion of cultural relativism emerged as a necessary counter to
the racism and jingoism that was common in America and Britain in the early
twentieth century. In America, for example, myths of superior and inferior races,
of dying races and progressive races, accompanied the final defeat and restriction of Native Americans to small reservations. (Note: in the 1900 census, there
were only 100,000 Native Americans left out of the more than 50,000,000 who,
in 1492, lived in the area that later became the United States.) The myths of superiority were deployed to justify slavery, the establishment of Jim Crow laws,
the segregationist policy of "separate but equal," the founding and revival of the
Klu Klux Klan, and the anti-immigration sentiment that led to the passage of
migration quotas in 1924. The Immigration Act of 1924 was the first attempt
by the federal government to limit immigration. It stopped Asian immigration
and limited immigration from southern and eastern Europe, while permitting
immigration from northern and western Europe. Known as the Johnson-Reed
Act, its supporters were influenced, as were many Americans, by Madison Grant's
The Passing of the Great Race. Grant himself contributed to the Act, as well as to
Virginia's Racial Integrity Act of 1924 with his "racial hygiene" theory. Both Franz
Boas and Madison Grant served on the National Research Council's Committee
on Anthropology after WWI, and each tried to take anthropology in a different
direction. In this, they were bitterly opposed. Adolph Hitler wrote to Grant saying, "This book is my Bible." The book was itself a remake of an earlier work by
the Comte de Gobineau (1816–1882), *An Essay on the Inequality of the Human
Races* (1853–1855). De Gobineau introduced the concepts of "black," "white,"
and "yellow" races, and argued that "race mixing" breaks down barriers and leads
to chaos. These ideas converged also with Francis Galton's (1822–1911) work on
"eugenics" and "nature versus nuture," terms that he invented. (See also Lothrop
Stoddard *The Rising Tide of Color against White World Supremacy* [1920], a
popular rewrite of Grant's book). In all these works it is assumed that culture is
based on race. As you can see, the same tired old arguments are constantly being
rehashed, and new believers fall for the lie.

The founder of American anthropology, Franz Boas, himself a Jewish
immigrant from Germany, spent his life work countering racial myths
of superiority and inferiority. One of the themes in his work in physical anthropology, linguistics, and cultural anthropology was the "plas-
ticity" or flexibility of the human body as well as the human mind. His
work with body measurements and intelligence tests demonstrated
that it was environment (food, health, nurture) that made a difference and not what was then called "race" (the contemporary "white,"
"black," and "yellow," which have no scientific standing). Eventually,
anthropologists found so many problems with the term "race" that
they have dropped it altogether, and thus you will not find the term

hereafter in this book except in its adjectival form describing the prejudices that we call "racism."

This is the context, then, in which the concept of cultural relativism developed. It was, and still is, a necessary counterproposal to the many forms that racism and prejudice can take. However, it is not the last word in dealing with other cultures. In its extreme form, a principle of cultural relativism would prevent criticism even of Adolph Hitler and the practices of Nazi Germany, or the Rwanda genocide, or the Cambodian reign of terror, or any such atrocity. Even anthropologists have been unwilling to dismiss Nazism by saying, "Its OK, that's just their culture." So, in fact, a kind of relative relativism prevails.[35]

One form could be called "methodological relativism," and the argument for it would run like this: One cannot know and understand another culture while at the same time judging and condemning it. Therefore, these things should be taken in stages. One should withhold judgment at least for a given period of research and study until the culture is described, analyzed, and understood. There will be a proper time for evaluation of the practices of the culture. There will also be a proper place and community in which to conduct an evaluation. Methodological relativism insures that prejudices do not warp the processes of understanding in the first place. There is a time and place for supporting justice and righteousness and for condemning abuse and oppression. It is premature judgment that is the problem, not judgment.

---

35. Nida, *Customs and Cultures*, 50.

Table 5. Romans 14 and Cultural Relativity

Romans 14:13–23
Let us therefore no longer pass judgment on one another, but resolve instead never to put a stumbling block or hindrance in the way of another. *I know and am persuaded in the Lord Jesus that nothing is unclean in itself; but it is unclean for anyone who thinks it unclean.*ᴬ If your brother or sister is being injured by what you eat, you are no longer walking in love. Do not let what you eat cause the ruin of one for whom Christ died. So do not let your good be spoken of as evil. For the kingdom of God is not food and drink but righteousness and peace and joy in the Holy Spirit. The one who thus serves Christ is acceptable to God and has human approval. Let us then pursue what makes for peace and for mutual upbuilding. Do not, for the sake of food, destroy the work of God. Everything is indeed clean, but it is wrong for you to make others fall by what you eat; it is good not to eat meat or drink wine or do anything that makes your brother or sister stumble. The faith that you have, have as your own conviction before God. Blessed are those who have no reason to condemn themselves because of what they approve. But those who have doubts are condemned if they eat, because they do not act from faith; for whatever does not proceed from faith is sin.
A. Some translations say "no food is intrinsically unholy," but there is no such limitation in the text, and the co-text talks about food, drink, and days. My italics here and also in Table 6 below.

The meaning of behavior, therefore, is *not* in the people's genes or skin tone; *neither* is it in the structure of their brains; *nor* is meaning embedded in the behavior itself. Meaning is symbolic, and thus meaning is not connected inherently to the form of speech or form of behavior. Instead, the meaning of a people's behavior is to be discovered in the people's culture itself, not imputed from the outside.

Culture is a way of understanding and responding to the world around us. Cultures differ from place to place. Cultures differ not just because the environment differs; though it does take different skills and tools to live on the plateau, in the rainforest, or in the desert. Cultures differ because people's perceptions differ. How people see the world is shaped by culture, which in turn shapes culture in the next generation.

Table 6. 1 Corinthians 8 and Epistemology

1 Corinthians 8:1–13
Now concerning food sacrificed to idols: we know that "all of us possess knowledge." *Knowledge puffs up, but love builds up. Anyone who claims to know something does not yet have the necessary knowledge; but anyone who loves God is known by him.* Hence, as to the eating of food offered to idols, we know that "no idol in the world really exists," and that "there is no God but one." Indeed, even though there may be so-called gods in heaven or on earth—as in fact there are many gods and many lords—yet for us there is one God, the Father, from whom are all things and for whom we exist, and one Lord, Jesus Christ, through whom are all things and through whom we exist. It is not everyone, however, who has this knowledge. Since some have become so accustomed to idols until now, they still think of the food they eat as food offered to an idol; and their conscience, being weak, is defiled. "Food will not bring us close to God." We are no worse off if we do not eat, and no better off if we do. But take care that this liberty of yours does not somehow become a stumbling block to the weak. For if others see you, who possess knowledge, eating in the temple of an idol, might they not, since their conscience is weak, be encouraged to the point of eating food sacrificed to idols? So by your knowledge those weak believers for whom Christ died are destroyed. But when you thus sin against members of your family, and wound their conscience when it is weak, you sin against Christ. Therefore, if food is a cause of their falling, I will never eat meat, so that I may not cause one of them to fall.

Paul first establishes that our knowledge is never complete enough to make final judgments, and the use of knowledge alone tends to inflate one's sense of importance. The use of love in a context of knowledge makes a contribution to the community of the King. What we know about "food sacrificed to idols" is contradictory, because, on the one hand, we know that "no idol . . . really exists," but on the other hand, idols are a reality for some new converts. If no idol exists, then eating food that has been sacrificed first to idols is of no consequence and thus not a sin. However, it is of consequence for someone with a weak conscience, so much of consequence that causing them to fall by eating meat sacrificed to idols in their presence is a sin. This is the relativistic line that Christians have to walk.

Where is the meaning of behavior, then? Is it in the behavior itself? As an example, consider two men walking down the street holding hands and talking. If this happens in the Pacific Islands, most cultures there interpret it as friendship, nothing more. Now consider a man and a woman walking along holding hands and talking. In most Pacific Islands cultures, this is taboo.[36] Men socialize with other men,

36. An appropriate word, since *tabu* (Tahitian) or *kapu* (Hawaiian) is the source

and women socialize with other women, but the two do not mix. On a Sunday morning, men will walk to church together, women and children walk in another group. Some churches, adapting the early New England Congregational practice, have separate doors and separate sides of the church for men and women. The meaning of holding hands is in the minds of the observers.

Table 7. Ethnocentricism: Humorous or Deadly?

> December 7, 2008. Brothers Jose and Romel Sucuzhañay were walking down a street in Brooklyn, arm in arm as is customary among brothers and friends in Ecuador, the country they had immigrated from to New York. Jose was a real estate broker. It was cold, so one brother stopped to give the other one his coat. At that point, four men in a Ford Explorer jumped out and used a bottle and a baseball bat to attack the brothers. The men shouted anti-gay and anti-Hispanic slurs, having mistaken the behavior of the two brothers for the behavior of a couple of gay men. Jose was declared brain dead at the hospital and died five days later.[A] An isolated incident? In 2008, there were 830 hate crimes against Hispanics reported in the U.S., a growing trend from the 595 five years before.[B]
>
> A. "Attack on Ecuadorean Brothers Investigated as Hate Crime," New York Times, December 8, 2008, online: http://www.nytimes.com/2008/12/09/nyregion/09assault.html; "Ecuadorean Man Dies from Beating before His Mother Arrives to See Him," New York Times, December 13, 2008, online: http://www.nytimes.com/2008/12/14/nyregion/14ecuadorean.html.
>
> B. "Ecuadorean Killed in New York Buried at Home," MSNBC.com, December 20, 2008, online: http://www.msnbc.msn.com/id/28329089.

Here is an analogy: Culture is like a pair of glasses. Some prescriptions are for nearsightedness, some for farsightedness, some are just sunglasses, and some are rose-colored glasses. We all grow up seeing the world through lenses that make the world clear to our group of people. However, these lenses bring clarity to some aspects of reality while distorting or blurring others. Both anthropologists and missionaries want to understand how other people view the world, but neither can take their own glasses off. The best they can do is to craft a pair similar to the ones the others are wearing and try to put them on. However, when they do, the picture they get is not the same one that the other people see because the anthropologist or missionary is now seeing through two pairs of glasses. Imagine the distortion. What can the anthropologist or missionary do? First, they can be self-aware and account for their own lenses, that is, their concepts, values, and

---

of this now Anglicized concept.

biases. Second, they can learn as much as they can about the lenses that belong to the other people. Do you see what I mean?

Stop for a moment. Much of culture is in our way of thinking and perceiving, and thus much of culture is itself unseen. For example, in American culture, in the English language, there is a cultural bias in favor of seeing, which is privileged over the other four bodily senses that Western culture tends to recognize: hearing, touching, tasting, and smelling. Indeed, Americans often say:[37]

> Seeing is believing.
> Observe the law.
> See the point . . .
> My view is . . .
> Another viewpoint is . . .
> It all depends on how you look at it.
> I'll believe it when I see it.
> I can't see that.
> See for yourself.
> It's out of sight.
> I'd like to catch her eye.
> I have to go see the doctor.
> She is a woman of vision.
> He has foresight.
> She has insight.
> What is your outlook?
> Lets look it over.
> Can't you see through her?

By contrast, American English tends to displace the other senses:

> We can't accept that, its hearsay evidence.
> That's too touchy-feely for me.
> Would you buy it sight unseen?
> He's a soft touch.

Human beings are unaware of many of their cultural biases. Culture is subtle and, as such, is more often caught than taught. For example, who teaches children and newcomers about supermarket behavior? Do you have cart ownership? Is it temporary but real? Can you take something out of someone else's cart since they haven't bought it yet? Are there rules for packing a cart? Rules for standing

---

37. Adapted from Dundes, "Seeing is Believing," 14–19.

in line? Rules for the express lane? You may not think so, but ask an international student if they had to learn these things.

Here is an exercise in discovering your own culture: Find a student from a different country than you, and ask them to talk about the little things that they had to figure out when they moved to your country. They may have had to learn things like how to line up at a bank or for a bus, how to read road signs, how to order at a fast food restaurant, how to greet people in passing, or whether or not to hold hands during a conversation.

Culture Shock

Culture shock is the disorientation that we feel when all the cultural maps and guidelines that we learned as children in our own society fail us miserably in our new situation. Culture shock is characterized by confusion, anger, and anxiety. We are confused because we do not even know what we did wrong. We are angry because we suspect that someone could have warned us. We are resentful because we think that these people could help but seem not to care. We are afraid, because we do not know what to do next. Then we are paralyzed, because we think that sitting at our apartment doing nothing will be the best option.

Kalvero Oberg (1901–1973) talked about the "anxiety" that people visiting another society feel as opposed to the "peace of mind" that they experience at home.[38] This anxiety creates a series of responses. There may be a honeymoon period when everything is new and exciting, but before long the visitor moves toward "rejection," a response that follows the logic: "the ways of the host country are bad because they make us feel bad." Another response or phase is "regression," where one's home country is idealized and idolized. It may take a trip back home to restore reality here. Some responses are physical as the visitor exhibits symptoms of headache, loss of appetite, and depression. When these responses pile up, the visitor may develop hostility. However, if the visitor moves to a learning phrase, and is persistent with the language and culture, it is possible to become accustomed to life in a new place and avoid going home in a straightjacket.

38. This concept was introduced by Kalvero Oberg, who was trained by A. R. Radcliffe-Brown and Edward Sapir at the University of Chicago.

Others have added to Oberg's original concept such notions as *reverse culture shock*. This is the experience of missionaries and others who have lived in a different culture for a number of years and then return to their home culture. Sometimes the simplest things seem overwhelming, such as all of the choices one has to make on the spot when ordering lunch at a fast food restaurant. Sometimes behavior that seemed normal and even natural when the missionary left home now seems odd or even scary, things such as driving down a freeway that has six lanes in both directions. Sometimes the home culture clearly has changed during the missionary's absence, such as coming back to find that there is an NFL football team in Tennessee or that people are driving while holding a cell phone in one hand and talking away as if their lives depended on it.[39] Now the missionary is in the odd position of not fitting in the home culture and feeling vaguely ill at ease about it. Patience, cultural relativism, and an attitude of learning are the answers to reverse culture shock as well.

Table 8. The Stages of Culture Shock

1. Tourist stage. Everything is fascinating, and we easily show good will. Usually lasts 1–3 months.
2. Disenchantment. Frustration and anxiety set in, and then stress follows. Usually lasts 3–6 months.
3. Resolution. Humor develops, as well as renewed appreciation for the local scene. Usually occurs sometime between 6 and 12 months; or not at all if the person stops trying.
4. Adjustment. We learn to function and grow in the culture. Usually develops after a year in the field.
5. Reverse culture shock. When we return home we find that we have changed in one direction and the people back home have changed in another direction.

What concerns Americans most about living in other cultures?

Language. We can't communicate. We communicate well at home, and we suspect that those symbol systems are innate (that is, there is a built-in connection between symbols and their referents). So, we shout louder in an effort to make English heard. We try to use distance (proxemics) and body language (kinesics) as we did at home,

39. My family and I returned from Papua New Guinea to the States in January of 2000 to find a Super Bowl between the Tennessee Titans, a new team to us, and the St. Louis Rams (last we looked, they were in Los Angeles). We were also shocked to see cell phones in such widespread use.

again not realizing that meaning is arbitrarily attached to symbols. We come closer to talk, and people back up. We raise our eyebrows in disapproval, and people take that as a "yes."

As we try to learn the local language, we find it frustrating, embarrassing, or boring. We can say "good morning," "good afternoon," and "good evening," but then the conversation stops there. Even the children laugh at us because they have learned the language and we have not. We sense rejection, so we study less, find more English speakers to complain to, get sick and make up excuses for not engaging the local people. Finally, we feel trapped. The only way out of the trap is to keep pushing in the same direction: learn, practice, be patient, don't judge; learn, practice, be patient, don't judge.

Time. We develop a schedule because it is efficient and convenient for us. We get things done this way. We plan out shopping, banking, cooking, laundering, mailing, doctoring, playing, eating out, and going to church. All that can be accomplished in one day at home, if everyone shows up on time and the encounters are efficient. However, in this new place, we are not sure how to do each of these things. We don't realize that some activities take twice as long to accomplish. For example, shopping at the open market is different from shopping at the supermarket. There is a lot of walking, looking at produce in the stalls, waiting to buy separately from each vendor, stopping and talking with acquaintances.

Then we go to the bank to replenish our money, and find a long line, or, worse yet, no line at all, just a bunch of people standing around the perimeter leaning against the walls. Where is the line and where is our place in line? Who's next? It turns out that there is a different perspective about schedules and about running these errands. People do not "run" at all. In fact, a trip to town is a social occasion in itself, not something to be hurried but an occasion to be savored slowly. The people standing around the wall are enjoying their conversations. Noticing that you are an American, they motion you to the teller when there is a vacancy, because they know that you are not like them, and suspect that, maybe, you even don't like them since you do not place relationships above keeping a schedule.

Sunday morning comes, and finally something familiar will happen: a church service. The advertised time for worship is 10:00, so you arrive fashionably at 9:50, only to find that there is no one in the church

but a few children who are playing around the outside. You sit down on a bench, and watch as, over the next hour, people wander in, greet one another, and sit down to wait. Finally, at 11:15, the pastor comes over from his house. After another 15 minutes of greeting, arranging lectern and music, and looking around to see if everyone has arrived, the service starts. The singing, praying, special music, Bible reading, preaching, offering taking, and announcements take up the next two and a half hours. Finally, at 2:00 the service is over, but people leave the building slowly and gather in groups in the yard. People sit down, take out betel nut to chew and some snacks to eat, and hang around for another hour or two. Church service takes all day.

We do not realize that some jobs take a lot of energy. For example, doing the laundry without a machine takes three times as long. Even doctoring takes a lot of energy, if you have to search for a doctor. So, again we are frustrated, depressed, and struggling to survive. And, other people do not seem as concerned about the situation as we are. For example, you can arrive on time, but the church service will not start until everyone gets there. That means an hour wait from the posted start time, and then two to three hours for the service to be over.

Relationships. Relationships contribute to our identity, reinforce it at times, and change it at times. However, it turns out that other people have their own ideas about our identity. We might be a *Nordamericano*, an American, a missionary, a "white-skin," an outsider, or a "boss." Our identity seems greatly reduced, almost to a caricature. When people greet us, we find a formal deference that is difficult to break through. We suspect that people are not responding to us as individuals, but to us as a class of others about whom they have already decided. They do not know who we really are. We have a hard time finding a role that makes sense in this society. Whatever status we are ascribed, we find that it conflicts with who we think we are at home.

Stress. The result is stress and eventually health problems. A sense of failure creeps in when unrealistic expectations are not met. We are unable to cope, overwhelmed by constantly facing new situations. People back home expect us to succeed and we will with patient persistence.

Culture in Postmodern Perspective

Modernist tendencies in the social sciences often led to the reification of analytic concepts. That is, anthropologists tended to treat culture as if it really exists apart from the human beings who are seen as displaying the effects of culture while not suspecting its presence. In the 1930s and 1940s this issue took shape in discussions about the "superorganic" nature of culture. Alfred Kroeber argued that things like fashion in dress displayed long-term patterns (the hemline of dresses went up and down over time) independent of any individual's control. So, for some anthropologists culture existed above humans, the hidden hand of tradition directing people's behavior.

By the 1950s and 1960s, some anthropologists were locating culture inside the heads of people, in the concepts and language that people use. An approach called "ethnosemantics" or "ethnoscience" explored the nature of categories, attributes, and taxonomies as they revealed culture in people's minds. By contrast, anthropologists who studied binary structures in the mind or symbol systems were less likely to place these under people's conscious control. Yet, for most, the prevailing belief was that culture was primordial, that is, situated deeply within or around persons so that people had little choice but to act in certain ways.

The postmodern turn deconstructs the concept of culture by first returning agency to human beings. It is not culture that does this or that, but rather it is human beings who act. Yet, human beings in a particular place at a particular time do not just do anything nor do they act randomly. What they do is *contingent* on what is at hand in their environment. Here environment is used in the broadest sense: physical (soil, flora and fauna, water, air), social (family, neighbors, village, city block), and spiritual (ghosts, spirits, gods, God). A person is not likely to wake up one day and decide to go fishing if there is no local body of water with fish, there is no one around with expertise in fishing, and there is no appropriate ritual for fishing. What a person decides to do is contingent on the physical, social, and spiritual resources available to him or her.

Culture, then, is *constructed* out of the materials, ideas, social relations, and spiritual resources at hand. People do not do the same thing every day, but go through the day making (in a fuller sense than the way this word normally is used) a living, developing relationships,

and pursuing meaning in life. Within a society, there are still a number of choices about how to live one's life; more in some societies, fewer in others. Whether a man in the Marshall Islands decides to go fishing, build a canoe, cut copra, or plant taro, he is still a Marshallese person. Even within these categories of activities, there are a number of choices. He can fish for tuna trolling a lure through flocks of seabirds in the ocean, he can sit anchored in the lagoon and use a drop line, he can gather a group of men and boys to use a surround net, he can throw a net by himself, he can skin dive with a spear during the day or during the night, he can search for sipunculoid worms when the tide goes out on the lagoon beach, or use a number of other methods. On any given day, he may use only a small percentage of the cultural resources available to him to construct culture.

However, he is not alone. What he has in mind for the day or what he contends is the right thing to do can be *contested* by other Marshallese in his family or on the atoll or in the community of all Marshallese. He claims that the season is right for planting taro while his brother claims that the time has passed. He claims the right to gather coconuts on a particular piece of land, but a neighbor counters that he has no such right. He claims ties to the land through his adoptive mother, but the neighbor claims that a chief gave that land to his lineage. He decides that there are better economic opportunities in the capital, but a cousin who just returned from the capital says that all the good jobs have already been taken by the people who live there. Every step of the way there are alternatives, and others will construct culture in ways that suit them.

This constructivist view of culture does not replace the more traditional view, but it does add a new perspective and some additional questions about why people do the things that they do. If culture is powerful, and it is when it directs what people see as possible, it is also *contingent* on the materials at hand, *constructed* on a daily basis, and *contested* by others in the same society.[40] It is important to learn culture but also to avoid essentializing culture as if everyone agreed. It is important to discover where the disagreements are, what people's hopes are, and where there are opportunities for the gospel.

---

40. See Rynkiewich, "World in My Parish."

Gospel and Culture

H. Richard Niebuhr's *Christ and Culture* is the classic representation of a persistent concern for Christians: What is the relationship between Christ and culture? What is the appropriate place for Christ in my life and what is the appropriate place for culture? Niebuhr framed the issue in several ways: Christ and culture in opposition, Christ as the converter of culture, Christ in tension with culture, Christ as the fulfillment of culture, and Christ in agreement with culture.

Many people read Niebuhr as if they had to make a choice among these ideal types, but Niebuhr was more descriptive than prescriptive. D. A. Carson reminds us that there is some biblical support and, thus, some truth in all of these perspectives.[41] Kenneth Cauthen argues that Jesus was shaped by culture and ministered in culture, otherwise he would not be human; so the dichotomy is false or lacking in this sense.[42] There is no "culture-less Christ" and thus no clear opposition to human culture. The Gospels present Christ-in-culture (he lived, spoke, and made friends the way people in first-century Palestine did), but also show the reader Christ-against-culture in some ways ("Woe to you . . .") and Christ-in-agreement-with-culture in other ways ("Blessed are you when . . .").

Menuge argues that the notion of separating oneself from culture is idealistic, does not consider the reality of sin, and thus asks the impossible.[43] This reflects his Lutheran view of the persistence of original sin and the necessity of settling for a dual life. Menuge also critiques Niebuhr for not clarifying when one type or another is applicable.

Yoder argues that Niebuhr's equation of "culture" with "the world" is unwarranted. "(W)hen the New Testament speaks of 'world' it precisely does not mean all of culture. It means rather culture as self-glorifying or culture as autonomous . . ."[44] For example, when Paul says, "Put to death, therefore, whatever in you is earthly,"[45] he goes ahead and defines "earthly" not as everything in this world, but as "fornication, impurity, passion, evil desire and greed (which is idolatry)."

41. Carson, *Christ and Culture Revisited.*
42. Cauthen, "H. Richard Niebuhr Revisited and Revised."
43. Menuge, "Niebuhr's *Christ and Culture* Reexamined."
44. Yoder, "How H. Richard Niebuhr Reasoned," 70.
45. Col 3:5.

Remember that there is culture in the Bible too. In fact, we do not have a pure gospel anywhere. The gospel only comes to us wrapped in culture, or, as Kraft says, *"God-Above-but-Through-Culture"*[46] The question then is: Whose culture? That question looks like it was settled in Acts 15 when the Gentiles asked, "Do we have to become Jews in order to become Christians? Do we have to learn Hebrew language, learn Jewish rituals, think in Jewish cultural terms?" The answer at that time, after much debate, was a qualified "no." However, that question has continued to haunt us down through the ages.

Table 9. A Quick Quiz on Biblical Behavior. Do you . . . ?

1. Greet one another with a holy kiss.
2. Settle disputes out of court.
3. Share all goods equally.
4. Abstain from eating blood.
5. Use only real wine and unleaven bread for communion.
6. Anoint people with oil for healing.
7. Refuse to braid your hair or wear pearls or gold (if you are a woman).
8. Refuse to have long hair (if you are a man).
9. Treat your slaves well.
10. Drink wine for an upset stomach.

Contextualization of the Gospel

Contextualization is, in some ways, the opposite of ethnocentrism. The process recognizes up front that people must be able to understand the gospel in order to consider the claims of Jesus Christ. For the Holy Spirit to invite people to faith in Jesus, the gospel must be communicated in symbols, metaphors, words, and deeds that convey God's intentions to a local population. Every culture, indeed every generation, deserves a fresh reading of the gospel in their language and the context of their culture.

The theological basis for contextualization is the incarnation. As Paul says in Philippians 2:5–11, the second person of the Trinity did not claim the privileges of position but "emptied"[47] himself. He travelled to the place of mission, arrived in a non-threatening manner,

---

46. Kraft, *Christianity in Culture*, 113.

47. *Ekenōsen* in Greek, and that is why this is called the "Kenosis Passage."

and labored for 30 years to learn the language, find his place in the society, and imbibe the culture before he began to teach and heal. When he did, he was able to call on proverbs, metaphors, similes, stories, and histories to speak to the people's contemporary social, economic, and spiritual condition in words and deeds that they could understand. In this, Jesus is our example even though we are less than perfect in our practices.

Compare this with a twenty-first-century Christian disciple who fills himself up, expects people to come to him, takes no time to learn people's language and culture, does not work to earn a place for himself in their society, and does not listen to the stories of the people in order to speak to their needs. He has all the answers to questions no one is asking.

Contextualization of God's mission has a long history, even in the Old Testament. God spoke with Adam and Eve, even walking in the garden with them, and dealt with them in ways that they could understand. God spoke with Abram and Sarai, then Isaac, then Jacob, all in ways that they could understand. As God formed Israel, he had some special things in mind for them, and did not want them to be like other people, in some ways. In other ways, they could not help but be like other people, else they would not have understood God. Hebrew places of worship looked like Canaanite places of worship, not like Mesopotamian places of worship. The big difference was a commitment to a universal God who could not be represented in images made by mankind.

Contextualization in the New Testament is more obvious. Dean Flemming has done a masterful job of revealing not only shifting metaphors for who Christ is and what salvation means, but also reveals the use of different rhetorical styles for different audiences.[48] It is clear, for example, that there are four Gospels because four authors were writing to four different audiences and had different practical and theological agendas. The author of the Gospel according to John speaks to a Greek audience that was familiar with contemporary philosophical work on the priority of the divine word. Knowing that this was what some Greeks were searching for, the author claims, "Jesus is the Logos." A Hebrew audience reading this would wonder why John did not just say, "Jesus is the Messiah," but the problem with this was

---

48. Flemming, *Contextualization in the New Testament.*

that a Greek audience did not necessarily know what a Messiah was and was not looking for a Messiah, so the claim meant little to them.

The development of the Greek term *kyrios* likewise shows an attempt to contextualize the gospel for a new audience. *Kyrios* is a multivocal word, having different but related meanings in different contexts. It could mean "teacher," as a substitute for rabbi. It could mean "master" in recognition of an unequal social relationship. It could refer to the emperor, and, as such, was a dangerous claim about allegiance. Finally, it was also a religious concept brought from the East by Greek soldiers and traders in the three hundred years after Alexander. In this context, *kyrios* applies to a particular god or goddess to whom one wants to devote himself or herself. Thus, the declaration that "Mithra is Lord" or "Serapis is Lord" meant that the devotee wanted to have a particular relationship to that god or goddess. It was a bold claim, then, for the disciples to say, "Jesus is Lord, Jesus is the Lord that you are looking for."

The letter to the Colossians provides another example, although there are many more. The primary message of the letter is that "the fullness [*pleroma*] of God is in Jesus Christ" and "the fullness [*pleroma*] of Jesus Christ is directly available to you." What few recognize is that *pleroma* was a technical term as used in the first century and takes full shape in the second century AD in a system of thought called Gnosticism. The theology of Gnosticism posited an unmoving God at the center of all things. As God thought wonderful thoughts, shells or *eons* were formed around him: Wisdom, Beauty, etc. One time God began a thought, but then aborted it. That accounts for the shell called Matter. The challenge to the believer in this system is to break through the shells to reach the fullness of God, the *pleroma*. Paul speaks directly to these people when he says that the *pleroma* of God is in Jesus Christ and thus is directly available to you. Paul saw that the cosmic significance of Jesus' birth, teachings, death, and resurrection was much greater than fulfilling the needs of the one group of people, the Jews. He told the emerging Gnostics that Jesus fulfilled their needs as well. "Jesus is the Pleroma, Jesus is the Pleroma that you are looking for."[49]

The problem seems to arise when Christianity gets stuck in a particular culture so long that the church forgets that the forms that it uses to identify Jesus Christ are not universal and thus not appropriate for

---

49. See Allmen, "Birth of Theology"; and Walls, "Old Athens and New Jerusalem."

other cultures, and perhaps not even appropriate for the church's own youngest generations. Some Jewish Christians tried to keep the new faith in Christ as the Messiah in the old wineskins of Jewish culture, but the Jerusalem council made a courageous decision to release Jesus to Greco-Roman culture. Greco-Romans eventually forgot that Jesus came in their concepts for them but these hard-won understandings did not answer other people's deepest needs. The Germans and the English had to ask, "Do we have to become Greco-Romans in thought and behavior in order to become Christians?" At first, the answer, just as at the Jerusalem council, was "no." For example, Pope Gregory the Great instructed Augustine to observe the rites of the various local churches and choose the best for inclusion into worship.[50]

> My brother, you know the customs of the Roman Church in which, of course, you were brought up. But, it is my wish that if you have found any customs in the Roman or the Gaulish church or any other church which may be more pleasing to Almighty God, you should make a careful selection of them and sedulously teach the Church of the English, which is still new in the faith, what you have been able to gather from the other churches. For things are not to be loved for the sake of a place, but places are to be loved for the sake of their good things. Therefore, choose from every individual church whatever things are devout, religious and right. And when you have collected these as it were into one bundle, see that the minds of the English grow accustomed to it.

Later, the church at Rome decided that Roman theology and Roman rites must be followed.[51] When missionaries left Europe for Asia, Africa, and the Americas, they once again brought the gospel wrapped in their own culture. Native Americans had to ask, "Why should we exchange our own sinful culture for someone else's sinful culture?"[52]

The question remains: How can the next group of people (culture, generation) best hear the gospel so that they have a fair chance of responding?[53]

---

50. Recorded in the Venerable Bede's *Ecclesiastical History of the English People*, book 1, ch. 27.

51. See Hunter, *Celtic Way of Evangelism*.

52. Twiss, *One Church, Many Tribes*, 79.

53. For a helpful account of current contextualization issues, see Whiteman, "Contextualization."

3

Language, Symbols, and Cross-Cultural Communication

These are the descendants of Japheth in their lands, with their own language, by their families, in their nations. . . . These are the descendants of Ham, by their families, their languages, their lands, and their nations. . . . These are the descendants of Shem, by their families, their languages, their lands, and their nations. (Genesis 10:5, 20, 31)

Language and Culture

THERE IS NO END TO THE CLAIMS THAT ONE THING OR AN-other actually makes us human. However, those who say that it is the *use of symbols* that makes us human do have a compelling argument. While some of this capacity may be shared, no animal uses signs and symbols to create complex layers of meaning the way humans do (or, at least, we do not think they do). Communication, itself, has many layers, from spoken words to facial expressions, body distance, body posture, movement, and gestures. All are part of an interpretative dance in which two or more people create, dissolve, and recreate meaning. Further layers are added with the use of media that separate symbols from the person in disembodied forms of printing and recording.

The study of language and communication by anthropologists developed out of the European tradition of linguistics, which usually

is associated with disciplines in the classics and humanities departments of universities. However, the concerns of anthropologists were primarily with the diversity of languages that they were encountering in the world, not just Indo-European languages, and the necessity of learning local languages that had not been reduced to writing in order to do good ethnographic fieldwork. For most of the world's languages at the end of the nineteenth century, very little historical and comparative work had been done because the basic descriptive work on phonemics and syntax had not been done. Anthropologists began to apply to unwritten languages the same methods that helped describe and compare Indo-European languages, thus creating the fields of historical linguistics and descriptive linguistics as applied to non-Indo-European languages. As anthropologists studied the relationship between language and thinking (cognition), as well as the relationship between language and behaving, the fields of ethnolinguistics and sociolinguistics developed.

The Greeks, particularly Plato and Aristotle, recognized early on the difference between the signs that are found in nature and those signs that are created by and recognized by humans. The latter, called "conventional signs," or publically agreed-upon signs, were declared by St. Augustine to be more significant for an understanding of communication and for the development of theology and philosophy. By the end of the Middle Ages, a further distinction had been made between spoken words and mental categories.

However, it was Ferdinand de Saussure (1857–1913) who named the physical sign (sound waves hitting the ear or the marks on a piece of paper), the "signifier," and the mental image or concept, the "signified," and then made the claim that the relationship between the signified and the signifier is an arbitrary one. Further, he claimed that both sides of the sign, the symbol and the concept, are separable from the actual thing itself. The European linguistic tradition had searched for the origin of language in some natural connection between an exclamation, such as "Wolf!," and the mental image of a wolf, but Saussure said that there was none. In addition, both the exclamation and the mental image have an arbitrary relationship with the living, breathing wolf itself.

There is no reason that, when someone says "Wolf!," listeners should conjure up the image of a wolf, except when the speaker and

listener are both members of a linguistic community that has agreed about the connection. If the speech community were in Spain, both speaker and listener would agree that the cry "Lobo!" will communicate. The connection is arbitrary and yet, within a particular group, the sum total of what the speech community agrees on becomes a system of signs that seems very real. That is, for indigenous speakers, the connection is not exactly arbitrary because it is learned from birth. This system Saussure called *langue* (Saussure was a French-speaking Swiss), while language in use (speech acts) he called *parole*. Speakers in actual situations make choices about sounds and words that can be slotted into particular places in the structure of an utterance, and they do this by making selections from the existing system.

People who spend their lives in one speech community tend to think that there is a natural connection between, for instance, the word *bird*, the mental image of a bird, and the physical bird itself. However, even within the same language family, different root words may be selected that over time develop into different concepts. As close as German and English are, if an Englishman and a German observe an animal flying, one will say "bird" and the other will say "*Vogel*." A Lithuanian standing with them might say "*paukštis.*" All three are Indo-European languages, but these three words have different roots. If, for some reason, a person from the Highlands of New Guinea who speaks Karam, which is not an Indo-European language but rather is in the non-Austronesian family,[1] were standing there with them, he might point and say "*yakt.*[2]"

All of these words are connected arbitrarily to the mental image of a bird and to the actual bird that is passing by. Further, not only are the words different, the items that properly fit in the category, as well as the characteristics that define the category, also differ. That is, the constellation of meanings associated with these concepts do not overlap completely. If these four people were standing in the forest in Papua New Guinea and a cassowary[3] walked into view, the three

1. Austronesian is a widespread language family encompassing the languages of the Philippines, most of Malaysia, most of Indonesia, Madagascar, half of Melanesia, and all of Polynesia and Micronesia, with a few representatives in Taiwan (thought to be the origin of this family), Vietnam, Cambodia, and Thailand.

2. Bulmer, "Why Is the Cassowary Not a Bird?"

3. A large flightless bird, one of four left in the world along with emus (Australia), rheas (South America), and ostriches (Africa).

Europeans, steeped in the Linnaean system of classifying animals, would apply the generic term *bird* to the cassowary, but the Karam man would not. The cassowary does not fit into the category of *yakt*. He would see something different and say instead "*kobtiy.*" This particular word is also a classificatory term, but the category it designates lumps together human beings and cassowaries. Of course, the Karam do not see this as lumping together two things that do not go together; it is the European language speakers who wonder what he is talking about.

Ralph Bulmer (1928–1988) wrote what is now a classic article whose title states the question: "Why Is a Cassowary Not a Bird?" On the surface, the Karam put humans in the same category because a cassowary walks upright, as human beings do. A little deeper meaning is that cassowaries are dangerous; they can kill a man, as can other men. A little deeper meaning yet identifies cassowaries with relatives, particularly with affines.[4] A still deeper layer of meaning identifies cassowaries with those outside the village, as opposed to consanguineal[5] relatives, particularly agnates,[6] who belong to the village. Then it gets even more complex concerning who can hunt cassowaries, how they may be killed properly, and where they may be eaten.[7] None of these meanings are applied to the category *yakt* but only to the category *kobtiy*.

The linguistic domain of *yakt*, then, is not the same as the linguistic domain of *bird*, nor *Vogel*, nor *paukštis*, nor are any of these exactly like the others. Germans, after all, do not "flip the *Vogel.*" It turns out that the category of *yakt* includes flying birds and bats, but does not include cassowaries. The layers of meaning around *yakt* and *kobtiy* are not the same as those surrounding *bird* and *cassowary* in English, nor *Vogel* and *Kasuar* in German. If this is true about things we can see, then how much more is it true of things that we cannot see, such as spirits, viruses, and love?

---

4. Affines are relatives by marriage.

5. Consanguineal means "related by blood."

6. An agnate is a relative on a person's father's side of the family.

7. Please read Bulmer's article for rich detail.

Language Acquisition

It has been a commonplace observation that children seem to learn languages easier and quicker than adults do. Recent research gives some weight to this folk belief.[8] Older theories argued either that language or the categories for language are innate, as Noam Chomsky claimed, or that language is completely a learned faculty based on stimulus and response, as B. F. Skinner claimed. It turns out that there are not innate categories, but rather built-in abilities to categorize sounds, recognize boundaries between phonemes, and mimic stress and intonation patterns characteristic of any language.

In the model based on the most recent research, as presented by Kuhl et al., infants in the first six months of life are able to discriminate all of the phonetic distinctions that are made in human languages. From six to twelve months there is an increase in the infant's ability to perceive distinctions that produce vowels and consonants appropriate to one's native language (the language the baby hears constantly). In other words, the child is actively learning what is important as a native speaker and, at the same time, is slowly losing the ability to distinguish phonemes that are not recognized by their parents.

The differences that are recognized begin to shape the brain; that is, repeated recognition and use of these distinctions tends to build up some connections and allow other connections to wither. Certain sounds are linked into tight networks of sounds, and those are distanced from other sounds that are distinct in the language being learned. The process is well on its way by nine months and nearly complete by five years. Once this happens, it is not impossible, but certainly becomes difficult, to learn a new language because the brain is now wired for the peculiarities of the first language. The emphasis on the "heart language" by SIL/Wycliffe Bible Translators and others is correct, although perhaps one's "mother tongue" should be called instead one's "brain language."

This means that not only is the child learning its first language, it is creating a particular "architecture" in the brain so that reality is perceived in a particular way. The child has gone from a universal ability to a particular expertise, and that expertise has shaped the brain. It takes a lot of learning for mature Japanese speakers to hear the difference between an [r] and an [l]. It takes a lot of learning for a mature

8. The following discussion is based on Kuhl et al., "Phonetic Learning."

English speaker to hear the difference between an [l] and an [ł].[9] And, this applies not just to language, but also to the problem of new categories of wider experience as well, and gives support to the claim that linguistic categories really do help shape people's reality.

Languages in the World

The biblical story of the dispersion of languages and peoples because of the pride of the builders of the tower at Babel, though it did give us the English word for talking nonsense, is not the only story about languages in the Bible. Earlier, God invited Adam to name the animals "to see what he would call them,"[10] and in the process, language became a gift for humankind to use. Before the Babel story, the text describes the separation of peoples according to geographical area, ecological adaptation, and diversity of languages.[11] Anthropologists observe the same thing: There are people indigenous to a place who are adapted to their environment, linked by their concepts and assumptions (local knowledge embedded in local language), and organized according to local notions of family and polity.

At the time that Columbus sailed from Europe to America, it is estimated that there were well over 10,000 languages in the world. Linguists now estimate the number of separate languages at just under 7,000 and dwindling fast.[12] Of course, the size of the linguistic communities varies considerably. There are nearly a billion Mandarin Chinese speakers, but only 250 speakers of Mamaindě, who live in four villages between the Cabixi and Pardo Rivers in the state of Mato Grosso in western Brazil.[13] While the Ethnologue, a project supported

9. This [ł] is a lateral [l], technically a voiced fricative alveolar lateral. The point of contact, as with the [l] that Americans do pronounce, is the tip of the tongue with the ridge of bone just behind the upper front teeth. The sound is voiced, that is, there are vibrations, such as the one Americans recognize in the difference between [p] (unvoiced) and [b] (voiced). However, the voicing is done with the sides of the tongue, not the tip. See Smalley, *Manual of Articulatory Phonetics*, 217–31.

10. Gen 2:19–20.

11. Genesis 10. This has led some commentators to reread the Babel story as a narrative of empire; that is, that the movement in the text from many languages (ch. 10) to one language (ch. 11) reflects the rise of a centralized power that forces people to speak one language.

12. The Ethnologue claims that there are 6,906 existing languages (see http://www.ethnologue.com)

13. Eberhard, *Mamaindě Grammar*, 9–14.

by SIL/Wycliffe, identifies 116 language families in the world, it also notes that just six of those language families contain 66 percent of all the languages in the world and 83 percent of all the speakers in the world (that is, over four-fifths of the total population of the world).[14] That means that the remaining third of the world's languages are divided into 100 families of languages that are spoken by only about a fifth of all the world's speakers (and signers).

These data point to a number of "endangered languages," communities that contain too few speakers to pass along the richness of the language to the next generation and/or are losing out in competition to more dominant or national languages. There are about 500 languages in the world now classified as "nearly extinct."[15]

Sometimes this is the result of an intentional national policy, as when the United States government forced Native American children into government-run and/or mission-run boarding schools, forbade the children to speak their native tongue, and forced them to speak, read, and write in English.[16] In fact, in the United States, 73 languages are listed as "nearly extinct." Another 19 in Canada, 8 in Mexico, and 7 elsewhere in Central America are classified as "nearly extinct," bringing the North American total to 107 languages that are "nearly extinct," a condition that is primarily the result of colonial practices carried out by European immigrants. Similar colonial practices in Australia have brought 97 Aboriginal languages to the brink of extinction as well.

Sometimes the community seems to have more agency, and it decides for itself, or is lured into deciding, to abandon its own language. For example, the youngest generation of Mamaindě speakers prefers to learn Portuguese, read Portuguese, and sing Brazilian songs in Portuguese, as well as live in Brazilian cities.[17] Overall, there are 37 languages in Brazil that are "nearly extinct." The dominance of a few languages in the area of advanced technology is the most recent in a series of forces that pressure people into abandoning their mother tongue for English, Spanish, or Mandarin Chinese.

14. Http://www.ethnologue.com/ethno_docs/distribution.asp?by=family.

15. Http://www.ethnologue.com/nearly_extinct.asp.

16. Adams, *Education for Extinction*.

17. Eberhard, *Mamaindě Grammar*, 32–36.

Table 10. Top Twenty Languages by Population[18]

Language	Home Region	Number of Speakers
Mandarin Chinese	China	845,000,000
Spanish	Spain	329,000,000
English	England	328,000,000
Arabic	Middle East	221,000,000
Hindi	India	182,000,000
Bengali	India	181,000,000
Portuguese	Portugal	178,000,000
Russian	Russia	144,000,000
Japanese	Japan	122,000,000
German	Germany	90,000,000
Javanese	Indonesia	85,000,000
Lahnda	Pakistan	78,000,000
Telegu	India	70,000,000
Vietnamese	Vietnam	69,000,000
Marathi	India	68,000,000
French	France	68,000,000
Korean	Korea	66,000,000
Tamil	India	66,000,000
Italian	Italy	62,000,000
Urdu	India	61,000,000
Top Twenty Languages. . .	*Spoken by a total of. . .*	*3,313,000,000*

Nearly half the world's population belongs to the 20 largest language communities. Of course, English as a general category is not the same as English in a local context. I was travelling down a road in Papua New Guinea when I read a sign on a store that read, "Children, we have rubbers now!" I wish I had taken a picture because this illustrates regional variations in language use. "Rubbers" in Australian/ Papua New Guinean English refers to what American English speakers call "erasers." Such variations exist within a country as well. In fact, there are only regional dialects of English; there is no standard English, contrary to what you were taught in school. I have lived in three locations in the US: rural southwestern Indiana; Pittsburgh, Pennsylvania; and St. Paul, Minnesota. The elastic loop that expands to hold something together is called a "rubber band" in southern Indiana, a "gum band" in Pittsburgh, and a "rubber binder" in the Twin Cities.

18. Adapted from the Ethnologue, but rounded to whole millions (see http:// www.ethnologue.com).

Class Exercise

Find out what people from different regions of the US call the sweet carbonated beverages that are so popular in America: pop, soda, sody, soda pop, or coke. Yes, "coke." In some parts of the country, a person may say, "I'll have a coke," and the waitress will say, "What kind of coke?," and neither one necessarily means the Coca-Cola® brand of soft drink.

Comparative and Historical Linguistics

Although Saussure dismissed the diachronic study of language because he thought that it could not be systematic, in fact the comparative study of languages would lead to the discovery that not every change is possible. Changes in sounds, in words, in grammar, and in meaning do occur in patterns. Linguist Roman Jakobson demonstrated in his study of the relationship between Russian and other Slavic languages that languages have a history "governed by internal laws, and not as a fortuitous agglomerate."[19] For example, in the Polynesian family of languages, there are regular shifts from [t] to [k] and from [b] to [p]. Thus, the Tahitian word for a restriction on behavior is *tabu*,[20] but in Hawaii one will notice that "no trespassing" signs read "*Kapu!*" This, and a thousand other points of comparison in addition to phoneme shifts, shows that the Hawaiian language is descended from an Eastern Polynesian forbear closely related to Tahitian, and that both are more distantly related to Central Polynesian languages such as Samoan and Tongan.

The Brothers Grimm, well known for their collections of folk fairy tales, were primarily interested in historical linguistics. They identified regular shifts from Proto Indo-European to Proto Germanic, and this was later formulated as "Grimm's Law." For example, Sanskrit, classical Greek, Latin, and Lithuanian[21] all have a word for foot that begins with [p], while German and English have similar words that begin with [f].[22]

19. Jakobson, "Remarks on the Phonological Evolution of Russian," 7.

20. Which has come over into English as "taboo."

21. Lithuanian is the oldest spoken Indo-European language and is related to Sanskrit and classical Greek, which are represented by written texts only.

22. Campbell, *Historical Linguistics*, 49.

Table 11. Sound Shifts in the Indo-European Language Family[23]

Sanskrit	Pāda	German	Fuss
Lithuanian	Pėda	English	Foot
Greek	Πούς	Swedish	Fot
Latin	Pēs	Dutch	Voet

While several scholars and dilettantes proposed relationships among European languages in the 1700s,[24] Sir William Jones (1746–1794), a British judge appointed to Calcutta, first published the claim concerning the relationship between Sanskrit, Greek, and Latin.[25] He assumed the evolution of languages, that is, descent with modification from an original early language. His comparative work was the basis for the idea of language families. Later authors developed the notion of the Indo-European language family to include most of the languages of Europe as well as languages in Iran and India, and the theory of linguistic change from a proto-Indo-European ancestor that gave birth to ancient languages, such as Old-Germanic, which became the sources of contemporary languages.

Table 12. The Twenty-Third Psalm in English through Time[26]

Old English	Drihten me ret, ne byth me nanes godes wan. And he me geset on swythe good feohland. And fedde me be waetera stathum.
Middle English	Our Lord gouerneth me, and nothing shal defailen to me. In the sted of pasture he sett me ther. He norissed me upon water of fyllyng.
Early Modern English	The Lord is my shepherd, I shall not want. He maketh me to lie down in green pastures. He leadeth me beside the still waters.
Modern English (NRSV)	The Lord is my shepherd, I shall not want. He makes me lie down in green pastures; he leads me beside still waters.

Later work by anthropological linguists has explored the relationships among languages on all the inhabited continents. Several anthropological linguists refined the methods of comparing languages. Morris Swadesh (1909–1967) in the 1950s worked out a method called "lexicostatistics" where a list of around two hundred common words is used to measure the degree of relationship of two or more

23. Adapted from ibid.

24. For example, Parsons, *Remains of Japhet*.

25. Jones, *Sanscrit Language*.

26. Adapted from Mallory, *In Search of the Indo-Europeans*, 22.

languages. Isidore Dyen (1913–2008), using the established rate of change in Indo-European language studies, which is approximately 20 percent every thousand years, attempted to apply a time factor to the relationships in an approach called "glottochronology."

Descriptive Linguistics

While there is a long history of the study of grammar among certain Indo-European languages, as any student of Latin and Greek will tell you, most of the world's languages were yet to be described at the beginning of the twentieth century. Anthropological linguists and Bible translators, among others, developed ways of analyzing and describing the sound systems and the grammatical systems of languages previously unknown to Europeans.

The researcher begins by making a phonetic analysis that involves isolating every sound made in speech. The sounds made by English speakers, for example, constitute only a small section of the range of human sounds. A variety of clicks made by smacking the tongue against the front, side or back of the mouth serve as consonants. One click resembles the sound that American English speakers make when they cluck, "tsk, tsk." Even the closing of the glottis at the back of the throat may serve as a consonant. This is the sound that American English speakers make when they say, "Oh, oh!" The glottis closes before each "oh." Sounds may be made by inhaling air, by not moving much air at all, or by exhaling air even to the point of an explosive rush of air. Try saying "ana" and "afa" slowly and feel the difference in the flow of air. Sounds may vary as well by whether they are voiced or voiceless. Try saying "apa" and "aba" slowly and feel the difference in the vibration of the lips.

When the phonetic analysis is complete, the researcher moves on to a phonemic analysis. Humans make many sounds in speech, but not all of those sounds signal a difference in meaning to the speaker. The researcher works toward a shorter list of phonemes, which are the minimal units of meaning in a language. Thus, "we may define a phoneme as a minimum feature of the expression system of a spoken language by which one thing that may be said is distinguished from any other thing which might have been said."[27]

---

27. Gleason, *Introduction to Descriptive Linguistics*, 9.

A non-English speaker doing descriptive linguistics in America may have identified two sounds. She hears people saying [b] and [p], but does not know whether or not the distinction is meaningful. By finding two words that place the consonants in similar environments, the researcher can discover that English speakers do distinguish "bet" from "pet" and "bat" from "pat." Since the only difference is between [b] and [p]; they are phonemes, or meaningful sounds, in English. Not everyone in the world hears this difference or, another way of saying it, not everyone in the world assigns meaning to the distinction.

On the other hand, English speakers do not distinguish "/ʔand/"[28] from "/and/." The first involves a hard glottal stop at the beginning, and the second can be made by pausing in conversation, taking a deep breath and, with a sigh, starting a column of air in order to say /and/ without beginning with a glottal stop. The word with a glottal stop (the usual way that it is said) and without a glottal stop still means the same thing. This is not true in Hawaiian, where a glottal stop serves as a consonant. You may have noticed that the state name has changed from Hawaii to Hawai'i in recent years and should be pronounced with a bit of a hiccup between the two i's.[29]

Phonemes can range from 15 to 100 in a language. James and Anne Henderson report that the Yele language spoken on Rossel Island at the eastern end of Papua New Guinea has over 95 phonemes, including explosive varieties that sound like a sneeze.[30]

The next step for the researcher is to move to higher-level structures—what in English might be called words, phrases, and sentences. While a phoneme is the smallest unit of sound that makes a meaningful distinction to native speakers, a morpheme is the smallest unit in the structure of a language.[31] Thus, the English word "running" contains several phonemes, but just two morphemes: "run" and "ing."

28. In the International Phonetic Alphabet, this sign [ʔ] indicates a glottal stop. It is not used in written English because a glottal stop is not a consonant in English. However, in some languages, like Hawaiian, that are written in English characters, an apostrophe has come to represent a glottal stop.

29. Perhaps the most famous use of the glottal stop is in the name of the small reef fish, the *humuhumunukunukuapaʻa*. This word shows also the CV (consonant-vowel-consonant-vowel) structure of Hawaiian words, and the importance of reduplication.

30. Jim and Anne Henderson, personal communication, 1998. See Henderson and Henderson, "Yele," as well as idem, *Rossel Language*.

31. Gleason, *Introduction to Descriptive Linguistics*, 52–53.

Only "run" can stand alone, but both may be joined with other morphemes, following the rules of grammar, to make other compounds, such as "overrun" and "walking." These may be combined, following the rules of syntax, to form phrases and sentences.

However, the terms *phrase* and *sentence* may not be appropriate for all languages. Some languages, called polysynthetic or agglutinative, tend to keep adding suffixes to root words until the meaning is complete. For example, consider the Mamaindě "word" *daongayeyekso'geuhgidaleknanwa*, which is pronounced "da-onga-yeyek-so'geuh-gi-da-lek-nan-wa." The morphemes are, in English, "cause-do-ugly-probably-for." The "word" or "sentence" means, "He probably caused me to do something bad awhile back."[32]

The work of descriptive linguistics is long and tedious, but necessary for both anthropologist and missionary. SIL/Wycliffe Bible Translators typically take twenty years from beginning to learn an unwritten and undescribed language to having a full New Testament translation in hand.[33] The early anthropologist Bronislaw Malinowski printed texts in his ethnography, and this practice has been followed by many.[34]

Linguistic Relativity

The relationship between language and cognition (thought) has been a subject of philosophical and linguistic interest for several centuries. At issue here is the nature of reality, or rather the human ability to experience reality then represent and communicate that experience to another. When we strike our hand on the wall, there appears to be no difference between our experience and reality. However, if later we tell someone about it, then the experience is mediated by language and/or thought, and then the connection with reality is not direct.[35]

32. David Eberhard, personal communication, 2004.

33. Bill and Sandra Callister arrived on Misima Island in Milne Bay in 1978 to work on Misiman. In 1998, I was privileged to witness a triumphant parade as copies of the New Testament in Misiman, the *Bateli Vavaluna*, were carried on the shoulders of the elders down the road to the church, with villagers and visitors dancing alongside. Following SIL tradition, neither their names nor the names of the local translation committee appear in the book.

34. Malinowski, *Argonauts of the Western Pacific*.

35. The argument could be made that there is a difference between our hand hitting the wall and our brain's immediate construction of the experience. In that case,

Edward Sapir (1884–1939) was a student of Franz Boas and followed his claim that there is no such thing as a primitive language, that is, one that is simpler, has a smaller vocabulary, and operates in a more direct fashion than metaphorical or philosophical associations. Boas sent him to study Native American languages, particularly in the Athabaskan language family. Later, Sapir had a student who had worked in industry for a number of years, Benjamin Lee Whorf. Whorf studied Hopi and began to conclude, extending his mentors' ideas, that the structure of a language has an effect on the structure of people's thought or cognition. Sapir and Whorf's ideas were summarized by their students and called the "Sapir-Whorf Hypothesis."[36] The hypothesis, if it is such, will likely never rise to the level of theory, because it proposes something nearly impossible to test.

> Human beings do not live in the objective world alone, nor alone in the world of social activity as ordinarily understood, but are very much at the mercy of the particular language which has become the medium of expression for their society. It is quite an illusion to imagine that one adjusts to reality essentially without the use of language and that language is merely an incidental means of solving specific problems of communication or reflection. The fact of the matter is that the "real world" is to a large extent unconsciously built up on the language habits of the group. No two languages are ever sufficiently similar to be considered as representing the same social reality. The worlds in which different societies live are distinct worlds, not merely the same world with different labels attached.[37]

Of course, this is a statement that concerns the absoluteness or relativity of reality as well. The hypothesis is as much about sameness as about difference. That is, language lumps together certain perceptions and experiences that would not necessarily or naturally be linked together, except that the linguistic concepts that a person uses lumps them together. So, perception, conceptualization, and cognition are linked by what they split (the categories that are created, such as trees separated from bushes, fish separated from lizards) as well as

---

the gap is there from the beginning.

36. Hoijer, "Sapir-Whorf Hypothesis."

37. Sapir, "Status of Linguistics," 69.

by what they lump (the items and experiences that are placed in the same category).

Color categories provide one of the central data sets for supporters and for critics of this view. Note from the outset that extracting color as a way of separating the sky, trees, water, plants, animals and earth in people's environments already involves lumping together things that are different. For example, why should one lump together a tree and a car just because they are both a particular hue of green? It is an American practice.

A prism breaks a beam of white light up into a rainbow. American English speakers learn at an early age the acronym "Roy G. Biv" for the seven colors red, orange, yellow, green, blue, indigo, and violet. Of course, in a rainbow, there is an unbroken range of colors with no dividing lines in reality. Other people looking at the same rainbow see three colors, four colors, or fourteen colors. What people see is not entirely relative, as there do seem to be some universal tendencies,[38] but, as it turns out, that makes color terminology not the best choice for testing this hypothesis. Other categories, such as the animal taxonomy discussed at the beginning of this section, are more telling.

Dorothy Lee argues that the structure of a language affects how people connect things and events. The Wintu, Native Americans of California, use one root word (*puq* or *poq*) to construct these:

> *Puqeda*: I just pushed a peg into the ground.
> *Olpuqal*: He is sitting on one haunch.
> *Poqorahara*: Birds are hopping along.
> *Olpoqoyabe*: There are mushrooms growing.
> *Tunpoqoypoqoya*: You walk shortskirted, stifflegged ahead of me.[39]

While we may not see it, the Wintu observer tends to stay outside the event and, rather than identifying with action, tends to talk about the shape of the activity or object. Thus, a fist holding a tent peg, a man leaning on one leg, a bird hopping, round mushrooms standing on one stem, and a person walking stiff-legged all suggest the same shape.

In another example, Lee notes the Western tendency to make patterns, to connect the dots, to see connections where there are no obvious ones. Using Malinowski's linguistic notes on Trobriand life, she observes that the language does not lead speakers to link things

38. Berlin and Kay, *Basic Color Terms.*
39. Lee, "Codifications of Reality."

or events together in patterns. When a canoe voyage is described, the narrative proceeds in punctuated phrases that are not connected. While Malinowski drew sketch maps of villages and gardens, and noted that villages were built on concentric circles, the language only refers to a village as an "aggregate of bumps" that might be better "felt" than "seen."

At higher levels of abstraction, George Lakoff has demonstrated that the use of metaphors tends to shape thought in particular ways.[40] This work, combined with the work in neuroscience and language learning cited earlier, pushes us closer to the notion that language, and even language learning, shapes the structure of the brain and thus the form of people's thinking and discourse.

Paralinguistics

Speaking is not the only way that people communicate. Just sit and watch people talking around tables in a restaurant or at a picnic and you will see much more going on than spoken words.

Edward T. Hall (1914–2009) pioneered an area of study called "proxemics," which focuses on the use of space in communication. Beginning with *The Silent Language*, Hall created and shaped the field of intercultural communication. Part of the cultural context of communicating is the distance at which people feel comfortable in conversation. Of course, it depends on what kind of conversation, as well. In general, North Americans feel comfortable in public at a conversational distance of about twenty-two inches, while Latin Americans feel comfortable at fifteen inches, and people in Middle Eastern societies feel comfortable at just under ten inches apart. One speaker moving in closer than the perceived bubble of personal space may make the other person nervous about a physical or sexual attack. There is much to learn from this book and Hall's second book, *The Hidden Dimension*.

Raymond Birdwhistell (1918–1994) pioneered an area of study called "kinesics," which focuses on the use of facial expressions and body language in communication. Persons visiting another society often find it difficult to read facial expressions and body gestures, and thus to understand fully what is being communicated. Classic cases

40. Lakoff, *Women, Fire and Dangerous Things*. See also Lakoff and Johnson, *Metaphors We Live By*.

involve the use of the American sign for "OK," which involves flashing a circle made out of the thumb and first finger. In many cultures, including many in the Pacific Islands, that is the sign for "vagina"—probably not what an American would mean by it. In conversation in the Marshall Islands, I had to learn that quickly raised and lowered eyebrows is a sign that the listener agrees with the speaker, that is, it means "yes." Quickly inhaled air, a gesture an American might use to signal surprise, means in Marshallese, "Keeping talking, I am listening." The sound of clucking that involves pulling the tongue down quickly from the aveopalatal ridge behind the upper teeth—what Americans hear as "tsk, tsk" and usually interpret as a sympathetic response, i.e., communicating agreement with the speaker—for the Marshallese it mimics the sound of sexual intercourse and may be used as an invitation for such. Again, not exactly what an American would mean by making that sound.

Among the people of New Hanover, an island on the north edge of Papua New Guinea, the lower lip may be used to point in a direction or point to an object. So, the person is not "making a face" but is responding appropriately to a question when he sticks his lip out.

Socio-Linguistics

Dell Hymes (1927–2009) pioneered an area of study that focuses not just on what is said, but on the social context of the speech act,[41] that is, who is speaking, who is listening, what their relationship is, and what their social setting is. How does discourse contribute to the creation, maintenance, and modification of political, economic, and religious relationships among people? The behavior of the speaker can be termed a "performance," and the function of the performance is construed to accomplish some social objective. Thus, speech performances can be rated by their impact.

One has only to follow another person on his or her daily rounds to catch a glimpse of this area of study. A student in seminary may wake up to talk with her husband, then, in a different tone and with different words, to her children. Next, she goes to her job, and switches from Korean to English, affecting a form of office-speak appropriate

41. See Hymes, *Language in Culture and Society*; Hymes and Gumperz, *Directions in Sociolinguistics*; Hymes, *Foundations in Sociolinguistics*; and Hymes, *Ethnography, Linguistics, Narrative Inequality*.

to being a receptionist in a dentist's office. While having lunch with an American friend, she switches to a more casual English style. In the afternoon she has a seminar, at which she uses more formal and respectful language for Dr. Rynkiewich, who understands that his Korean students cannot call him Mike. In the evening, she attends a Bible study at the Korean United Methodist Church and speaks a more formal Korean with the pastor and her husband. Thus, during the day she has spoken in a variety of social situations which required three different forms of Korean and three different forms of English.

Intercultural Communication

What we have learned about culture, perception, ethnocentrism, values, and worldview all help us communicate with people in our own society, but these same things can be barriers to cross-cultural communication. The context of communication includes many assumptions about shared understandings of history, geography, religion, politics, and economics, as well as about what makes for appropriate conversation, a reasonably convincing argument, and a proper accompanying paralinguistic performance. The wonder is not that we communicate so well, the wonder is that we communicate at all (attributed to Samuel Johnson).[42]

Summary

Communication is no longer conceived as a process for transferring information from A to B. Rather, communication is project shared by speaker and listener, an ongoing project of constructing meaning in the midst of dialogue, then deconstructing the meaning, and then building it up again. This is a *constructivist* view of communication.

Here are some questions for evangelism, ministry, and mission. For the purposes of communicating the gospel, who has to master the foreign language? Is it up to people to master the foreign language of an evangelist in order to be able to understand him or her? Or, is it up to the evangelist to master the foreign language of a people in order to communicate to them? Too many evangelists, pastors, and missionaries expect the people to whom they would minister to make the adjustment. For a missionary or a pastor, language learning is a

42. See, among others, Samovar and Porter, eds., *Intercultural Communication*.

necessary step toward being in mission, whether it is in a different society or a different generation. Learning must happen in a social context of respect for the speaker and the language. Learning involves reaching many plateaus, but also gearing up to climb the next slope.

Second, who is in a position to communicate the gospel? The constructivist project of communication only comes to maturity in a long-term relationship. Jesus was able to communicate as well as he did because he took 30 years learning the language and developing relationships in society. Though it looks like Paul is breaking new ground, and he likes to claim that he is, in fact, he goes to cities where he can find Jews speaking Aramaic and Gentiles speaking Greek; and he knows both languages well. He gets into trouble when he goes to a place that depends more on Lycaonian (Acts 14:11), and the miscommunication there nearly cost him his life (Acts 14:19).

Finally, is communication limited to language? In the case of both Jesus and Paul, their demonstration of the good news accompanies their rhetoric, and it is the combination of words and works that communicates the gospel.

4

Self, Society, and Behavior

Culture, Society, and Ecology

WHILE THE CONCEPT OF CULTURE IS ANTHROPOLOGY'S PRI-
mary contribution to the social sciences, anthropologists usually are
not cultural determinists, though that tendency exists in the subfield
of cultural anthropology. That is, most anthropologists do not believe
that culture is the only concept one needs in order to explain other
people's behavior. There is a school of anthropology, British in origin,
called social anthropology. There is another subdiscipline, with adherents in various national versions of the discipline, called cultural
ecology. A more complete model for explaining a people's way of life,
or even a multicultural community where several kinds of people are
living, would include culture, society, and ecology.

There are a number of ways of observing and explaining people's
lives. First, the cultural perspective directs the researcher to ask how
these people perceive the world around them, how they feel about the
things they see, and how they prioritize or value these things. Second,
the social perspective directs the observer to ask how these people
actually behave, and in particular, how people acquire an identity, negotiate social relations, and form groups. Society is a pattern of institutions and institutionalized behavior that has emerged at a particular
point in time. Third, culture and society emerge for a reason, so that
a people can live in a particular environment. The ecological perspective directs the questioner to consider the range and types of resources

available, the perception and use of those resources, and how people produce, distribute, and consume products from the environment. Finally, the historical perspective considers antecedents to the current cultural, social, and economic adaptations that a people have made, the patterns of change that have taken place, and the continuing effects of the past on the present for the future.

So, at base, if one wants to understand a group of people, and that is certainly an initial goal of the missionary, one would have to look at them through the lenses of culture, society, ecology, and history. While it is difficult enough to do this at one point in time, for example, a Chinese neighborhood in the city of Chiang Mai, Thailand, in the year 2015, the truth is that time does not stand still. Neither does culture.

There is no static culture, anywhere, contrary to reports in the popular press. You should be quite critical of sensational stories about a people who have not changed in 10,000 years, or who are living in the "Stone Age." Everybody changes all the time, though the rate of change differs from people to people. All people have a local history, including a variety of traditions that come from the ancestors and are deployed to shape the future. In addition, there is interaction over space. These people, whoever they are, are not completely isolated, even if they live on an island. They have had and continue to have encounters with other people marked by cooperation and conflict, and linked in a web of exchange, and thus in a network that includes the diffusion of innovations. So, although the culture, society, ecology, and history of a people constitute a local system, that system is also part of a larger system of social relations.

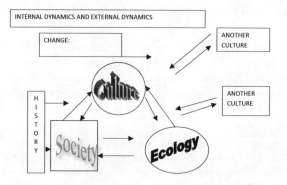

Figure 2. Causality in Anthropology (arrows show lines of influence, not determination)

Person in Culture and Society

As a Western social science, the product of the Enlightenment and its emphasis on the person as an individual, anthropology has only recently begun to examine its assumptions about what a person is or how a person is constructed in a particular society. In the past, anthropology tended to ask the same kinds of questions that the other social sciences were asking, such as: Given the existence of an individual, for example, a new born baby, how does that person grow to become a member of society? What are the developmental steps? What are the pitfalls? What happens when things go right and the person is socialized? What happens when things go wrong and the person becomes a deviant? How can the individual negotiate society's attempt to proscribe behavior and make the individual conform to society's norms? These are all good questions for Western society, but not necessarily applicable for other cultures.

Much work was done following this paradigm, particularly in the 1930s and 1940s in an anthropological school called "culture and personality." Margaret Mead (1901–1978) went off to Samoa to see if Samoan girls[1] experienced the same kind of angst over sexuality that American girls did while growing up.[2] She came back claiming that there was no *sturm und drang* during maturation because Samoan girls were free to experiment sexually. While this contributed to the sexual revolution in America, under the misguided equation, "If it is all right for them to do it, then it is all right for us to do it," it also became a hotly contested claim in anthropology.[3] Perhaps the girls were telling stories that actually had the opposite meaning. Other anthropologists studied the socialization of children, the development of a personality, and the relationship of the individual to society.[4]

1. Note: Teenager, as a social category, originated in the United States after 1900; before that there were no teenagers. Instead there were children who married and entered the labor force between 14 and 18 years of age, that is, they became adults, unless their parents were rich enough for them to pursue other interests, such as higher education.

2. Mead, *Coming of Age in Samoa*.

3. See Freeman, *Margaret Mead and Samoa*; Freeman, *Fateful Hoaxing of Margaret Mead*; Holmes, *Quest for the Real Samoa*; Shankman, "History of Samoan Sexual Conduct." There are many other articles and books on this fascinating topic.

4. For example, Benedict, "Anthropology and the Abnormal"; Erikson, *Childhood and Society*; Kluckhohn, "Influence of Psychiatry on Anthropology"; Sapir, "Why

However, the question of what a person is, and how a person is constructed in a particular society has yet to be fully probed by anthropology and is almost completely ignored in missiology. Mary Douglas declares that anthropology has "no adequate conception of the individual."[5] Kennelm Burridge attempted to distinguish the "individual" who was striving for autonomy from the "person" who was learning how to fit into society.[6] On the contrary, Marilyn Strathern, who, like Burridge, worked in Papua New Guinea, countered that "we must stop thinking that at the heart of these cultures is an antinomy between 'society' and 'the individual.'"[7]

Anthropologists have discovered that, in some societies, perhaps the majority, people assume that social relations exist prior to the person and thus persons are constructed later as a product (even a byproduct) of social relations.[8] Persons may not be conceived as being constructed of body, soul, and spirit (the modern Christian conception), but rather some combination of heart, shadow, essence, spirit, face, and a number of other characteristics that are partible (able to be detached and exchanged with others), dependent (linked to others through dyadic relationships and thus not constitutive of an independent person), and/or transformable (persons may appear in different forms, including those of an animal or spirit being).[9]

In sum, the nature of sociality, what relationships are about, and how persons are constructed is always an open question that must be pursued within the culture and society of the local people. This is the reason anthropologists work so hard to do particular ethnographic studies that do not depend on assumptions drawn from their own culture.

Personal and Social Identity

Modernist anthropology begins with the notion that an individual, that is, a person who enters society as a baby, spends the rest of his or her life negotiating relationships, linking up in networks, and forming

---

Cultural Anthropology Needs the Psychiatrist."

5. Douglas, "Cultural Bias," 5.

6. Burridge, *Someone, No One*, 5, 6, 30, 150.

7. Strathern, *Gender of the Gift*, 12, 26, 269.

8. For example, Iteanu, "Concept of the Person."

9. See Rynkiewich, "Person in Mission."

groups. Traditionally, social theory distinguishes *ascribed status*, attributed to the baby from birth, from *achieved status*, that is attributed to a person as he or she acts out a number of *roles* in *social relations* with others.

A *status* is a position in society: a mother, a doctor, a secretary, a quarterback, a pastor. A *role* is the expected behavior of a person with a certain status: a mother nourishes, a doctor cures, a secretary assists, a quarterback passes or hands off the ball, and a pastor ministers. A status is actually one pole of a dyad; that is, it is acted out toward specific other statuses: a mother nourishes a child, a doctor cures a patient, a secretary assists a manager, a quarterback throws passes to an end, and a pastor ministers to a congregation.

Of course, it is more complex than that, because a person of a particular status may relate to several others in several different ways: in a given day, a mother may feed her son, punish her a daughter, and protect a baby against the weather by dressing it properly. As a mother, she represents one child at a Parent Teachers Association meeting, signs off for medical care for another child for a field trip to the zoo, and pays for car insurance to add the oldest child to the number of drivers in the house.

Every person occupies several statuses in life over time. In American society these may include: child, teenager, college student, working adult, retired person, nursing home occupant. Other societies name statuses according to function: herdsman, warrior, elder. Every person also occupies several statuses at a given time in life: daughter, wife, mother, volunteer fireperson, office manager, youth leader, neighbor, tennis player.

Some societies are more insistent and more rigid than others in ascribing status. Status may be ascribed by age, by gender, by family affiliation, or along other lines. Some argue that the trajectory of American society has been in the direction of identifying, struggling with, and finally rejecting ascribed statuses; or at least that is the myth. The message proclaimed in such diverse venues as Disney movies and Protestant pulpits is, "You can be anything you want to be; what other people think about you will not hold you back." It is true that race, ethnicity, gender, age, and family background have been used to ascribe statuses to people, and that, one after the other, these have been resisted in American society to the point of going to court to establish

"rights." Yet, certain ascribed statuses are useful, as when children are singled out for protection from sexual predators. Whatever society you come from, there is a tendency to think that ascribed statuses are somehow innate or built into biology.

In some societies, statuses are like stages that a person moves through in life. For example, East African cattle herders, like the Lmaa, institutionalize generations by inducting boys approximately every seven years into a named *Olporror*, or age set, that is linked with the next set into *Olaji*, fourteen-year paired groups. Members of these age sets are expected to display respect and obedience toward their sponsoring elders and to continue to associate all of their lives in solidarity with their own age set. The formation of a new age set involves a process of instruction and initiation so that the young men know how to act in society. That does not mean that the system works smoothly, as the protection of one's own group always means defense against another. In addition, there is subdued resistance to the elders from the older age sets when warriors think that they are now ready to take over as elders themselves.[10]

Every society also has another class of statuses that are *achieved* or earned by persons or groups. While outsiders tend to think of a Polynesian chiefs as an inherited position, and thus ascribed, in fact, in Samoa the position is linked to a title that is owned by large family units, and particularly promising young men are selected to bear the title of a *matai*. People can claim membership in a number of named units, *aiga*, if they can trace ancestry to a title holder in that group.[11] The tradition of the title would identify the holder as an *ali'i*, "chief," or a *tulafale*, "talking chief," since in Samoan society the role of decision maker has been separated from the role of orator.

When a title holder or *matai* dies, the *aiga* meets to name a successor. The process is not a matter of simple inheritance, but rather of choosing the right person from a list of qualified candidates. The *matai* manages the family land (but may not alienate the land forever from the family), organizes labor for various social functions (the young men are organized as the *aumaga* and the young women as the *aualuma*), and represents the family in village councils.

A young *matai* told Margaret Mead:

10. Galaty, "Maasai Expansion," 80–81.

11. This is an example of a *cognatic* descent principle, a topic to be discussed later.

I have been a chief only for four years and look, my hair is grey, although in Samoa grey hair comes very slowly. . . . But always, I must act as if I were old. I must walk gravely and with measured step. I may not dance except upon most solemn occasions, neither may I play games with the young men. Old men of sixty are my companions and watch my every word, lest I make a mistake. Thirty-one people live in my household. For them I must plan, I must find them food and clothing, settle their disputes, arrange their marriages. There is no one in my whole family who dares to scold me or even to address me familiarly by my first name. It is hard to be so young and yet to be a chief.[12]

All societies have ascribed statuses and all societies have achieved statuses, but the emphasis put on each and the balance between the two varies greatly. It is part of the metanarrative of America that a person can become anything, even president of the United States. We think that there is no limit to what one can achieve. Yet, at the same time, there is a strong feeling that "it is not what you know but who you know that helps you get ahead." So, the privileges associated with ascribed status remain strong in American society, thus illustrating the difference between the *ideal* and the *real*.

Multiplex and Simplex Roles

Missionaries often assume that sociality, that is, how people are positioned in society, is the same everywhere. That is not true. In the West, people tend to have a great number of relationships, each with a different person. These relationships are likely built on a single strand: kinship, economics, religion, or politics. Thus, a person tends to have one relationship with his or her boss, another with his or her pastor, another with his or her doctor, and so on. Each relationship is rather simple and straightforward, and complications occur if one relationship spills over into another.

In other societies, people are involved in relationships with others, but often with fewer others, and the relationships are more multi-stranded and complex. A person tends to have several kinds of relationships with other persons. Thus, one person may relate to a single other person as clan member to clan leader, as patient to healer, as nephew to uncle, as warrior to war leader, and as gardener to crop

12. Mead, *Coming of Age in Samoa*, 36–37. See also Holmes, *Samoan Village*.

manager. The roles carried out by either person toward the other are multiple or multiplex.

What difference might that make to the persons? Persons who live in societies with simplex roles are able to negotiate (add, subtract, enhance, diminish) those roles without endangering their larger social support system. If the doctor does not pay enough attention to your complaints, then you may simply find a new doctor. If your pastor seems interested in adding sex to the relationship, then find a new church. If the boss expects you to attend his church, then find a new job.

The number of roles between two persons can be increased, but in the West, this often leads to *role confusion*. For example, Bob works for Roy during the week, so Roy is Bob's boss. However, on weekends they both serve in the National Guard. In the Guard, Bob is a sergeant and Roy is a corporal, so Bob has authority over Roy. Such "role reversal" may be fun once a year, e.g., for "Turn About Day," but cannot be sustained without some difficulties in the relationship.

On the other hand, people who live in societies with multiplex relations are locked into those relationships, for better or worse. There is security in a system where one's uncle takes responsibility for one's daily life by providing work, land, and protection, and secures a proper spouse. A person has a place, an advocate, and a purpose. But to the Western observer, there may be a lack of freedom in such an arrangement. Insiders might come to see things this way if their society is shifting toward the "modern world." The duties and obligations that in traditional society bind the person securely in a social network may, in an urbanizing, capitalizing, globalizing society, seem restrictive or even oppressive.

What difference might what we have just learned about the construction of persons, the ascription of statuses, and the nature of role relationships (multiplex and simplex) make to a missionary? When a missionary makes her appeal, if she listens closely enough, she might hear the classic gangster movie line, "Who do you think you're talking to?" Are the people in the audience persons in the Western sense, i.e., individuals with simplex ties to others? If so, then making a decision to turn from traditional beliefs to Christianity might be painless enough to contemplate.

At the other extreme, are the people in the audience persons in some other sense, i.e., "dividuals"[13] (dependent persons) with multiplex ties to others? If so, then decision making itself usually resides elsewhere, outside the person. Deciding to turn from traditional beliefs to Christianity might not be a matter of easily breaking a simplex tie to a disposable person or group while maintaining a number of ties to other persons and other groups. The decision may require breaking multiplex ties and thus separating from all groups, something that is never required of Western converts.

Perceiving this difficulty dimly, some missionaries in the past tried to create new villages or towns where only converts lived in order to pluck the convert out of his or her society and create a new "Christian" society. Jonathan Edwards's "praying villages" among Native Americans is an example. Other missionaries created a mission compound that became the center of a new village that operated outside the traditional system of kinship, economics, and politics.

Missionaries from Christian Keyyser[14] in the nineteenth century to Fr. Vincent Donovan[15] in the late twentieth century have had a different vision. They claim that a proper approach to people in such societies is to present the gospel to whole sections of society: clans, villages, barrios, etc., and make an appeal for a group decision that is taken in traditional ways. Then the village, for example, as a whole decides to become Christian. While this approach grates against American concerns for individual autonomy, to other people in the world it makes a lot of sense. One still hears, on a regular basis, of an Indian caste from a particular region deciding to adopt, *en masse*, Christianity or Buddhism rather than continue to suffer their low status under Hinduism.

Honor and Shame, Sin and Guilt

In the 1960s model of anthropology, people were divided into *guilt societies* and *shame societies*. Thus, Japan was seen as an honor-and-shame society, and that posed a problem for missionaries. Europeans and Americans, on the other hand, were said to live in a sin-and-guilt

13. A term introduced by Marilyn Strathern to reference a person who exists in dependence on other persons.

14. Keysser, *People Reborn.*

15. Donovan, *Christianity Rediscovered.*

society, not a problem for missionaries, but certainly a profitable concern for psychologists whose solution was psychoanalysis.

The distinction comes from Ruth Benedict's work in *Patterns of Culture* and later in *The Chrysanthemum and the Sword*. She argued that the Japanese, and by implication Chinese and other Asian cultures, were not bothered when they did something wrong unless and until someone else discovered the fault and revealed it to the public. Then the person felt shame for the wrongdoing, a loss of face, but not guilt. As Benedict explained:

> True shame cultures rely on external sanctions for good behavior, not, as true guilt cultures do, as an internalized conviction of sin. Shame is a reaction to other people's criticism . . . it requires an audience. Guilt does not.[16]

The key characteristics were that the person was concerned with "saving face" or "maintaining face" by adopting a certain posture toward those in society who mattered most to him or her. This so affected social relations that saving face for someone else often overruled what Americans might call "doing the right thing" no matter what the consequences.

The problem that this understanding caused for missionaries may be clear. Protestant missionaries steeped in the penal substitution analogy of atonement expected to see a clear case of the consciousness of sin, that is, a conscience with the same sensitivities as a Western conscience. Missionaries assumed that without a sense of personal sin that has broken one's relationship with a personal God, the gospel offer of forgiveness fell on deaf ears. The argument that "Christ died for your sins" is not a convincing appeal for a people who feel shame at a loss of face when a particular deed is revealed but do not live in the torment of guilt for sins committed. The missionary solution to all this was to teach people that they are sinners.

The early separation of cultures into shame cultures and guilt cultures has failed under the impact of more recent research. Christopher Flanders concludes that "current empirical researchers patently reject the traditional notions that the difference between shame and guilt rests in the context of experience (e.g., a putative public-private dif-

---

16. Benedict, *Chrysanthemum and the Sword*, 223.

ference) or the types of causes (e.g., particular shame-inducing acts versus guilt-inducing acts)."[17]

Instead, guilt is the feeling one has when a rule is broken, while shame involves a failure of character. That is, either the act is wrong (guilt) or the person is wrong (shame). In the first case, the act must be corrected or paid for, and in the second, the person needs to be transformed from a failure into a success. Guilt involves behavior that requires punishment or payment, while shame involves a fundamentally defective self that requires a remaking of the self. Shame "is an inner experience of self as an unattractive social agent, under pressure to limit possible damage to self via escape or appeasement."[18]

Flanders offers a helpful reworking of *face theory*. This implicates missionaries who have failed to do the research themselves. Using a dated framework from the standard anthropological model of the 1960s, missionaries have proceeded as if there were shame cultures and guilt cultures, as if they knew the meaning of these terms, and as if a whole society could be one or the other. If they had the skills of a historian, they would have realized that, in Western culture, honor and shame dominated up until the Reformation and Enlightenment periods, and then sin and guilt eclipsed these as dominant forces in Western society as well as theology.

Flanders argues that both shame and guilt exist in every culture, though the priorities given to each vary greatly, and that all peoples concern themselves with the presentation of self or "face."

> Self-presentation is not something *some* of us do *some* of the time. The presentation in social space of symbolic information about the self is a dynamic process that is both enduring and ubiquitous. We are always encoding information about the self into our relationships. Thus, human relationality inevitably involves self-presentation.[19]

In other words, it is not possible to "just be yourself," because everyone works to present a particular version of their self, even if it is studied casualness.

17. Flanders, *About Face*, 59. I am indebted to Flanders's work for much of my discussion here of shame and guilt.

18. Gilbert, "What Is Shame?," 22. Quoted in Flanders, *About Face*, 64.

19. Flanders, *About Face*, 80.

The study of the presentation of self, or "face-work," in Western social science, comes from the school of social psychology,[20] founded on the work of George Herbert Mead (1862–1931) and the work of Erving Goffman.[21] Goffman conceived of social interaction as a drama where actors presented themselves in carefully managed ways for maximum effect. What we know of another person depends on what that person projects to us, what we think about that projection, and how we respond to that projection in sustained interaction. Face, as much as any concept of person and culture, is a socially constructed reality.

One mistake that missionaries often make is to interpret face, say in Thailand, in a context of Western notions. There are several questions that help frame this problem, such as where face comes from, where it resides, how it works, and who it serves.[22]

Table 13. A Simplified Version of Face Attributes[23]

FACE	WEST	SOUTH/EAST
Where does it come from?	Generated inside the individual	Generated in social interaction
Where does it reside?	Deep within the person (essential)	In between persons (constructed)
What is its function?	Protects individual autonomy	Promotes group cohesion
Who does it serve?	Personal values or religious commitment	Societal values and commitments
What does it create?	An independent self (individual)	An interdependent self (dividual)[A]

A. This term is not adapted from Flanders, but from the work of Marilyn Strathern cited above.

20. Mead, *Mind, Self, and Society.*

21. Goffman, "On Face-Work"; idem, *Presentation of Self in Everyday Life*; idem, *Stigma.*

22. I want to make a disclaimer here. I try not to generalize about Western and non-Western characteristics in an "us vs. them" fashion, in part because I do not like the term "non-Western" since it defines a large group, about five billion people, by what they are not. We might as well call the West the "non-East." In addition, "the East" has its own history and problems as a concept (see Edward Said, *Orientalism*). The term "Global South" is on its way in, but may just as quickly accrue unintended meanings and be on its way out.

23. Adapted from Flanders, *About Face*, 77–102.

The social institution of honor and shame is central to understanding New Testament cultures and the practices of Jesus and the early church.

> In the ancient Mediterranean as a whole, and Palestine in particular, scholars have focused upon the "honor/shame complex" as the base values (Peristiany 1965; Gilmore 1987; Malina 1993). Briefly, the honor/shame complex implies that the maintenance of honor—for one's self, one's family, and one's larger groups—is absolutely vital to life. This entails reputation, status, and sexual identity. The vocabulary of honor and shame is extensive in Hebrew, Aramaic, Greek, and Latin.[24]

And, I would claim, understanding the "honor/shame complex" is central to understanding some of the metaphors for salvation used by Jesus as represented in the Gospels, and in the writings of Paul, Peter, James, and John.

So, why would contemporary missionaries writing about face tend to evaluate it negatively, wanting to eliminate it in favor of "directness," that is, replace it with the way that they perceive that Westerners approach social relations? Flanders cites several such approaches that assume that face-work is detrimental to the spread of the gospel, and that also assume, falsely, that Westerners speak directly without resorting to the deceptive mask of face.[25] The result is that missionaries tend to offend people by damaging their face (self) and then turn around and ask them to accept Jesus' sacrifice for their sin (behavior).

This standard missionary practice of teaching people that they are sinners continues even outside of Asian cultures. Joel Robbins has recounted how the Urapmin, under the tutelage of missionaries, embarked on a journey of *Becoming Sinners*.[26] The Urapmin adopted a form of Christianity in which "people spent a lot of time talking about what bad people they were, how they were lawless and could not get along with one another and live good Christian lives."[27] When a dispute arose between different parts of the village, the people tried to settle the dispute in a traditional way by "having them exchange

---

24. Hanson and Oakman, *Palestine in the Time of Jesus*, 6.

25. See Flanders, *About Face*, 148–67, for a critique of missionary and secular social science approaches.

26. Robbins, *Becoming Sinners*.

27. Ibid., xx.

equivalent goods with each other in order to 'buy the shame' or 'buy the anger' of the other party," but the results still left the Urapmin in "moral torment."[28]

Summary

There is no one vantage point that gives us a privileged perspective to understand a people. I have argued that it takes at least a cultural perspective, a social perspective, an ecological perspective, and a historical perspective. We have discussed various construals of the person or self in society, personal and social identity, statuses and roles, the difference between simplex and multiplex roles, and the differences between societies that emphasize honor and shame and those that emphasize sin and guilt. We have only touched on some of the ways in which people are different. In the next chapter, we will examine the concept of society more closely, working out how people sort themselves into social categories and groups, and how people develop or fit into networks.

28. Ibid., xxi–xxvii.

5

Marriage, Family, and Kinship

PEOPLE IN DIFFERENT CULTURES TEND TO ORGANIZE THEM-
selves in patterned ways that give social life a distinctive look and feel.
For the most part, people are just trying to accomplish personal and
group goals. People use given rules and strategies to modify or extend
certain relationships, groups, and networks that often predate the person in society. An account of the way people visualize society is called
"social structure." An account of the outcomes of these activities for a
particular point in time is called "social organization."

One way to view social structure is to see it as a given. That is,
society is already based on certain categories of people (a set of statuses), who have a range of options in their relationships and activities
(roles). On the ground, some people in these categories actually meet
and interact or perform some task, so they form predictable groups
(family, lineage, clan, village, chiefdom). There is a certain amount of
truth to this view. After all, society comes before babies and society
persists after individuals die.

Another way to view social structure is to see it not as a given
but as something that is constantly negotiated. That is, society is a
set of imagined outcomes, each under construction, but some more
dominant (successful?) than others. In this view, more than one social
order is envisioned by the people of a particular culture.[1] The existing

1. This point was made in Edmund Leach's *Political Systems in Highland Burma*
where he described two ideals: *gumsa* and *gumlao*, roughly a polity with a centralized hierarchy and a polity with a decentralized democracy. The political history of

collection of rules, narratives, and social strategies can be deployed in ways that lead to one or another outcome, depending on the choices of agents who are cooperating and competing with one another. There is a certain amount of truth to this view as well. After all, some babies do grow up to become innovators and adapters, and societies do change, sometimes gradually and sometimes radically.

An anthropologist or missiologist must consider the weight of tradition in shaping people's behavior, but also consider that people are skilled at selecting and deploying the resources that culture provides in order to influence the form and function of relationships, groups, and networks. Both the primordialist (it was there from the beginning) and the constructivist (it was made up on the spot) perspectives are needed to help explain people's behavior.

Kinship Systems

Kinship is a system of terminology with associated rules for behavior that frames relations with certain others who are thought to be biologically linked (consanguineal relatives), or associated by marriage (affinal relatives), or linked by adoption or fosterage (adoptive kin), or associated by co-residence, joint defense, common labor, shared worship, shared food, or any other relationship that leads people to treat others "as if " they were kin (fictive kinship).

The traditional use of "brother" and "sister," sometimes modified as "brother in the Lord" or "sister in the Lord," has long been common in the church. The addition of newly created relatives may be what Jesus meant when he said, "Whoever does the will of my father in heaven is my brother, and sister, and mother."[2] Further, "And every one who has left houses or brothers or sisters or father or mother or children or lands, for my name's sake, will receive a hundredfold, and inherit eternal life."[3] Nothing seems to undermine biological relationships as much as Jesus' words about discipleship: "If any one comes to me and does not hate his own father and mother and wife and children and brothers and sisters, yes, and even his own life, he cannot be

---

the Kachin reveals an oscillation, back and forth between one ideal and the other. Americans familiar with the Republican and Democratic visions, and the oscillation of our politics toward one pole then the other, will understand.

2. Matthew 12:50; Mark 3:35.

3. Matthew 19:29; Mark 10:29–30.

my disciple."[4] But, in the rhetoric of the time, "hate" in this context implies a comparison, meaning something like "love less." It is a matter of priorities, and both are possible. After all, Jesus' own mother and aunt (mother's sister) were at the foot of the cross[5] and Jesus' brother James took a leading role in the early church.

The Apostle Paul commonly refers to fellow believers as his brothers (13 times in Romans alone), and tries to regulate behavior according to kinship principles that would apply to brothers and sisters. In fact, Paul instructs Timothy to treat older men as fathers, younger men as brothers, older women as mothers, and younger women as sisters.[6]

Paul specifically refers to the following as his brother (*adelphos*) or sister (*adelphe*) at least once.

Table 14. Paul's Use of Kinship Terminology for Non-Biological Others

Phoebe	Romans 16:1
Quartus	Romans 16:23
Sosthenes	1 Corinthians 1:1
Apollos	1 Corinthians 16:12
Timothy	2 Corinthians 1:1
Titus	2 Corinthians 2:13
Tychicus	Ephesians 6:21
Epaphroditus	Philippians 2:25
Onesimus	Colossians 4:9
Philemon	Philemon 1:7

The use of kinship terminology implies certain behavior that is expected of good brothers and sisters. A limited survey shows the following exhortations for or against certain kinds of behavior through the use of kinship terminology.

Table 15. Paul's Deployment of Kinship Terminology as a Rhetorical Device

To Avoid Immorality	1 Corinthians 5:11
To Deal with Divorce	1 Corinthians 7:15
To Offer Hospitality	2 Corinthians 8:18–24
But Not to be Exploited	1 Thessalonians 4:6

4. Luke 14:26.

5. John 19:25.

6. I Timothy 5:1-2.

The practice of using kinship terms for fellow Christians was apparently widespread in the Christian community because Peter, James, and John also employ kinship terminology to emphasize the affection and obligations of relationships and to denote the limits of proper behavior among Christians. In missionary communities, where children are away from their extended families but in face-to-face relationship with unrelated adults, the use of the terms "aunt" or "auntie" and "uncle" has been extended to other missionaries.

Kinship contributes to personal identity and establishes rules and guidelines for both informal and formal behavior. Kinship may define appropriate patterns for reciprocity and retribution, for marriage and exchange, and for residence and labor.

No kinship system has a separate term for each person, though the Sudanese system comes close. Systems extend the meaning of terms to others according to perceptions of the significance of generation, lineality, birth order, gender of the relative, gender of a connecting relative, or gender of the speaker. There are also usually separate systems for terms of reference ("My Father works at the newspaper") and terms of address ("Daddy, may I go to the park?").

Interestingly, there are only six general models for kinship terminology in the whole world. Though the terms differ, the practices of merging and splitting certain kin fall into six patterns.

Anthropologists call the predominant English-Canadian-Australian-American terminology system "Eskimo kinship."[7] In this system, one's biological mother and father are separated from parents' siblings, who are identified by gender but not by whether they are on the mother's or the father's side. So, in the first generation above "ego" (oneself), the English terms are "mother" and "father," then both father's and mother's siblings are called either "uncle" or "aunt." Siblings are separated from the children of aunts and uncles, who all are identified by the non-gendered term "cousin." So, in ego's generation, the English terms are "brother," "sister," and the inclusive "cousin."

Relatives of the grandparental generation, two generations up from ego, are identified by gender, and ego's parents' parents are identified by terms that separate them from their siblings. So, in the second

---

7. This notwithstanding that "Eskimo" is no longer the proper term for the people who live across the northern reaches of Alaska, Canada, and Greenland. Their term for themselves is *Inuit*, meaning "The People."

generation above ego, the English terms are "grandfather," "grandmother," "great uncle," and "great aunt." It is a system that should be
familiar to those who were raised in the English tradition, but will
seem unfamiliar and perhaps illogical to others.

Table 16. Eskimo Kinship Terminology, English Version

great aunt	great uncle	grandfather/ grandmother		grandmother/ grandfather	great aunt	great uncle
aunt	uncle	father		mother	aunt	uncle
cousin	cousin	brother	ego (oneself)	sister	cousin	cousin
cousin	cousin	nephew/niece	son/ daughter	niece/nephew	cousin	cousin
cousin	cousin	grandnephew/ grandniece	grandson/ granddaughter	grandniece/ grandnephew	cousin	cousin

The system foregrounds lineal relationships. Grandfather and
grandmother are separated from great aunts and great uncles. Father
and mother are separated from aunts and uncles. Brothers and sisters are separated from cousins. This creates a line of closer relatives
(grandfather, father, brother, son, grandson) and distinguishes them
from relatives who are one step removed from one's own line (great
uncle, uncle, first cousin, first cousin once removed, first cousin
twice removed).

The system is bilateral, that is, it represents both sides equally.
The line of close relatives could also be traced as grandmother, mother, sister, daughter, granddaughter. The term "grandmother" applies
to father's father as well as mother's mother, cousins on mother's side
are equivalent to cousins on father's side, and "granddaughter" applies
equally to son's daughter and daughter's daughter.

In addition, in this system, spouses are incorporated as kin: father's sister's husband is called "uncle," mother's brother's wife is called
"aunt." Brother's wife is called "sister-in-law," and son's wife is called
"daughter-in-law."

This system is not the most common one in the world (11 percent by society, but not by total population). It functions well in hunt-
ing/gathering societies, where the band has to break up into bilateral
family units in order to exploit scattered resources in their season.
Thus, the Inuit of Alaska, Canada, and Greenland and the Jutwase
of Namibia and Botswanna both have this system. Ironically, it also
functions well in industrialized societies, where both laborers and ex-
ecutives are required to be able to pack up and move with the job. In

either case, the family must be separable from larger social units, such as extended family, band, or clan, in order to be able to scatter to sites where there are adequate resources for surviving. In some societies, that means sites where trees are ripe with fruit, in others that means sites where herds of game thrive, and in other societies that means sites where a factory offers lots of jobs.

The least complex system of kinship terminology is the *Hawaiian kinship* system. This is more common; the system in use by 36 percent of the world's cultures, especially in, but not restricted to, Polynesia. In this system, all persons in ego's grandparents' generation are called by one term if they are male and another term if they are female. In the case of Hawaiian itself, *kapuna kane* for the male and *kapuna wahine* for the female.[8]

If the gloss for the term is "grandfather" or "grandmother," then to an English speaker it seems like people are mistaking their great aunt for their grandmother. Of course, this is a problem of translation, not an error of category. The gloss should not be "grandmother" but "female relative two generations above me."

The term for the males and females in the first generation above ego, in Hawaiian, are *makua kane*, "male of my parents' generation," and *makuahine*, "female of my parents' generation." Likewise, the term for ego's father should not be glossed in English as "father" since it also applies to father's brother and to mother's brother. The proper gloss would be "male relative one generation above me." This system places more emphasis on generation than lineality. Thus, kinship terms clearly show who gets respect and authority.

Early anthropologists, led by Edward B. Tylor's work, supposed that this was a survival left over from the time when people lived to-gether in hordes and followed group marriage, and thus did not know who their mother or father or grandparents really were. To have even imagined this explanation reveals *ethnocentrism* (cultural myopia or bias). It would be as if a Sudanese anthropologist wondered if those in the English tradition knew the difference between their father's sister and their father's brother's wife, since they are both called "aunt," and wondered if this was a survival from a time in the English past when brothers and sisters married.

8. Handy and Pukui, *The Polynesian Family System in Ka-'u, Hawai'i*, 42.

The Hawaiian system emphasizes generation but not lineality and thus functions in society to keep the greatest number of options open for residence and inheritance. This system serves well people who are on the move (voyaging, migrating, settling) because they can depend on others for help (e.g., in child rearing) and for resources (e.g., settling where other relatives have made a successful settlement).

The *Iroquois kinship* terminology system equates father with father's brother, and mother with mother's sister. It is a general-purpose system that can be modified to fit with any kind of unilineal descent. The people of the Marshall Islands feature an Iroquois system of kinship terminology along with a matrilineal descent system.

Table 17. Marshallese Kinship Terminology
(females are in **bold** face type, except from ego's own generation down, where it does not make a difference.)

jimau	**jibu**	jimau	**jibu**		jimau	**jibu**	jimau	**jibu**
jinu	jema		jema		**jinu**		**jinu**	uleba
jeu reliku	jeu jinu		jeu	ego	jetu		jeu jinu	jeu reliku
neju	neju		neju/ mangeru	neju	neju/ mangeru		neju	neju
jibu	jibu		jibu	jibu	jibu		jibu	jibu

In this kinship system, generation is important, and the terms are a guide to how one should act in the presence of persons of another generation. At the same time, the gender of kinsmen is not as important. In the second descending or one's grandchildren's generation, everyone is called by a single term, *jibu*, regardless of gender. This is not unusual, since an English speaker can call all of the children of his or her sons and daughters "grandchildren." However, in this system all of the grandchildren of one's first cousins are also called by this same term, *jibu*. For female speakers, the term is reciprocal; the one who is called *jibu* responds with the same term. Relationships between grandparents and grandchildren are free and open, though not as ribald as certain other relationships.

That gender is not a defining feature of this system is evident particularly in ego's own generation. In one's own generation it is birth order that makes a difference. Anyone who is born before ego, here represented as being on the left side of ego, is called *jeu*, which means something like "elder sibling" or "elder cousin." Anyone born after

ego is called *jetu*, which means something like "younger sibling" or "younger cousin." These terms are further nuanced by an important distinction for behavior.

For the children of father's brother and mother's sister, the term may be modified. A male ego would call father's brother's daughter or mother's sister's daughter *jeu jinu*. People related in this way are called "parallel cousins" in anthropological terminology because the connecting relatives are of the same (i.e., parallel) gender. In *manit in Majol*, "Marshallese custom," these people deserve respect and one's behavior must be quite circumspect around them. No joking, no sexual innuendos, nothing but proper behavior as locally defined.

For the children of father's sister and mother's brother, the term is modified in a different way. A male ego would refer to a female cousin as *jeu reliku*. People related in this way are called "cross cousins" in anthropological terminology because one must "cross" gender lines to get to this relative. In Marshallese custom, relationships with these people are free and open. Joking, especially the use of sexual innuendo, is appropriate, as long as none of one's siblings or parallel cousins are around.

While relations with members of the first ascending generation (mother, father, aunts, uncles) is restrictive, the most restrictive relationship of all is with one's mother's brother. In Marshallese, this is the *uleba-mangeru* relationship, defining how a mother's brother relates to his sister's son and vice versa. In Marshallese culture, it is not the biological father (*jema*) who is the authority over the child, but rather the mother's brother (*uleba*). This person is the disciplinarian, the source of clan and lineage wisdom, the provider of land and other resources, and the person from whom one will gain an inheritance. One does not mess around with a mother's brother, but offers proper respect at all times.

So, anyone using the Iroquois kinship system exists in a world where generation is important, but where certain relatives take on special meaning. The most important distinction is in ego's own generation between parallel and cross cousins.

It might seem obvious that people should recognize generations. However, there are kinship terminology systems that downplay generations and generational differences. In the *Crow kinship* terminology system, a male ego calls all males in father's lineage, regardless

of generation, by a single term, and all females in father's lineage by another term. On mother's side, many more distinctions are made. Children of one's mother's brother are called by the same term as one's own children, since both are children of, but not in, one's own lineage. All this attention to distinguishing among mother's relatives restricts the distribution of this terminology because it fits so well with people who use a matrilineal descent construct, but does not fit well with any other form of descent.

The *Omaha kinship* terminology system is the reverse: a male ego calls all males on his mother's side by a single term, and all of the females on his mother's side by another term. Thus, two kinship terms cover all the people in mother's lineage. Yet, on the father's side, there are separate terms for several classes of kin. This terminology functions well in a society that uses a patrilineal descent construct because it differentiates people in one's own patrilineage. But, it lumps people in mother's patrilineage because they all stand in the same relationship to ego.

This has led to a mistaken understanding of kinship relations among early anthropologists and missionaries. The early practice was to create a gloss for a kinship term based on the closest relative to whom that term applied. Thus, if one's biological mother was called *timbu*, for example, then the gloss (translation) for that term was thought to be "my mother." But when anthropologists and missionaries observed an old man calling a young girl *timbu*, they wondered why the man was calling a little girl "my mother." In fact, the problem was in the translation, not in the people. In the Omaha kinship system in this example, *timbu*, does not mean "my mother" but rather "female of my mother's patrilineage," and thus it applies perfectly well to one's mother and to a two-year-old cousin.

Finally, the *Sudanese kinship* terminology system has many more terms, nearly a separate term for every relative. Such specificity is not very common.

It should be clear by now that kinship terminology does not mirror genealogical relationship, as Westerners like to think, but always points to socially constructed statuses and roles. Americans split and merge in their own special ways. Think of the number of different referents for the Western term "aunt": mother's sister, father's sister,

father's brother's wife, mother's brother's wife, and close friend of mother or father.

How does a kinship system fit into society? Society is a concept we use to understand how people are organized into categories and groups, what statuses and roles they perform, and how their interpersonal relationships are worked out in terms of rights and duties, privileges and responsibilities, power and persuasion. The principles of society both give order to life and are used by people to achieve their cultural ends in life.

In fact, kinship can become a metaphor for social relations. When other people come to live in a place, a kinship connection is sought, but not always found. In many places, the rules are not as important as the practice. When people live together, they form bonds for protection, exchange, land use, and ritual. It is not difficult for people to extend the terms and relationships of relatives to non-relatives. Thus, social structure always has a degree of flexibility, and is often situational and open to constant renegotiation.

Descent

Descent is an ideology or set of rules that specify a series of genealogical links that establish the membership, composition, and identity of a particular group of relatives for some purpose in society.

When a society emphasizes a line of descent from a distant ancestor, then the term "lineal" is applied both to the emphasis of the kinship terminology and to the kinds of descent groups that are formed. By contrast, when a society emphasizes a broad range of kin on either side of the family and is concerned only about the generation above and below ego, then the adjective "lateral" is often used to describe the system of descent. Kin on the mother's side are called "matrilateral kin" and kin on the father's side "patrilateral kin." A system of descent that ensures inheritance equally from both mother's side and father's sides is called "bilateral."

Descent groups are units of society that hold and exercise certain rights, privileges, duties, and obligations as defined by a culture. These rights typically concern the place of the descent group in the social structure and the group's relationships with others in society regarding identity, power, property, and spirits. Descent groups are usually

exogamous (members marry outside the group) at lineage and clan levels, or at the *moiety* (society's clans divided into two halves) level.

Patrilineal Descent

Patrilineal descent is an ideology specifying genealogical links to ancestors through men only as a criterion for recruiting new members (male and female) to a group. Groups of kin may be termed "patrilineages," "patriclans," and/or "phratries" (allied "brother" clans). Patrilateral relatives are called "agnates," the relationship "agnatic."

Societies that use patrilineal descent as an organizing principle are as diverse as Chinese agriculturalists, Venezuelan gardeners and gathers, and east African cattle herders. The Nuer (or Nath) of South Sudan have, historically, been an expanding society of cattle herders.[9] They conceive of society as arranged from smaller to larger patrilineages, ranging from a local group up to several thousand people. Boys follow the line of their fathers, and the fathers their own fathers, and so on. Lineages are significant in the organization of work, marriage, and defense. Evans-Pritchard emphasized that the ecology and social structure mirrored each other. During the dry period, people broke up into small groups according to lineage divisions and cattle were spread far and wide in search of green pastures. During the rainy season, people came together in cattle camps, making choices that put them together with close agnatic relatives.

It may be necessary, in order to explain Nuer life in English terms, to talk about residence, work, marriage, economy, and politics as if they were separate institutions, but that is not the way that the Nuer themselves would conceive of society. It is the cattle that are at the center of Nuer concern, and it is patriliny that provides the model for social order. Nuer even know the lineages of their cattle and the way that those lineages are entangled in history with marriage, politics, and other human lineage dynamics. Marriage is a relationship between lineages solidified by the exchange of a certain number of cattle. Their political dynamics will be discussed in the chapter on politics.

9. This account depends on E. E. Evans-Pritchard's classic ethnography *The Nuer*. See also the excellent video *The Nuer* (1971).

Matrilineal Descent

Matrilineal descent is an ideology specifying genealogical links through women only for recruiting new members (male and female) to a group. Groups formed may be termed "matrilineages," "matri-clans," and/or "moieties." Matrilateral relatives are called "uterines," the relationship "uterine."

If an anthropologist asks a Marshallese man why he is living on a particular slice of land (a *wato*), he will usually say that this is *bwij* land. The term means "umbilical cord" and symbolizes a series of um-bilical cords linking the living with their ancestors. A *bwij* is a group of people who hold the majority of rights in an estate, i.e., certain pieces of land. If asked who belongs to this group, the man will begin with a female ancestor, as far back and he can remember (probably four generations). This is the founding ancestor, and he will list all of her children, both male and female. Then, as he moves down to the next generation, he will list only the children of the woman's daughters, but not the children of the woman's sons. The link is through umbilical cords, and umbilical cords link a mother with her children but not a father with his children. The man will complete the genealogy by listing his own sister's children and her daughter's children if there are any. His own children are not listed because they do not belong to his *bwij*. They belong to their mother's *bwij*, and they have a mother's brother who is their lineage leader.

Table 18. An Ideal Marshallese *Bwij* or Matrilineage

			founding female				
daughter	son	daughter	son	daughter	son	daughter	son
daughter's children		daughter's children		daughter's children		daughter's children	
daughter's daughters' children		daughter's daughters' children		daughter's daughters' children		daughter's daughters' children	

The anthropologist may ask about the ancestors of the first female, but the man probably does not have that information. Ask the name of the matrilineage and the man will say it is the matrilineage of the first female's name. Or, he may volunteer that this matrilineage is part of a larger category with a name. His people, he says, are *Ripako*, "Shark People." A few more questions reveals that this category is larger than

a matrilineage, that it is, in fact, the name taken by a number of matrilineages who assume that they are related though no one can recount
the genealogy any more. This category is called a "clan," in this case a
"matriclan."

The Marshallese matrilineage is significant as a land-holding corporation. The leadership is shared by the oldest female and the oldest
male. The oldest female has significant input into internal matters, and
the oldest male represents the lineage to other lineages and to chiefs.
The lineage heads will assign certain pieces of land to lineage members, their spouses and families, as places to live, garden, and fish, but
not places that they can alienate (give away or sell to others). The matrilineage holds ultimate rights in land.

Males in matrilineal societies are in a bind. They are responsible
for the welfare of their own lineage so they must take care of their sisters and sisters' children. But, they are also responsible for their wives
and own children. So, in most matrilineal societies, males split their
time between their family of origin and their family of procreation.
Brother-sister ties are stronger in matrilineal societies, in general,
than are marriage ties.

Cognatic Descent

Cognatic descent is an ideology specifying genealogical links through
ancestors of either gender to an apical ancestor who held a title or
property. If an ancestor held rights in a particular piece of land, a group
of descendants has probably already formed around that interest. A
man with limited access to land, then, might try to activate membership in that group. The ancestor may be his father's mother's father's
father or any other combination. Other members have activated other
ties and have a certain degree of veto power over his application for
membership, depending on the availability of land and their need for
new members.

Cognatic descent is a postmodernist's dream because it offers
choices, allows membership in multiple groups, and is ambiguous. It
is more agency than structure. Roger Keesing has described the Kwaio
of Malaita in the Solomon Islands.[10] Persons have many links to many
ancestors, but cannot belong to all possible groups. Groups formed

10. Keesing, "Statistical Models and Decision Models of Social Structure: A Kwaio
Case"; and "Shrines, Ancestors, and Cognatic Descent: The Kwaio and Tallensi."

are called ramages or cognatic descent groups. There is a premium on joining one's father's group, and some leverage is gained by joining the group where one grew up. However, one can establish membership in any group where one is able to trace back to the founding ancestor, and one can maintain membership in several groups.

Relatives on either side are called "cognates," the relationship "cognatic." This kind of descent is also called "ambilineal" or "optative" because there is choice of which ties to activate and which to ignore, as well as a choice of tracing descent through any of the possible lines to an important ancestor. This kind of descent is not common, but it occurs in Polynesia, Madagascar, Ethiopia, and Indonesia.

Bilateral Descent

Bilateral descent is an ideology for specifying genealogical links through both sides to delimit membership in small groups. This is not only non-unilineal, it is non-lineal. The beginning point in bilateral descent is ego; the beginning point in all kinds of unilineal descent is an apical ancestor. Descent is reckoned back to both mother and father, the founders of ego's nuclear family of origin. Of course, both mother and father had their own family of origin. Their inheritances are now combined and ready for ego and his siblings to inherit. The range of relatives with whom one might potentially develop a relationship is called a "kindred." The group of relatives who actually associate and work together is called a "band." Groups that use bilateral descent as a social principle include the Inuit, the Americans, the Jutwase of the Kalihari Desert, and the Dyak of Borneo.

Sex and Marriage

All societies have rules governing who may be a partner in sexual relations and whom one may marry. The rule against sexual relations, let alone marriage, between certain kinds of close kin varies by culture and by the size of the population. All societies have what has been termed an "incest taboo." There seems to be a universal rule against father-daughter, mother-son, and brother-sister sexual intercourse. However, in some societies, such as ancient Egypt and traditional Polynesian societies, for example, the chiefly or kingly family became so sacred that brother-sister marriage was accepted as a solution to the problem of pollution. Such marriages produced

even more sacred children. However, insofar as marriage is a form of making alliances, brother-sister marriage eventually isolates and weakens the ruling family.

The obverse of the incest taboo is a rule specifying acceptable marriage partners. For example, in the Marshallese case described above, a person could not marry anyone in his or her own lineage, even what Americans might call a "third" or "fourth cousin." Further, a person could not marry anyone else with the same clan name, whether or not a genealogical tie can be established. Thus, the Marshallese practice *exogamy*, marriage outside of the group, where the group is a lineage or a clan.

In some societies, there is a *preferential marriage* rule indicating who the most favored spouse would be. The most common rule, found in many societies, is that one must not marry parallel cousins, but one should prefer to marry cross cousins. Thus, mother's sister's child would not be considered a possibility for marriage, but mother's brother's child is a prime candidate. Note that parallel cousins would be in the same lineage as ego (at least on one side), while cross cousins are always members of another lineage. For some people with a lineage exogamy rule, parallel cousin marriage would be like incest while cross-cousin marriage serves to build alliances with other lineages.

This logic does not prevail in Middle Eastern societies, nor in many of the societies that have been influenced by Islam. There parallel cousin marriage is the preferred form. The result is not to build alliances, but to consolidate the wealth and influence of the descent group. Note that Abraham sought a wife for Isaac from his brother's family, and Isaac sought a wife for Jacob from his father's brother's son's family. Isaac was born late in life and so the people his age were in the generation beneath him. Though the ideal there may have been patrilateral parallel cousin (father's brother's child) marriage, no society can limit marriage choices this narrowly. While both patriliny and patrilateral parallel cousin marriage are important, these practices function within a larger context of *endogamy*, that is, marrying within one's own descent group.[11] This builds up resources and personnel at home instead of dispersing land, livestock, and warriors. Some studies show that bilateral ties are just as important in negotiating daily life.[12]

11. Ayoub, "Parallel Cousin Marriage and Endogamy."

12. Pastner, "The Negotiation of Bilateral Endogamy in the Middle Eastern Context."

Migration to the city puts different kinds of pressure on the family, and studies show that while the practice of cousin marriage remains high, strict patrilateral parallel cousin marriage is on the decline.[13]

Marriage is a socially sanctioned relationship established between families or lineages that involves obligations and duties for the exchange of men and women, goods and produce, or other valuables, and thus regulates sexual relations, procreation, and rights over children. This definition may grate Americans who believe in romanticism and individualism, but it fits most societies in the world. Even Americans recognize that "the marriage of *Name* and *Name* unites their families and creates a new one."[14]

As an institution, marriage provides a relatively long-lasting, stable environment for relations between men and women, including sexual and labor relations, for the reproduction of children, for the socialization of children into society, and for the long-term care of family members. Rules against sexual relations within the family, except for husband and wife, contribute to the stability of the family as a unit. Cooperation, rather than competition, makes the family stronger than any individual can be. That is why weakening the family threatens both individuals and societies. Rules like the incest taboo also force families to make alliances with other families, thus strengthening society as well.

For these reasons, *arranged marriage* provides a powerful platform for social stability and cohesion. This is such serious business that families often hire a third party to find the right partner. Criteria begin, in India, with caste, but move on to include education, reputation, congeniality, and overall attractiveness. This can be difficult enough in India or Pakistan, but for people in diaspora, it becomes more complex yet. Wolfe and Gudorf provide an interesting case in ethics for a young Indian man raised in America by his immigrant parents, on his way to a career in finance, and then blindsided by the announcement that his family has found a spouse in India who is just right for him.[15] Or so they think. Since he was raised in America, the young man thinks differently.

13. Klat and Khudr, "Cousin Marriages in Beruit, Lebanon: Is the Pattern Changing?"

14. United Methodist Church, *Book of Worship*, 117.

15. Wolfe, "Marriage is for Life."

Marriage involves an exchange, at least of rings in American society, but of much more in other societies. In some societies, it is appropriate to give some valuables as a gift to accompany the bride. The *dowry* ensures that the young couple will be well endowed (pun intended), that the bride will be treated properly (or else she can take her dowry and go home), and that the bride receives at least some inheritance from her father (she likely will receive no more at his death).

In some societies, it is women themselves who are exchanged, a brother giving his sister in exchange for the sister of the groom. This is what the prince of Shechem suggested to Jacob: "Make marriages with us; give your daughters to us, and take our daughters for yourselves. You shall live with us; and the land shall be open to you; live and trade in it, and get property in it."[16] Even in this kind of exchange, *bride price* may be appropriate or expected. The son who caused the problem was not a great negotiator. "Shechem also said to her father and to her brothers, 'Let me find favor with you, and whatever you say to me I will give. Put the marriage present and gift as high as you like, and I will give whatever you ask me; only give me the girl to be my wife.'"[17] The story also shows what happens to society if marriage practices are not well established. Jacob's sons convinced the men of the city that they had to be circumcised, then killed them when they were incapacitated. Jacob had to leave the area because his sons had caused such a stink in the land.

Particular kinds of exchange, such as matrilateral cross-cousin marriage in a patrilineal society, or patrilateral cross-cousin marriage in a matrilineal society, as Levi-Strauss argued, stitches together at least three lineages in a small-scale society.[18] One lineage gives women to a second lineage, which gives women to a third lineage, which gives women to the first lineage. This is just one way that marriage practices function to integrate societies.

In some societies, the exchange is unidirectional: women either marry up (*hypergamy*) or marry down (*hypogamy*). The first tends to correlate with giving a dowry, and the latter with receiving a bride price. In a system, a marriage does not stand alone, but rather a mar-

---

16. Genesis 34:9-10.

17. Genesis 34:11-12.

18. Levi-Strauss, *The Elementary Structures of Kinship*.

riage is only one of a series of exchanges between long-established groups.

Polygamy is marriage with multiple spouses. If a man takes several wives, that is *polygyny*. If a woman takes several husbands, that is *polyandry*. While everyone has heard of the first—and missionaries are notorious for opposing it—very few have heard of cases of polyandry. The classic cases are the Toda of southern India, the Nayar of the Malabar coast in India, and isolated examples from Tibet and the Marquesas in Polynesia. While some traditional practices, such as female infanticide (not enough adult women), the rotation of professional warriors (men are not always around), or scarcity of land (brothers stay together and thus keep the estate intact) push people toward polyandry, in fact, this rare practice is now nearly extinct.

Polygyny is widespread, meaning that many societies permit it, but in no society is polygyny the practice for any more than the elite. Polygyny is a sign of wealth, and commoners are not usually in a position to practice it. The initial reaction of early missionaries was to label polygyny as a sin, but this was based in part on Western Enlightenment values concerning women and marriage. When Africans began reading the Bible in their own languages, they discovered that there is polygyny in the Old Testament (one reason that Africans tend to identify more closely with the Old Testament) and there is no prohibition against it in the New Testament, except in the case of church leaders. Disciplining men in polygynous marriages cost the early African missions the support of leaders in society. When some men complied and put away any wives beyond the first, then another problem arose: Where do those wives and children go? Many missions moved to a compromise position: When polygyny exists, let it play out for the older generation, but prohibit new church members from having more than one wife.

Yet, some of the causes of polygyny still press people in that direction. Auli Vähäkangas has described the issues for the Lutheran church in Tanzania.[19] She notes:

> Many female theologians in Africa criticize polygyny as being
> a way to exploit women. The findings of the model narrative
> on formal polygyny suggest, however, that there are some good

19. Vähäkangas, *Christian Couples Coping with Childlessness: Narratives from Machame, Kilimanjaro.*

aspects of traditional polygyny, even for women. The way parishes deal with polygyny often brings problems to Christian couples. Church discipline does not relieve the pressure of the traditional Chagga community toward procreation.[20]

In changing times (are there any other kind?), "Urbanization, labor migration, and changing gender roles have influenced the dynamics of marital life in the area."[21] In effect, the context for polygyny has changed, but pressures are still there, and it is still an issue for the church.

Finally, descent groups often govern marriage and postmarital residence with rules specifying where a newly married couple should live. A couple may follow the male (*virilocal*) or the female (*uxorilocal*) in choice of residence. A couple may live with his patrilineage (*patrilocal*) or her matrilineage (*matrilocal* or *avunculocal*, "with the uncle"), or in a new place (*neolocal*). Though Genesis seems to specify uxorilocal residence,[22] Americans tend to prefer neolocal residence.

American Kinship Terminology

Americans are a diverse group, including those from the First Nations (Native Americans) to recent Sudanese immigrants. Thus, there is a lot of variation in how Americans address and refer to kinfolk, and the terms "relatives" and "family" are themselves flexible in use. Some variations occur between the standard regions of the United States: East, South, North, Midwest, and West. For example, whether it is females only or both males and females who use the term "Daddy" varies by region of the country.[23]

Americans of European descent tend to recognize relatives by nature, by blood, and by law.[24] Americans speak of a "natural child" or, in the past, an "illegitimate child," and a child's "natural mother" or "natural father." The common terms are "father," "mother," "brother," "sister," "son," "daughter," and "cousin," with the modifiers "grand-" and "great-" being applied to more distant generations. When new

20. Ibid., 109.

21. Ibid., 109.

22. Genesis 2:24: "Therefore a man leaves his father and his mother and clings to his wife, and they become one flesh."

23. Schneider, *American Kinship*, 70.

24. Ibid., 29

relatives are added by marriage, adoption or fosterage, or modified by divorce, other adjectives are added, such as "in-law," "step-," "half," "adopted," or "foster."

Relations by blood would seem to be defined by actual biological connection, but even this is nuanced. If the speaker has a relative whom he or she has never met, who may be still alive, but has no social relationship with the speaker, then the speaker may not even claim that person as being among his or her relatives. This is certainly true as generations pass by. Americans tend to know four generations of relatives, and tend to forget who came before that, unless that person was a "famous relative," another cultural category.

The number of people included in the category of cousin is so large that other modifiers are used to differentiate those in social relationship from those rarely seen and those never seen. "Kissing cousins," a term used primarily in the South, refers to those who are known and deserve the greeting of a kiss when met.[25] "Shirt-tail relatives" are lesser-known relatives of closer relatives, that is, brought in on someone else's shirt-tail.[26] This larger sense of family, brought together not just by certain ancestors but also by marriage, materializes primarily at weddings, funerals, holidays, and family reunions.[27]

Whether or not the dead are still relatives is questionable for some Americans, though most people elsewhere in the world tend to think of them as alive and well and part of the crowd. The problem is, in part, that death changes relationships. A wife becomes a widow with no husband, a child becomes an orphan with no father.

Historically, in the English system, and other European systems (French) that have contributed to the American kinship system, kinship terminology emphasized certain features that were important in law and politics. Succession to a title, inheritance of property, responsibility for a kinsman's debt, and eligibility for marriage are all embedded in the American kinship system.

The system recognizes lineality by layers, that is, relatives in a specific line as opposed to relatives off to the side of the line. Thus, Anglo-Americans have referred to the "distaff side" (the line coming from the mother). The system isolated great-grandfather (GGF),

25. Ibid., 70.
26. Ibid.
27. Ayoub, "Family Reunion."

grandfather, father, son, and grandson as a direct line of ancestors and descendants. These are separated, in terminology, from great-great-uncle (GGU, GGF's brother), great-uncle, uncle, and cousin (the next line out, parallel to one's own line). The next layer out is a variety of first cousins; first cousin three times removed (GGF's first cousin), first cousin twice removed, first cousin once removed, and first cousin. The next layer is second cousins, and so on.

Notice that "removed" means "above or below ego's generation." A cousin once removed is either in ego's father's generation or ego's son's generation, but not ego's own generation. Notice also that the terms are reciprocal. If ego calls a person "second cousin once removed" then that person likewise calls ego "second cousin once removed."

Table 19. Lineal and Lateral Lines in American Kinship Terminology

Direct line of descent for ego (oneself)	Closest lateral line	Next lateral line: first cousins	Next lateral line: second cousins	Next lateral line: third cousins	Next lateral line: fourth cousins
GGGGF[A]					
GGGF	GGGU				
GGF	GGU	1stC3[B] GGGU's son			
GF	GU	1stC2 GGU's son	2ndC2 1stC3's son		
F	U	1stC1 GU's son	2ndC1 1stC2's son	3rdC1 2ndC2's son	
Ego	B	1stC Uncle's son	2ndC 1stC1's son	3rdC 2ndC1's son	4thC 3rdC1's son
S	N	1stC1 1stC's son	2ndC1 2ndC's son	3rdC1 3rdC's son	4thC1 4thC's son
GS	GN	1stC2 1stC1's son	2ndC2 2ndC1's son	3rdC2 3rdC1's son	4thC2 4thC1's son
GGS	GGN	1stC3 1stC2's son	2ndC3 2ndC2's son	3rdC3 3rdC2's son	4thC3 4thC2's son

A. G=great- or grand-; F=father; U=uncle; C=cousin; B=brother; S=son; N=nephew.
B. 1stC3, for example, means first cousin three times removed.

Table 20. Another Way to Visualize American Kinship Terminology (this time with a female ego and female relatives)[28]***

GGGGM					
GGGM					GGGA
GGM				GGA	1stC3
GM			GA	1stC2	2ndC2
M		A	1stC1	2ndC1	3rdC1
Ego	Z	1stC	2ndC	3rdC	4thC
D	N	1stC1	2ndC1	3rdC1	4thC1
GD	GN	1stC2	2ndC2	3rdC2	4thC2
GGD	GGN	1stC3	2ndC3	3rdC3	4thC3

While few Americans today would even recognize a cousin beyond second cousin or beyond once removed,[29] this system served in the past to establish legal obligations for inheritance and for debts incurred, and to establish clear lines between who was marriageable and who was not.

Summary

Marriage, kinship, and descent continue to function to structure relationships, form groups, and define society even in the face of urbanization and globalization. They are not the only forces operating, however, they function to establish identity, to determine access to resources, and to prepare people for engaging larger political, economic, and religious structures. Marriage, kinship, and descent language provides as well models and metaphors for the many other relationships that people develop, including relationships within the church.

28 *** Rows indicate generations. M=mother; A=aunt; D=daughter; Z=sister; N=niece, C=cousin.

29. Since my Mother's family has been in our farm community since the Civil War, my children do know some of their Second Cousins Once Removed and Third Cousins Once Removed.

6

Economics, Development, and Mission

The Anthropology of Economics

ECONOMICS, LIKE OTHER SOCIAL INSTITUTIONS RECOGNIZED in the Western social sciences, is not necessarily a separate social and cultural domain in other societies. Therefore, we will hold lightly to the academic approach that separates economics into a compartmentalized social field.

Economics is the knowledge, values, and structures used to organize the production, distribution, and consumption of goods, services, and ideas in a social group or network, in a whole society, and between societies. At base, all this depends on notions of ownership and use.

Land and Resources

Property is not simply "things." Things become property when they become the subject of relationships between people. No one can own a piece of land. The land does not do the bidding of the person. What a person holds is rights in land in cooperation with certain people and as opposed to other people. Rights come in two varieties: *demand rights* and *privilege rights*.[1] Demand rights create duties in others to respond. Privilege rights mean only that others have no right to interfere.[2] For

1. See Hohfeld, *Fundamental Legal Conceptions*, 35ff.

2. These are often confused in modern American society, as if a privilege to do something creates a duty in others to make it possible, which it does not.

example, I have the right to be secure in the use of my farm in southern Indiana. You have a duty not to trespass on the land. I also have the privilege of using the national parks in America and, while you do not have to pay my way, you have no right to stop me. I open myself to liability when I advertise that my land is for sale and, while you have no duty to make an offer, you have the power to activate the liability by making an offer on the land. All ownership of property involves a bundle of rights, duties, powers, and liabilities.

That bundle of rights may be held by an individual or by a group, but some rights are also distributed among various levels of society. For example, contrary to the American myth of private property, I am not the only owner of "my" farm. First, my siblings and I inherited the farm from our mother, who inherited it from her father. Now my wife and I have bought out my siblings, and both of our names are on the title. Second, various levels of local government have certain rights: they collect taxes every year and they have zoning laws that restrict what I can do with the land. For example, I cannot decide to put in a landfill since no land in our county is zoned for that use. Third, the state has certain rights: five years ago the state of Indiana exercised the right of eminent domain, taking eight acres out of the middle of the farm even though I did not want to sell it. The state rerouted a highway through the middle of "my" farm and I had no right to stop them. The federal government also has rights. The United States Department of Agriculture permits me to participate in farm programs, but only as long as I follow certain farming practices and do not cut down the acre of woods on a corner of the farm. There is no such thing as an individual holding absolutely all of the rights in land, not even in America.

How rights are held depends on the social position of persons in that society. How rights are inherited also follows local rules. My farm can be inherited by my five children as a legal corporation, or each could inherit a certain number of acres. In some societies, the land would be inherited by my sister's children, while in other societies the land would be inherited by my sons but not my daughters. In ancient Israel, the eldest son would inherit twice as much as other sons. In many societies, residual rights in land (the right to ultimate disposal of the land) would be held by a larger descent group (a lineage or clan), while the individual and his or her family hold use (usufruct) rights.

Some churches in America have begun to question the biblical propriety of the major investment in property that most American churches have made. Many emerging and/or missional churches rent abandoned buildings and even whole shopping malls. They are then free to spend the bulk of their budget on ministry and mission. This is a prophetic challenge to the American imagination of what it means to be a church.

In recent times, indigenous people have begun to question the ownership of land by mission groups and churches.[3] One of the reasons that indigenous rights in land—for example, the rights of Native Americans in the United States or the rights of the Lmaa/Maasai pastoralists in Kenya—have not held a high priority for missions and churches is that Western Christians usually lack a biblical theology of land. Several theologians have raised this issue and thus exposed the secular ideology toward land held by many.[4]

Still, it is not just the concept of rights that defines material things or even immaterial things. To talk like this is to look through a legal and commercial lens. For some people, things in the environment cannot belong to persons. People use resources as they come across them, that is, because they are there, and/or because God or the spirits have provided them. In one passage, God claims, "The land is mine; with me you are but aliens and tenants,"[5] obviating any sense of ultimate human ownership.

The Organization of Production

The organization of production involves a method of gaining access to land and other resources, a particular division of labor in society, and technology for turning raw materials into finished products. The organization of production differs according to the environment, social structure, and ideology of the people.

---

3. See, for example, Rynkiewich, ed., *Land and Churches* (2001); and idem, *Land and Churches* (2004).

4. Habel, *The Land Is Mine!*; Brueggemann, *The Land*; and Wright, *God's People in God's Land*.

5. Lev 25:23.

Hunters and Gatherers

At one time in prehistory all humans were hunters and gatherers. In the last fifty years the number of groups employing this kind of economy has dwindled significantly. The few remaining groups are in the plains of Botswana and Namibia, the rainforest of Venezuela and Brazil, the plateaus of western Papua New Guinea, and central Australia.

Until recently with the Mabo case,[6] Australian Aborigines' rights to land were not recognized by the state. In fact, the concept of *terra nullis*, or "empty land," was a legal reality, as if the British had arrived in Australia and found no humans living there. Yet the Aborigines were there and they have not gone away. The Jigalong Mob (Mandjildjara speakers),[7] for example, live in the Western Desert near the Jigalong Mission. This environment did not look promising to British immigrants, but "Aborigines sustained a hunting and gathering adaptation that allowed them much leisure time for social and ceremonial activities."[8] As Tonkinson notes, recent work-time studies show that hunters and gatherers actually spend only a few hours a day collecting food, and this because their detailed knowledge of the landscape, plant recognition and use, and animal behavior helps them survive where others would die.

> An observer who travels with Aborigines through their home territory is soon aware that perceptions of the desert differ. The Aborigine sees his home as a marvelous, supportive place, full of waterholes and with some kind of food always available. It is composed of physiographic features that abound in religious significance because he knows how they came into existence during the great formative period, the Dreamtime. Because all these landforms were created by ancestral beings with whom he strongly identifies as relatives and supporters, the Aborigine feels secure in his homeland.[9]

It is for this reason that the Jigalong Mob has not accepted Christianity, at least the fundamentalist type that characterized their local mission, because it offers them little in the way of survival skills.

6. *Mabo v Queensland (no. 2)*. 1992. High Court of Australia.
7. Tonkinson, *Jigalong Mob*.
8. Ibid., 13.
9. Ibid., 19.

They may enjoy the isolation and security of living near the mission, accept periods of work on stations handling cattle or sheep, or even send their children to school when it is convenient, but they retain control over their own lives, performing their own rituals and living, in part, off of the desert, as their ancestors did in the past.

Pastoralists

The Nuer are a nomadic cattle-herding people living in South Sudan.[10] Young men working with others of their own age set move with the cattle and care for the cattle. Younger boys and girls milk cattle and collect dry cattle dung for fires. There are few trees in the environment and thus little firewood available. Women pound grain into flour and prepare food. Men who are elders work on alliances, political strategies, dispute settlement, and marriage arrangements, including establishing bride price. Specialization occurs by age set and gender. Both households and patrilineages also have their areas of responsibility.

The system is organized as an efficient way to produce usable goods given the limitations and possibilities of the environment. Thus, as in any economic system, behavior is goal oriented. However, the definition of goals changes from society to society. Here cattle are valued highly, not only as a form of wealth and a symbol of well-being, but cattle also have an aesthetic value. They are named, and poems and songs are written about them. Cattle are also worth fighting for, though the group that fights is not a standing group, but rather is organized according to the segmentary lineage system. That is, the group that is formed depends on how closely related the disputants are.

The Nuer in some ways mirror their environment in their social structure. During the rainy season they gather together in large cattle camps, which they can do because there is plenty of water and fresh grass for the cattle. In the dry season, they break down into smaller groups and scattered across the land in constant search for water and grass. When they are together in large camps, ages and genders come together, but when they are scattered, young herdsmen group together to care for the cattle while children, elders, and women form "family" units elsewhere.

10. Evans-Pritchard, *Nuer*.

Gardeners

The Dani are a gardening people who live in the Highlands of Papua,[11] Indonesia.[12] Among the Dani, labor is organized around household and gender. Men clear the land, dig drainage and irrigation ditches, and defend the gardens. Women prepare the soil, plant, cultivate, harvest, and prepare the food. They also collect salt. Children herd pigs, while women prepare sweet potatoes and other foods. Men maintain alliances, defend the frontier, and hunt. Men engage in long-distance trade for shells and other items of importance to the local economy. Men also weave and prepare decorative funerary belts.

The system functions to make settled life in the highlands environment possible. Until the arrival of the sweet potato, about 350 years ago, New Guinea people went into the highlands to hunt, but could not stay because yams, taro, and manioc, as well as other minor root crops, did not grow well there. The sweet potato changed all that, providing a year-round food source for humans and pigs. The gardens that the Dani have developed are extensive, all supported by a grid of irrigation and drainage ditches. Gardening is a daily activity for both women and men. When enemies raid gardens and steal pigs, then local alliances form to protect their property.

Agriculturalists

Intensive agriculture, including irrigation agriculture, arose independently in the Ancient Near East, in China and Southeast Asia, and in Central and South America. As crop production and animal domestication spread, so did cultural innovations in Europe and Africa. Farmers provided the basis for the establishment of cities, long-distance trade, political hierarchies (kingdoms and empires), and regional religions.

While competitive, market-orientated agriculture dominates America and Europe, there are societies with other values and farming practices. The Amish in America organize themselves around the

11. The western half of the island of New Guinea was claimed by the Dutch in colonial times. The people are Melanesians (Pacific Islanders), but in 1962 the area became a province of Indonesia. It has been known as Irian Jaya, and is now divided into two provinces: Papua and Papua Barat (West Papua). Papua is the site of a well-known revival, described by Hayward in *Vernacular Christianity among the Mulia Dani.*

12. Heider, *Grand Valley Dani.*

values of *Gemeinde*, "the redemptive community," and *Ordnung*, "the rules for how to live different from the world."[13] The Amish do not farm to make money, but rather farm to live their "preferred way of life."[14] Contrary to most Christians, they do have a theology of land. The land belongs to God, and humans are to manage and protect the land as the "steward of an absentee landlord."[15] Thus, Amish farmers do not strive to profit from the most land that they can farm, but rather build up and sustain an appropriate amount of land for a family to work on.

The family is the work unit, and both crop production and husbandry require heavy inputs of manual labor—the more so because, for the most part, tractors and other machines are eschewed. The soil is improved through the use of manure for fertilizer, selected minerals, and crop rotation. A couple raises a family, then retires early to support their children in farming.

The Amish want to live in an environment without depleting the resources, so they have what others would call a small "ecological footprint." They make minimum use of fossil fuels, they fertilize with manure (one of their complaints about tractors is that they do not produce manure), they do not produce waste by doing paperwork (another complaint concerns government regulation), they restrict consumption, and they accomplish most of their tasks with manual labor, which, with a little food and sleep, is quite renewable. Production involves practices that lead to sustainability and self-sufficiency.

These practices contrast with the farming of the larger community. Farm production in Pennsylvania and the Midwest is competitive and individualistic, not cooperative, and is driven by "market realities." The focus is on farming more acres with large machines and fewer farm laborers. In the whole US, according to the 2007 USDA Agricultural Census, the average farm size is 418 acres. In Illinois it is closer to 500 acres, while the Amish in Illinois have an average farm size of 85 acres.[16] Farmers in the Midwest, the closer they are to the

13. This section is based primarily on John A. Hostetler's life work of studying Amish, Mennonite, and Hutterite communities, in particular, his book *Amish Society*.

14. Ibid., 117.

15. Ibid., 114.

16. Ibid., 121.

Mississippi, Illinois, and Ohio Rivers, tend to limit their planting to corn, soybeans, and wheat, and to not have animals. Livestock have high labor costs and, when the export and domestic milling markets push the price up, corn and soybeans have too much value to be invested instead in cattle, hogs, and chickens. Throughout the Midwest there are good rail lines to river terminals and/or to the Southeast (millers and chicken feeders), and the rivers have barge traffic that carry grain to New Orleans. There are nine export elevators on the lower Mississippi, and during the winter months their bids are usually high in order to serve the export market. The price of grain, then, is determined by what the futures are doing on the Chicago Board of Trade, what the export market or Southeastern feeders are willing to pay, and what the cost of moving a farmer's grain to a river or rail elevator is.[17] This system pushes farmers to be in competition with each other to rent ground and to make the land produce the most for the least input, but at the same time it puts farmers at the mercy of a world market such that any change in the condition of crops in other countries—for example, wheat in Australia or soybeans in Brazil—as well as the import needs of other countries—for example, Japan and China—makes the price of grain fluctuate regardless of the input of materials and labor of the American farmer.

Industrialists

Long ago, through irrigation and intensive agriculture, farmers began producing more than they themselves, or their family and kinfolk, could eat. This began to free up some people for specialization. Some specialized in religious functions and thus there arose a priestly class, but others specialized in the production of tools and luxury items.

17. The Chicago Board of Trade deals in units of 5000-bushel contracts for certain months (March, May, July, September, and December for corn and wheat; January, March, May, July, August, September, and November for soybeans). This becomes the standard for hedging grain, though traders reverse those hedges before delivery in Chicago comes due. So, an elevator on the Ohio River sells grain to an exporter in New Orleans according to a basis (amount under or over the Chicago futures) called CIFNOLA (Cargo, Insurance, and Freight delivered to New Orleans Louisiana). When delivery occurs, both will turn their contract into a flat price at an agreed upon futures price plus or minus the previously agreed on basis. Barge freight also trades daily, so keeping up with the market requires close monitoring. I worked as a grain merchandiser at a major elevator on the Ohio River for ten years (1981–1991).

Even in hunting and gathering communities, older men who were failing on the track were able to continue to contribute through the production of spear points and spears as well as arrow points, arrows, and bows. Agricultural production has taken specialization to a new level so that, today, most people make their living off the farm in factories and other kinds of businesses.

While there was a time when laws restricted the movement of people from the villages to towns and cities in China (particularly the 1950s and 1960s), and even a time when city dwellers were sent back to the farm (during the Cultural Revolution), the move from the farm to the factory has continued. For example, Half Moon Village, one of many villages in the Red Flag Commune just outside Beijing, was organized around collective farming until recent decades brought a more individualistic form of ownership and labor. Work brigades were formed to plant and harvest wheat, rice, corn, peanuts, rapeseed (the source of canola oil), and a wide variety of vegetables. Some of the harvest was "sold to the state, some distributed to the villagers, and some set aside for seed and as a reserve."[18]

At the same time, some individuals were looking for ways to migrate to the city for work, while the commune itself was searching for new means of production. At different times, Half Moon Village attracted to itself a jade-carving factory, a kiln for making bricks, a candy factory to produce for a Beijing exporter, and a factory to make fire-retardant paint spray. Some of these initiatives required negotiation through endless governmental bureaucracy, some required *guanxi*, that is, bribes. Increasing privatization of ownership, local control over production, and exposure to the marketplace continue to change the lives of Half Moon Villagers away from the farm and toward industry and business.

The Organization of Distribution

Producing commodities is one thing, but, as any factory owner knows, one must also get them to the right place at the right time. There are several general ways of accomplishing the distribution of commodities.

---

18. Chance, *China's Urban Villagers*, 59.

Reciprocity and Exchange

At the base of economics, or as some would argue, at the base of social relations, is reciprocity. Reciprocal exchange involves the flow of
goods, services, and ideas between two or more persons that blos-
soms into a network of relationships. There is a variety of systems of
exchange in the world, each contributing to a different social order.

In a seminal work titled *Essai sur le don* ("Essay on the Gift")
Marcel Mauss (1872–1950) laid the foundation for the study of exchange in sociology and anthropology. Mauss surveyed the extant
literature on archaic societies as well as the ethnographies that anthropologists were writing, particularly the work of Bronislaw Malinowski
on the Kula Ring[19] in the Massim (islands at the east end of Papua
New Guinea) and the work Franz Boaz on the Potlatch among the
Native Americans along the northwestern coast of North America.[20]
Impressed with the lavish attention that people gave to producing
and giving gifts, Mauss concluded that "prestations" were the center
around which social relations, the circulation of goods, and the production of meaning revolved.

Mauss observed that there were three obligations in these systems of exchange: the obligation to give, the obligation to receive, and
the obligation to repay.[21] Thus, the system keeps going, carrying with
it symbolic, social, and economic value. When the exchange occurs
among equals with items of equivalent value, the exchange is called
"balanced reciprocity." However, this may be a bit of a misnomer. If
the two parties want the relationship to continue, the exchange is
never exactly balanced. Someone owes and someone is owed. This
leads to the next exchange. If the two parties want the relationship to
grow, then the obligation to repay is handled delicately. In Marshallese
society, for example, a quick return of items with exactly the same
value is a signal that the recipient of the first gift does not want to pursue the relationship. The relationship is finished as quickly as it began
because the gift has been repaid and no one owes anything further. In
American society, this is the way market exchange occurs: we select

---

19. Malinowski, *Argonauts of the Western Pacific*.

20. Boas, *Social Organization and Secret Societies*. See also Drucker, "Rank,
Wealth, and Kinship."

21. Mauss, *The Gift*.

an item, pay the price, and there is no lingering relationship between seller and buyer.

Ancient Greco-Roman society was structured by patron-client relationships based on balanced reciprocity. The other major system was that of honor-shame, and it too was based on balanced reciprocity, including *negative reciprocity*, where when a family was shamed that shame was removed by injuring or killing the person who caused the shame.[22] Joel Green suggests that Jesus' Sermon on the Plain (Luke 6) specifically targets this system.[23]

> Do to others as you would have them do to you. If you love those who love you, what credit is that to you? For even sinners love those who love them. If you do good to those who do good to you, what credit is that to you? For even sinners do the same. If you lend to those from whom you hope to receive, what credit is that to you? Even sinners lend to sinners, to receive as much again. But love your enemies, do good, and lend, expecting nothing in return. Your reward will be great, and you will be children of the Most High; for he is kind to the ungrateful and the wicked. Be merciful, just as your Father is merciful. Do not judge, and you will not be judged; do not condemn, and you will not be condemned. Forgive, and you will be forgiven; give, and it will be given to you. A good measure, pressed down, shaken together, running over, will be put into your lap; for the measure you give will be the measure you get back.[24]

Green argues that Jesus offers, instead, a form of *generalized reciprocity* in which followers of Christ give gifts without expectation of a return, thus rejecting the trap of debt and obligation that Greco-Roman and even Hebrew society had become.

Indeed, there are other exceptions to the rule that a gift must be reciprocated. Recent work in India has highlighted a particular kind of gift, called an *asdăn* or *dana*, which is a gift given to a priest to bear

---

22. See Hanson and Oakman, *Palestine in the Time of Jesus*, 70–82.

23. Green, *Luke*, 269–71.

24. Luke 6:31–38.

away pollution.[25] No one would want a return for this gift, just as no one would want to be reciprocated for giving up a scapegoat.[26]

Reciprocal exchange is the most widely used method of moving goods; it is found in every society, though sometimes it is overshadowed by redistributive systems or markets. Even a gift in Western society is a statement about the relationship between giver and receiver. The gift is a symbol of the relationship, and thus has value and meaning beyond its appearance. We say, for example, "It's the thought that counts," when a small child (or clueless husband) gives an obviously inadequate gift. Gifts may express equality and solidarity, as when children exchange Christmas gifts. Or, gifts may express hierarchy and dominance, as when a political leader gives a follower a large gift for which the receiver can reciprocate only by giving service (or votes).

Reciprocal exchange can be the basis for large scale trading systems. Archaeological research in Melanesia reveals obsidian (volcanic glass) from New Britain in Papua New Guinea as far away as Fiji and Indonesia, and this at three thousand years ago. That means the system was working over a range of several thousand miles. The Kula Ring, again, involved a great number of islands, languages, and cultures. Yet, it worked and it not only moved goods around, but also created the desire for peace so that men could trade armbands and necklaces.

Redistribution

The second general category of exchange found in the world is not between persons of relatively equal status, but rather the movement of goods toward a center, and the subsequent movement of other goods out from the center. While specific prestations might occur face to face, the whole system is far from face to face. A contemporary case is the way that taxes are supposed to work in modern society. People pay taxes, and in return the government provides services, such as building roads, getting rid of sewage, picking up garbage, providing law enforcement, building schools, supporting a standing army, and so on.

25. Raheja, *Poison in the Gift*. See also the introductory text by Hendry that uses the theme of gift giving to examine all of societies institutions.

26. Lev chs. 5, 9, 10 , 16, 23; Num ch. 7.

Redistributive economies circulate goods to a central person or structure, and then receive back things from elsewhere in the system. A redistributive chiefdom, common in Micronesia and Polynesia, involves tribute given to a chief who is then obliged to make return prestations from his storehouse of tribute from other regions. Thus, goods are moved around from one ecosystem to another.

For example, Marshallese society, more so in the past, was organized politically and economically by a royal *bwij* ("matrilineage") from which an *irooj lapalap* ("paramount chief") would be selected according to specific rules of succession. At the head of related or noble matrilineages would be an *irooj iddik* ("lesser chief"). The *kajur* ("commoner") lineages were each led by an *alap* ("lineage head"), usually a brother-sister team who took care of the inner workings and outer relationships of the matrilineage. Beneath them were the *rejerbal* ("workers") or regular lineage members. It was the job of the lineage head to assign plots of land to various branches or families of the lineage.

At certain times of the year, when certain fruits were ripe or certain fish were running strong, or when a particular kind of craft production was underway, it was the responsibility of the lineage head to gather up the firstfruits and take them to the lesser chief. The lesser chief, when a number of lineage heads had signaled their readiness, led them to the paramount chief and the items were offered as gifts, perhaps even tribute, to the paramount chief and his family. However, this was an exchange, so the gift giving did not stop there. From his stores, usually of some items from another part of the atoll or another atoll altogether, the paramount chief drew some gifts to give back to the lesser chief, who passed them along to the lineage heads. In this way, goods from a variety of ecological niches were redistributed around the chiefdom (an atoll or several atolls) so that everyone benefitted from the broader production of goods in the islands: fish from here for pandanus pudding from there, breadfruit from the larger islets for thatch from the smaller islets, arrowroot floor from the poorer soils for taro from the swamps.

Market Exchange

The third general category of exchange is rapidly spreading in this globalizing world. In this system, persons bring their goods to a common

place, a market, whether it be in the middle of town or online, and offer goods in exchange. If the exchange is for other goods, it is called *barter*, but this practice has been on the decline for a number of years. Money, standardized tokens that may be exchanged for any good or service, is rapidly becoming accepted in all forms of exchange.

Goods are moved around in society, from persons or areas of surplus to areas of scarcity, in several different ways: by reciprocal exchange, by centralized redistribution, or by market exchange. Markets are by no means restricted to Western societies, and reciprocity is not limited to non-Western societies.

Market economies are common in many societies, though the method of trade is usually bartering. The Igbo of Nigeria had a four-day week, and every fourth day was a market day when people brought their produce and crafts to certain market towns.[27] In a monetary market economy, there is a separate measure of value, money that can be traded for any of the goods for sale. One result of the use of money is the commodification of life; soon anything and everything becomes a commodity for sale: labor, sex, votes, etc.

The Organization of Consumption

Until recently, the role of production has been of special interest to Marxists and the role of distribution (markets and marketing) has been of special interest to capitalists, but few had examined the role of consumption as it relates to culture, society, and the environment. Perhaps that is because, until recently, there was not enough density of population nor enough variety in the available goods, services, and ideas to warrant such concern. But now there is, on both counts.

As I have explained elsewhere,[28] anthropologists in the field often get strange requests for goods. A man on Arno Atoll, in the tropics where everyone wears sandals, shorts, and T-shirts, asked me to buy him a suit from the Sears catalogue. A young man in Papua New Guinea asked us to buy him a CD player, in a village without electricity. What drives consumer desire?

As media have globalized, so has marketing expertise reached out and touched every hidden corner of the world. The concern for basic needs has been overshadowed by a drive to satisfy wants. Of course,

27. Achebe, *Things Fall Apart*. See also Uchendu, *The Igbo*.
28. Rynkiewich, "Underdevelopment of Anthropological Ethics."

Thorstein Veblen, observing Europe and America, warned us years ago about "conspicuous consumption," a condition in which people consume in order to build up their identity, their status in society, and their prestige with others.[29] In other words, the meaning and value of consumption is, as the rest of culture, socially constructed.

Anthropologists have contributed to the study of consumption by providing accounts of groups that destroy valuable items as a form of consumption, and accounts of the circulation of valued goods without their permanent consumption (i.e., they remain for a while with one person, then circulate again in trade). Both forms are also found, but not often recognized, in Western society. For example, the destruction of guitars by rock bands sends a message that they are rich enough not to care about the cost of replacement. Another example is the continual circulation of a class of goods dubbed "antiques," which are not consumed but keep coming back to the market.

There are now studies about the affect of consumption on personality, that is, the role of goods in making meaning for persons as well as the role of goods in forming personal identity. There are studies about the affect of consumption on society, that is, the role of goods in establishing value, in creating class or ethnic identity, and in the display of prestige and power. The latter defines a new area of study called "social capital," the accumulation and deployment of prestige in the pursuit of ends.

Finally, given the size of the population in the world and the power of consumerism, scientists and social scientists have recently begun to ask about the effect of consumption on the environment. I say "recently" because this has been going on for years. Archaeological studies have shown that the arrival of the Iron Age in Europe can be marked by the sudden appearance of pollutants from the smelting process, concentrated in the areas of production but scattered as well all over Europe, in about 700 BC in Europe, which lagged behind the Middle East and Africa in this innovation. There, the production, distribution, and consumption of iron tools and weapons defined who would thrive and/or be dominant and who would not.

29. Veblen, *Theory of the Leisure Class.*

Economic Development and Mission

Missions work, particularly of those mission agencies that want to do social justice and work with the poor, has tended to buy into the theories of development current in the Western world. Yet, in the 1950s and 60s, there began a sustained critique of development theory and practice. The exposure began with Aime Cesaire and Frantz Fanon, then Kwame Nkrumah, Albert Memmi, and Andre Gunder Franke, and by now it has become clear that development, as a discipline, is shot through with Western values.[30]

There are alternative theories of change and development, but too infrequently has there been a Christian or missionary critique of development. Does the mission of God include social transformation? If so, what is the relationship between that and development? What is God doing in the world? Is the transformation of the world into the kingdom of God only a spiritual development?

The dominant paradigm arose in the 1960s to guide discussions about development. In that decade, the Peace Corps began, as did many aid programs for developing (newly decolonized) nations. This concept of development grew out of an interpretation of certain historical events in the West: the Industrial Revolution in Europe and the United States; the colonial experience in Latin America, Asia, and Africa; the rise of positivism in science (rational, objective, amoral); the spread of capitalism and opposition to communism; and the rise of modern nation-states and the spread of democracy.

Implicit in the emerging theories of development were certain assumptions that were not questioned until the 1970s and 80s: that development is the same as modernization, that the most important element in development is technology, that development can be measured by the gross national product index combined with per capita average income, and that nations can be ranked by degree of development.

The Industrial Revolution, not coincidentally, was concurrent with the emergence of colonialism. This ushered in rapid economic growth in Europe and the United States, and the implication was that industrialization was at the core of development. Less developed, or later, "underdeveloped" countries were advised to industrialize.

---

30. Cesaire, *Discourse on Colonialism*; Fanon, *Wretched of the Earth*; Memmi, *Colonizer and the Colonized*; Nkrumah, *Neocolonialism*; Frank, *Latin America*.

Find ways to generate electric power (hydroelectric dams, such as the Aswan Dam), then build factories to manufacture goods. Lower priority was given to agricultural development unless it involved the use of machinery, fertilizer, herbicides, pesticides, and industrially produced hybrid seed.

Although economic growth through industrialization was seen as the key to development, this process requires capital and technology. This seemed to make sense to the West, but it was not appropriate for the historical and social settings of the underdeveloped countries. It was also a misreading of what actually happened in the West. Critical to the emergence of industrialization in the West was the existence of cheap labor (farm hands in England and slaves in the colonies), cheap raw materials (extracted from the colonies), and markets (in the emerging middle class in Europe and sometimes forced on the colonies, as in the famous Salt Law in India). Contemporary nations in the Majority World do not have colonies.

After World War II, when social scientists looked around the world, it appeared that the more developed nations had capital-intensive technology, not labor-intensive technology. Less developed nations had less of it. The implication seemed clear: Developed countries have to export technology to underdeveloped countries. It was assumed that, with the introduction of material technology, the necessary social structures would emerge as well. When this did not happen, social scientists tended to blame traditional ways of thinking and behaving. Social scientists got to work identifying the various social, psychological, and cultural barriers to change.

Modernizing traditional individuals became a priority task for government agencies, NGOs, and mission agencies. This involved using mass media, changing literacy, and introducing a Western educational system to make people into "rational" decision makers. These efforts cost a lot of money. Where does the money come from to introduce capital-intensive technologies in underdeveloped countries? It can be built into national budgets, but countries with small budgets already would have to eliminate other items, such as infrastructure and healthcare. It can come from local entrepreneurs, but that sector tends to suffer from greed and corruption. It can come from international loans, but if the program does not work, or does not work

quickly enough, this can lead a country into massive debt. The quick fix with delayed obligations was chosen by most countries.

If the International Monetary Fund and the World Bank are involved, then this money comes with plenty of strings attached. The money can come as international aid from industrialized nations, but much of this money is tied to importing and using personnel and goods from the donor country. It can come from multinational corporations, but this is often the opening step toward segments of the local economy being owned and controlled by industries in the Western nations.

Gradually, the newly independent nations of Africa, Asia, and Latin America began to realize that their political freedom was not the same thing as economic independence. That is, the end of colonialism did not necessarily mark the end of financial dependence on the industrial West. Often, dependency increased because emerging nations were counseled to build a governmental structure that they could not afford. The bureaucracy, technology, and demands or desires for military spending soon bankrupted many nations.

Have Christian missions been influenced by the dominant paradigm of economic development? Here are some areas to consider. Some missions have bought into the idea that they have a dual goal of evangelizing and civilizing. Missions offered three programs, sometimes called "Bibles, books, and band-aids" or "soap, soup, and salvation." The assumption is that if the West has reached a developed status and has the proper model, then it should help other people reach that status by following the same route.

Many missions take an individualistic approach trying to remake persons into rational decision makers. They assume that when converts reach a critical mass, then society will change. Technical assistance, in the form of money, equipment, and personnel, is the way that Christians from the West tend to work on behalf of the people from the Third World, especially in relief work, theological education, healthcare, and even church planting and evangelism.

Some missions assume that the major function of Christian education is to socialize people into a Western worldview. In this top-down approach, educational needs are defined by experts. Learners become passive recipients of the truth. The inherent tensions of mission in

this mode are paternal and neocolonial attitudes, ethnocentrism, pale carbon-copy churches, and split-level Christianity.

The old paradigm implied that poverty was equivalent to under-development. The obvious way for less developed countries to develop was to follow the lead of the West and become developed countries. It was less obvious that the "rules of the game" of development were con-trolled largely by the industrial West. The scholars who studied and wrote about development were all from the West and had a Western worldview. The balances of payments, interest rates, and monetary exchange rates were largely determined in New York, Washington, London, Paris, and Zurich. Technical assistance programs tended to make the recipients, the poor, even more dependent on the rich donor nations.

The result has been that development projects have not worked very well. Now the question comes: Who is to blame? Some have blamed the people in underdeveloped nations themselves for not hav-ing a need to achieve, for being corrupt, or for having a traditional social system that prevents entrepreneurship. Few saw flaws in the system, especially that large loans to nations tend to produce depen-dency, not development. Few saw any value in traditional beliefs and practices. The dominant paradigm put the blame for underdevelop-ment on the developing nation and not on the policies and practices of the developing countries. A new realization dawned by the 1990s: People cannot be developed; they can only develop themselves. The new role of the change agent is to help facilitate this process, not to force a preconceived idea of development on people.

Colonialism continued in the form of neocolonialism (appar-ent political independence but economic control from the outside). Neocolonialism, in some senses, continues in the form of globaliza-tion. Even though Thomas Friedman talks about the "democratization of technology," other evidence shows that most of the world's people have never made a phone call and most people do not have access to the Internet.

Tom Sine, in *Mustard Seed vs. McWorld*, says:

> . . . we increasingly find ourselves contending not only with
> escalating global change but also with a system of values that
> is often fundamentally counter to the values of the gospel of
> Christ. . . . we also need to make a massive effort to assist the

marginalized to start small businesses and credit unions to help them move out of poverty and achieve a decent way of life for their families. But the efforts to create a one-world economic order are raising some new challenges that deserve a more thoughtful response by people of faith. I am concerned about some of the consequences of economic globalization, and I am particularly concerned about the values driving it. . . . early evidence suggests that globalization doesn't work as well for the global poor as for those who have resources to take advantage of the liftoff. More troubling is the centralization of economic power, which seems to be one of the consequences of the rapid creation of a global economy. . . . the aspirations and values driving globalization are a product of the Enlightenment and modernity and are in many ways directly counter to the aspirations and values of God's new global order. Therefore we Christians have a challenging task of finding a way to be part of this world, in all its dimensions, while doing battle with any values that we believe are contrary to God's new global order.[31]

By now, it should be clear that development is not industrialization, urbanization, modernization, or Westernization (all terms used in the past). Some have called for the abandonment of the concept of development and the adoption of a concept more appropriate to the church: transformation.[32] Transformation would be incarnational, indigenous, holistic, and integrated. This would be a process in which people gain greater control over themselves, their environment, and their future in order to realize the full potential of abundant life that God has made possible through creation, redemption, and reconciliation.

Business and Mission

A new departure in mission is called "business as mission," though its roots are deep. Paul, Aquilla, and Priscilla were tentmakers; Peter, Andrew, James, and John were fishermen; Jesus was a carpenter. Not all were called to "leave their nets." Ted Yamamori, among others, encourages the movement of mission in the direction of more holistic ministry through the inclusion of business.[33]

31. Sine, *Mustard Seed vs. McWorld*, 20.

32. See Samuel and Sugden, eds., *Church in Response to Human Need*.

33. See, for example: Yamamori and Eldred, eds., *On Kingdom Business*; Rundle and Steffen, *Great Commission Companies*; and Steffen and Barnett, eds., *Business as Mission*.

The notion of marketplace ministries is pushing Christians to ask about the connection between mission and work. Microeconomic development involves increasing small-scale production and/or giving small loans so that people can start businesses. Small to medium enterprise involves credit development for larger-scale capital investment. Business as mission ranges from an entrepreneur building a factory in order to provide an appropriate witness in that place and to lift the economic level of the people, to running a store that markets handicrafts and agricultural products that are fair-trade certified.

Summary

As much as anything else, if you read the Prophets and the Gospels, the kingdom of God is about the production, distribution, and consumption of goods, services, and ideas. There is no justice in a society where people are marginalized, disenfranchised, and enslaved by those who control these processes.

> Thus says the LORD: For three transgressions of Israel, and for four, I will not revoke the punishment; because they sell the righteous for silver, and the needy for a pair of sandals--they who trample the head of the poor into the dust of the earth, and push the afflicted out of the way; father and son go in to the same girl, so that my holy name is profaned; they lay themselves down beside every altar on garments taken in pledge; and in the house of their God they drink wine bought with fines they imposed.[34]

This is a picture of a society where the rich have forgotten that the poor cannot afford to provide a blanket for collateral because they only have one and will need it the same night to ward off the cold. This is a society where the religious leaders impose fines and then buy their luxuries with what they collect. This is a society that passes laws to secure the economic status of the upper class, not laws to protect the health and welfare of the poor and sick. Every economic system provides goods for some, and thus every economic system stands under prophetic critique.

34. Amos 2:6–8.

7

Politics, Power, and Law

Politics as Order

THERE ARE A NUMBER OF WAYS TO EXPLORE DIMENSIONS OF power, prestige, and social control. One could examine the nature of hierarchy. From the perspective of cultural evolution and cultural ecology in anthropology, the important question used to be: What is the origin of the state? This question assumed that the modern na-tion-state was the highest level of order and control.[1] The logical (by European assumptions) outcome of this line of research was a model of stages of development of political power.[2] Thus, there is the familiar evolutionary scheme of growth from band to chiefdom to kingdom to state, with the concomitant development of leadership from headman to chief to king to president or prime minister.

From the perspective of structural functionalism, the important question used to be: How do the means of instituting order and social control fit with other social institutions and what contribution does the institution of politics make to the overall whole? Both of these are

1. Actually, the nation-state of today is a modernist invention, the culmination of processes begun in the 1600s, reaching a high point in Europe with the formation of Germany as a state in the 1870s, continuing with the formation of a number of new states following the dissolution of empires after World War I and the demise of clas-sic colonialism in the 1960s. This perspective was successfully argued by Benedict Anderson in *Imagined Communities*.

2. Fried, *Evolution of Political Society*; Krader, *Formation of the State*; Service, *Origins of the State and Civilization*.

121

important questions, but neither exposes the dynamic of politics: the use of influence and power to decide "who gets what, when, and how."[3]

Headmen

Nomadic bands of hunters and gatherers or fishers usually do not have a complex political organization. With everyone in face-to-face contact and focused on the same goal of gathering enough food, water, and shelter for the day, there is little specialization of roles, accumulation of wealth, or insistence on personal property. The band considers their territory as the site of their wandering and not as a possession.

In such a society, kinship, economics, politics, and religion all overlap, and a multitasking headman is also a father, a good hunter, and a healer. Authority is based on prestige and the power of persuasion. Given the egalitarian nature of the band, leaders lead only as long as people agree to follow. Disagreement may result in the people following the advice of a different person in the same band, who then becomes, for a while, the headman. Conflict may result in people leaving and joining another band where they have relatives. If resources are scarce, the band may voluntarily split into extended family groups that go their separate ways until more resources are available in one place.

Bigmen

In Melanesia in the South Pacific, there is a type of leader called a "bigman" or "man of renown" or "centre man." In this environment, there are usually abundant resources; the people garden, herd pigs, and fish, so people settle into hamlets or villages. A bigman does not inherit his position. He is a person who creates his own organization out of standard relationships in society. A bigman is able to influence the behavior of others because of his skills in warfare, negotiation, gardening, pig raising, trade, oratory, and/or healing. Some have compared him to an entrepreneur who works his way up the chain.[4] A bigman develops a personal following rather than inheriting one. He creates a position of authority and influence by manipulating the wealth of others, not by being rich himself. This occurs in an arena of competition

3. Lasswell, *Politics.*

4. The classic study of Bigmen is Oliver, *Solomon Island Society.* See also Sahlins, "Rich Man, Poor Man."

where other rising bigmen are also trying to achieve a following. An aspiring bigman must have energy and creativity.

Among the Siuai (now Siwai) of South Bougainville in the Solomon Islands (politically in Papua New Guinea but culturally in the Solomons), this competition is expressed in competitive feasting. The bigman calls on kinfolk and village mates to contribute work, pigs, and vegetables to prepare a feast. When the food is ready, another bigman is chosen as the "guest" who receives this "honor." That man comes with his followers to receive the food. Then there is a waiting period to see if the recipient is able to organize his followers to provide an equal or greater feast in return.

Should he fail, then he has dropped a notch in rank and the giver has moved up. What do the kinfolk and village mates get? Renown, prestige, the privilege of associating with the bigman, the prestige of being in an important village—sort of "basking in the glow" of the bigman.[5] The problem for the bigman is that his rise means someday there will be a fall. The food, pigs, and other wealth that a bigman amasses for a feast are not his own, but rather the product of debts called in, cajoling, and borrowing. It gets increasingly more difficult to extract pigs and organize feasts. He is increasingly in the debt of his followers. This type of leadership, though traditional, still influences the way that members of parliament function today. Interestingly, the concern for one's position in an honor-shame system is reminiscent of first-century Palestine.[6]

Chiefs

By contrast, in Polynesia and Micronesia there are more classic leaders that we can properly call "chiefs." These are more or less hereditary leaders who come from a distinct class in society. While headmen have influence and bigmen have prestige, chiefs have power that functions in a different economic setting.

As described in the last chapter, traditional Marshallese politics provides a classic case of the *redistributive chiefdom*, a hierarchical system where goods flow from the lowest level to the highest and then

---

5. An excellent film illustrating the work of being a Bigman is *Ongka's Big Moka: The Kawelka of Papua New Guinea* (1976), in the Disappearing World Series.

6. See Luke 14:7–14.

back again, and where power has supernatural confirmation and can be exerted with real force.

Islands and coral atolls have a diversity of resources (gardens, trees, fish and other seafood) spread across a number of microenvironments (mountains, valleys, plateaus, swamps, shores, reefs, lagoons, and open ocean). Instead of moving those resources and products (such as pandanus mats, preserved breadfruit, preserved pandanus, thatch, tools, and weapons) through trade routes, the traditional system moved things through the central agency of a chiefdom.

As described elsewhere,[7] Marshallese society was divided into two classes, *kajur* ("commoners") and *irooj* ("royalty"). The *irooj* were a chiefly matrilineage that had achieved their status through organization and expansion (often through warfare) over an atoll or several atolls. The leader of the matrilineage became the "paramount chief" over the atoll or atolls. Leaders of junior lineages would be named as "lesser chiefs" in the districts in which they lived. The leader of a *kajur* matrilineage was called "lineage head." So, there was one "paramount chief" in a chiefdom, several "lesser chiefs," and many "lineage heads" under them—a classic pyramid hierarchy.

The "paramount chief" was responsible for protecting the people from other predatory chiefs, and for expanding the chiefdom when opportunities arose. The "commoners" were responsible for working certain pieces of land, called *wato*, and gathering resources on the reef and ocean in order to take care of their own families and keep the chiefdom productive. The firstfruits of any enterprise (fishing, gardening, collecting) were owed to the "paramount chief."

The system, like politics in the United States, could be open to abuse. Perhaps for that reason, succession to the position of paramount chief was not automatic. Matrilineal succession to chieftainship followed three rules:

- *bwij emman*, the senior branch of the lineage comes first;

- *ebeben emman*, the senior generation come first; and

- *memman emman*, a brother comes before a sister (in precolonial times).

There is an inherent contradiction in the system, such that when the last of a set of siblings of one generation dies there is always more

7. Rynkiewich, "Ossification of Local Politics."

than one person who seems to be able to make an argument that they should be the next paramount chief. Who actually becomes the chief depends on who can gather the most support, the most followers from among the *kajur*. The relationship between chiefs and followers is symbolized in the fact that *kajur* means "commoner," but it is also the word for "strength." Thus, the strength of the chief is the number of commoner followers he has. The number of followers he has depends on how generous he has been in redistributing resources.

In early colonial times, such leaders were perceived by missionaries and colonial administrators to be tyrants or despots. Such was rarely the case before the colonial administration arrived. In the traditional system, no despot would last very long but, like Rehoboam, would lose his followers to other chiefs. Instead of being lockstep, the traditional system of inheritance was more flexible and even democratic than imagined.

Politics as Conflict

From a functionalist perspective, conflict is dysfunctional. From the point of view of actors, conflict may be necessary to redress grievances or reorder society. The idea that conflict may have positive functions for the order of society was established in anthropology through the ethnographic work of E. E. Evans-Pritchard.[8] The Nuer are a nomadic cattle-herding people who live in the South Sudan. They are patrilineal and have age sets (named generational cohorts that perform different functions in society). There is no traditional central leadership or bureaucracy; every lineage owns its own cattle and conducts its own business of herding, managing households, and arranging marriages. If a dispute breaks out among cousins, then warriors and elders will take sides along lineage lines. If, days later, a dispute breaks out among more distant cousins, then the warriors and elders who had been opposed to each other will unite against their more distant agnatic kin. If, a month later, those people have to protect themselves from attacks from another patriclan not related to their own, then all the former disputants align themselves on behalf of their patriclan against the other clan. Thus, the political order is established according to the nature of the dispute, with people following their lineage links to form groups for political action.

8. Evans-Pritchard, *The Nuer*.

Evans-Pritchard called this political dynamic "segmentary opposition." Americans with a European ancestry have something similar in their history, preserved in the old saying, "My brother and I against our cousin; my brother, my cousin, and I against our neighbors; and all of us against the stranger." Political units are formed around issues and are not permanent. There is no one in charge, so it does not matter who is eliminated from this system, the response is structural not hierarchical. People know where their alliances lie without being told. The system organizes itself. This principle applies to more than Evans-Pritchard imagined.

Max Gluckman picked up on this idea and argued that it was more widespread in a book titled *Custom and Conflict in Africa*.[9] With the concept of "the peace in the feud" Gluckman sought to show how violence, while inherent in the system, was in fact limited by structural constraints embedded in custom or tradition. That is, there are forces pulling societies apart but also forces pushing them together. Gluckman was the first anthropologist at Manchester University, and there he founded what has come to be known at the "Manchester school" of thought based on conflict theory and extended case studies as a method.

At about the same time, Fredrik Barth was publishing studies linking segmentary opposition to the theory of games.[10] Barth's ethnographic fieldwork was conducted in the Swat Valley, which may have seemed obscure at the time but had come to center stage by 2010. Barth described a political system that was based less on bounded territories than on patron-client relations.[11] Khans developed a followership by getting clients into their debt and then expecting political support when issues arose. That meant that the domain of influence of a khan could not be defined unless there was a conflict and people had to take sides. It also meant that the followership of various khans overlapped, and the marginal followers could be pulled either way. The khan had to maintain relationships actively or his influence waned.

The idea that there might be more than one political system in the minds of people, and that politics might be the activity of people trying to install one model over another, also arose in the 1950s and

9. Gluckman, *Custom and Conflict in Africa*.

10. Barth, "Segmentary Opposition."

11. Barth, *Political Leadership among Swat Pathans*.

60s. Edmund Leach studied the Kachin of Burma before and during World War II, serving part of that time in the Burmese army. His ethnographic fieldwork demonstrated that the Kachin had two models, one more democratic and emphasizing autonomy (*gumlao*), and one more hierarchical and emphasizing hereditary chiefs (*gumsa*). He also showed that historically the Kachin cycled back and forth between their two political ideals.[12]

Leach's work, coupled with the studies of the Nuer and the Swat Pathans, undermined the functionalist's understanding of society because they introduced alternatives, strategies, cooperation, and conflict into our understanding of local-level politics. It was possible to have political dynamics (organization, opposition, outcomes) without leaders, without hierarchy, and without a single political order. This perspective on politics has become significant at the beginning of the twenty-first century.

Politics as a Game of Strategies not Territories

Today, there are very few full time nomadic hunters and gatherers anywhere. In addition, there are no villages, alliances, or tribes anywhere that are not encapsulated, to one degree or another, within a modern nation-state. No groups are able to operate as an independent political system. Local-level political styles may be practiced in larger political arenas,[13] but all political systems are enmeshed in larger political spheres.

In fact, in the twenty-first century, nation-states themselves are not the ultimate political units in the game anymore and thus cannot operate as independent nations. Many global corporations, businesses, and organizations operate in a parallel universe with little regard for the old national boundaries. The resurgence of a conservative and militant Islam carries a narrative that submits religious issues to no nation.

Political entities are arising that have no leader, no permanent organization, are composed of a network of loosely affiliated local groups, and are driven by a compelling ideology. Taking out the "leader" of such a group accomplishes nothing. Eliminating one cell of the group does not affect the others. Taking territory accomplishes little

12. Leach, *Political Systems of Highland Burm.*
13. Rynkiewich, "Big-Man Politics."

since these groups do not hold territory. The Christian movement was once like that. Today such diverse movements as Al-Qaeda, the Tea Party, and WikiLeaks thrive in a world filled with seemingly powerful nation-states.

In any case, the anthropologist or missionary is always challenged to understand the local political situation. These are some variations in leadership styles, but the truth is that there are many more varieties than normally identified by generalists. One must discover what an *alcalde* or *cacique* might do, or how a *matai* or *tulafale* might interface with church hierarchy.[14] Any anthropologist or missionary must explore the meaning of leadership in the society where they live.

What are the missiological implications of understanding local politics? In Romans, Paul says that God instituted governments for our own good. That means that every system serves purposes for the society and is not to be taken lightly or dismissed lightly. It is also true that every system is a fallen system because men and women are involved. While the particular system of government may not matter to God, the results of governance do. Every government is subject to prophetic critique based on kingdom values. At the center is the command to take care of the widow, the orphan, and the alien.

Finally, there is no reason to colonize others, to try to coerce others, or to export one's political system to others. God has ordained no system, but instead critiques them all—as Jesus did in his refusal of Satan's offer to give him all the kingdoms of the world. Jesus transforms all peoples with the fellowship of his suffering and the power of his resurrection.

Law as Conflict Resolution

Law is a form of social control that, ideally, works toward order, predictability, and social justice in society. This is achieved in different ways with differing measures of individuality and community, freedom and constraint, oppression and justice. In traditional societies, legal procedures tend to be lodged in generalized institutions rather than specialized courts and court officers. The goal of law in traditional communities is not to find the truth, however defined, but to restore relationships and preserve community. In the modern nation-state, legal procedures are usually located in specialized institutions

14. Tomlinson, *In God's Image.*

that pretend to serve all the people but end up privileging one group over another.

There is a great variety of legal models. Even in Scripture, there are examples of wandering nomads herding goats and cattle who live under the control of clan elders like Abraham, Isaac, and Jacob. There are examples of an immigrant people settling a land under the authority of judges, prominent men and women such as Samson and Deborah who rose to positions of leadership based on the observation over a period of time that God was indeed with them and thus they were worth following. There are examples of kings who ruled by succession, or by assassination, kings who could muster the power but through misuse of power lost the authority, kings who humbly came back to God's ways of justice and mercy, and kings who went down to defeat for the accumulated sins of the nation, as the prophets tell us. Finally, there are examples of empire, almost all of them evil, with exceptions such as God's anointing of Cyrus of the Persian Empire to come and release captive Israel so they could return to their land. It is empire that most often brings death, destruction, and misery to so many in the biblical narrative, and that trend continues. The truth is that God can work through a variety of legal and political systems. The difference is whether or not God's love, mercy, and justice are expressed in the performance of law and politics.

There was a time when Western anthropologists and missionaries alike dismissed some societies as having no law and no government. That was a mistake, as it has never been true of any people, or any that have survived. When I began graduate studies in anthropology at the University of Minnesota, my first advisor was E. Adamson Hoebel. He had been a student of Franz Boas, the father of American anthropology, and he was then chair of the department. Hoebel was a pioneer in demonstrating that every society had law.

In the past, people took an ideological approach to studying law. They looked for rules for controlling behavior, preferably a set of codes. Then, they looked for the structures that accompany Western law: a court, court officials, lawyers, plaintiffs, defendants, and juries. When they did not find law codes or courts, they declared that that society did not have law.

Hoebel approached it from a different perspective. He observed that societies have cases of dispute and yet, most of the time, societies

do not fall apart over the disputes. Instead, societies have ways of handling trouble when it arises. Hoebel shifted the focus to dispute settlement. He used a method familiar to any law student: the trouble-case method.

Hoebel lived and studied among the Northern Cheyenne in 1935 and 1936. He talked with the elders and tried to get to the time just before their wars with the US, that is, to around 1840–1860. He wanted to get an understanding of the ways of Cheyenne law. Hoebel found areas of social control within the kindred, led by elders, and within the larger band, which were larger named groups of relatives. Cutting across the bands were the military societies that became increasingly important in the mid-1800s. The five original societies were the Fox, Elk, Shield Soldiers, Dog Soldiers, and Bowstring or Contrary Society. Later the Wolfs and the Crazy Dogs were organized, each with a special set of rules. The point here is that law may be specific to social groups that are formed in society. For example, a student may be kicked out of a private church school for drinking alcohol, but, as long as she is of age, the general society has no sanction on drinking.

Over the tribe as a whole stood the Council of Forty-Four. Five head chiefs governed this organization, with two door-keeping chiefs and thirty-seven others who were all chosen/elected from the bands. Required personal qualities included: even-tempered, good-natured, wise, energetic, kind, courageous, generous, and concerned for the well-being of others. The council had a sacred origin and a founding narrative. The story makes it clear that the function of the council was to hold society together against the forces for division. As Hoebel says, "Cheyenne government . . . is highly democratic and representative of people's concerns."[15] The goals of Cheyenne law were to eliminate the desire to resort to feud and to regulate the annual communal hunt. The following case illustrates Hoebel's case-study approach.

> In a typical case the tribe was moving up the Rosebud River in Montana looking for buffalo in the direction of the Big Horn Mountains. All the hunters were in a line with the Shield Soldiers to restrain them until the signal was given, for the scouts had reported buffalo. Just as the line came over a protecting ridge down wind from the buffalo, two men were seen riding in among the herd. At an order from their chief,

15. Hoebel, *The Cheyennes*, 46.

the Shield Soldiers charged down on them. Little Old Man shouted that any who failed or hesitated to beat the miscreants would be beaten themselves. The first to reach the spot killed the two hunters' horses. As each soldier reached the criminals, he slashed them with his whip. Their guns were smashed.[16]

This was not the end of the matter as punishment is set in the context of social order, much as Jacob lectured his sons.

The offenders were sons of a Dakota who had been living with the Cheyennes for some time. He said to his sons, "Now you have done wrong. You failed to obey the law of this tribe. You went out alone and you did not give the other people a chance."[17]

Punishment puts the offenders in a liminal position: they have no status in society. That is followed by the recovery of order in society, and then by the re-entry into society of the chastened hunters.

The Shield Soldier chiefs took up the lecturing. The boys did not try to defend themselves, so the chiefs relented. They called on their men to consider the plight of the two delinquents, without horses or weapons. "What do you men want to do about it?" Two offered to give them horses. A third gave them two guns. All the others said, "Good!"[18]

Hoebel's conclusion could stand for most precolonial legal systems: "It is in facing up to new crisis situations . . . that the Cheyennes show their real legal genius and capacity for treating their culture as a working instrument for the realization of social ends."[19]

British social anthropologist Philip Gulliver studied among the Arusha, an agricultural Lmaa group in Tanzania.[20] They do have a formal judicial review system that resembles a court; Gulliver called it a "moot." The Arusha have age sets, a system where people move through the stages of life with their age-mates. These cut across the patrilineages that otherwise ordered society. Since the Arusha are

16. Ibid., 53–54.
17. Ibid., 54.
18. Ibid.
19. Ibid., 55.
20. While I was in graduate school at the University of Minnesota, I took a class from Gulliver, who was a visiting lecturer. Gulliver's account of the Arusha moot is available in Gulliver, *Social Control in an African Society*.

gardeners, residence in a territory, a "parish," is also significant. Most disputes were between members of different age sets. At a moot, supporters of each disputant would stand for their relative according to the closeness of the relationship. The goal was not to fix blame, but to fix relationships so that society would hold together and life would go on.

Crosscutting ties and multiple memberships contribute both to the formation of support groups behind the disputants in a moot, and to the likelihood that the matter will be settled. If people have an interest in both sides, then they will find a way to resolve disputes.

Here Gluckman's notion of "the peace in the feud" applies. As in the case of the Cheyenne and the Arusha, societies that are organized around institutions that cut across society in different ways tend to have forces that cause feud and forces for settling feuds. The Cheyenne are organized around bands, but cutting across these were the military societies. The Arusha have patrilineages, but cutting across these are the age sets. The point is that when there is a tendency for society to split one way, that tendency is countered by the fact that some of the people on one side are linked to people on the other side in another way. When a conflict breaks out, it is in their best interest to seek peace rather than fight.

What are the missiological implications of discoveries about law and dispute settlement? First, every society has its own ways of maintaining order and settling disputes. There are more models out there that work than just the Western one. An anthropologist or missionary who makes a long-term commitment to a community must learn to work within the system because it has been tested and served the people well over time.

Second, there is great danger in ignoring or attacking an existing system. The breakdown of the traditional system of social control may leave a vacuum that is not filled by a coherent and comprehensive system, and thus the breakdown of the traditional system may usher in a period of disorder. In the towns of Papua New Guinea there are roving gangs of criminals, called "rascals," who are young men who have migrated from the village and no longer operate under the authority of the elders. The state is a modernist fiction to them and, at any rate, does not have the resources to stop them.

Every system is biased in favor of some and tipped against others. That is, every system of justice contains the seeds of injustice. The prophetic voice of the church follows the lead of the prophets and Jesus. The rule of thumb for evaluating a society in the Old Testament is this: How are orphans, widows, and strangers[21] protected and cared for? How do the marginalized and poor fare in this society? Jesus came declaring that the Year of Jubilee (the Year of the Lord's Favor) had arrived with him, a year when debts were forgiven and the poor were restored to their land.[22] A missionary without a theology of politics and law, justice and reconciliation, as well as contextualization of the gospel for transformation of society runs the risk of simply imposing Western concepts and practices where they will not work.

21. Exod 22:22; Deut 10:18; 16:11–14; 24:17–21; 27:19; Pss 68:5; 94:6; 146:9; Isa 1:17; 10:2; Jer 22:3; 49:11; Ezek 22:7; Zech 7:10; Mal 3:5; Jas 1:27.

22. Deut ch. 25.

8

Religion, Belief, and Ritual

Introduction

THERE IS ALWAYS UNEASINESS IN WRITING ABOUT RELIGION OR comparative religion when one is a committed Christian, like walking a tightrope and fearing that one might fall off toward ethnocentrism on the right or liberalism on the left. Perhaps it is best to begin with the concept of religion as a subject itself.

Let's start with a bold claim: Hinduism is not a religion. Hinduism is a way of life, or a set of related ways of life that includes a variety of beliefs and practices, none of which can be isolated from the others. Hinduism became a religion when Europeans said, "We have a religion, so we wonder what their religion is?"

Christianity is not a religion. However, Christianity, in the post-Enlightenment world, increasingly has been defined as a religion. Christianity is often conceived as a social and cultural category of beliefs and practices that mostly belong within the institution of the church, but do not necessarily impact other areas of life (the separation of church and state) and can be rejected in some people's lives (non-believers). At the same time that Christianity was becoming distinct as one of many institutions in European society, researchers began to search for the equivalent in other cultures. So, the people of India were found to have a religion called Hinduism, except for those who were Muslim, Sikh, or Jains, and the Chinese were found to have a religion called Buddhism, except for those who tended more toward

Confucianism or Taoism. In the West, it was thought that society was made up of different parts or institutions, so everyone had a religion, except perhaps the isolated people on the lowest rung of humanity who did not have a religion. The world religions were Christianity, Judaism, Islam, Hinduism, and Buddhism.

However, as it turns out once again, the world is not like that. The conception of society constructed out of building blocks that are separable and replaceable is a new notion; a particularly Western schema for construing social order. Most of the people in the world most of the time think (or thought) about life in a more integrated fashion. For most people, beliefs and rituals are conceived as being more embedded in daily life, and what appear to be outside forces and influences, including spiritual forces, have been more imminent than these appear to be to Europeans and Americans today.

In many places in the world, if you asked people what religion they are, they would not know how to answer. That is because not everyone separates the spiritual from the material. In that way of life, everything is spiritual or religious. In fact, in earlier times, this was true for European Christians as well. Once the cracks began to appear, Europeans began to try to recover this monism. Brother Lawrence's *The Practice of the Presence of God* (seventeenth century) is a prime example of the genre.

Definition

Let us construct a definition of religion, then examine the reasons why it needs to be deconstructed.

Religion is a set of beliefs and practices that function to help people make sense of the world, answer life's questions, and deal with life's problems. This usually involves:(1) a cosmology—often, but not always, one that includes spiritual beings; (2) a concern with accessing spiritual power, sometimes to achieve life beyond this life, but more often to enhance life on this earth; (3) associated ritual practices that test or demonstrate these beliefs, especially rituals that activate spiritual power for the practitioners and petitioners; and (4) certain statuses and structural arrangements that order ritual performances and perpetuate beliefs and practices.

This definition tends toward the rational side, and does not deal adequately with the emotional side of life. It includes a note of

modernist skepticism, as if some of these beliefs might not be real, and assumes that cosmology, order, and hierarchy, which are evident in organized religion, is more common that it actually is. Perhaps the question should be: How helpful is it to have a category called "religion," and what have anthropologists and other social scientists discovered about religion in various cultural settings?

Evolutionary Anthropology and the Origin of Religion

Early anthropologists, both scholars and dilettantes during the nineteenth century, were concerned with the origins of customs and institutions. The underlying motivation for this quest for new foundations was the desire to bolster European cultural pride. The underlying assumption was that, if it could be shown that culture and society developed in stages from simple to complex versions, then it was but a short step to justifying why Europe was at the top of the ladder, as it certainly seemed to be in terms of political and military power. In addition, the church's version of history, one of devolution or a fall from a primal state of purity and innocence, would be undermined in favor of the new faith in progress. The idea of cultural and social evolution provided a narrative that justified colonial domination and economic exploitation. Finally, for some, an evolutionary perspective might liberate Europe from the metanarrative that grounded its story in the Old Testament version of Jewish history and the way would be open for the discovery of new ancestors in Assyrian and Babylonian texts and/or in Greek and Roman texts.

In this cultural context, a polymath named Herbert Spencer (1820–1903) drew together other speculations about the direction of human history and developed a theory of evolution that he applied to many fields. Spencer used the analogy of a biological "organism"[1] to talk about human society, imagining that they evolved by the same processes. He assumed, as did others of his era, that "primitive" societies exhibited a simple technology and a generalized social structure without specialization. So influential has this belief been that, today, even Christians who do not believe in biological evolution seem to believe in cultural evolution. Spencer introduced the famous phrase

1. He wrote textbooks in biology as well as sociology.

"survival of the fittest," and applied it to human societies.[2] The next step from this concept to the justification of the colonial enterprise is not difficult to imagine.

In this theoretical paradigm, Edward Burnett Tylor (1832–1917), whom one might say is the father of British anthropology, developed his ideas about the origin of religion. His minimal definition of religion, "belief in spiritual beings,"[3] is still widely quoted today, even though it leaves out Buddhism, which is more concerned with a path to a "place" beyond material or spiritual realms. What Tylor had in mind as the earliest form of religion was animism. The premise for animism is speculation about how early humans might have responded to the mysteries of nature. Tylor and others assumed that reflections about death, dreams, and visions led "primitive" philosophers to invent the idea of a soul. In death, something seems to leave the body. In dreams, people who have died seem to live again. In visions, whether induced by hallucinatory drugs or by psychological disturbances, one seems to travel to other places and meet people who are far away.

Once conceived, then the idea of a soul might be extended to other animate objects, such as wolves and cattle, or even to seemingly inanimate objects that still seem to affect human lives, such as rocks and trees. From this one could imagine the development of other concepts: an afterlife where dead souls live, the sacrifice of an animal in order to release its soul to go to the other world, and the idea that disembodied spirits might interact with this world by their own choice or by being induced or bribed by humans to do so.

Missiologists from the previous generation followed anthropologists by reifying a religion or religious category called "animism." Eugene Nida and William Smalley concluded:

> When confronted with the claims of Christianity, or even of other major religions, animistic beliefs have usually proved to be weak. They have capitulated to organized religious systems far more quickly than the more elaborate religions have given in to each other. There are several reasons for this inherent weakness in the primitive religions.[4]

2. This phrase does not appear in Darwin's *Origin of Species* until the sixth edition, published in 1872.

3. Tylor, *Primitive Culture*, 8.

4. Nida and Smalley, *Introducing Animism*, 56–57.

Nida and Smalley make other claims: that "there is no fundamental moral basis in animism," that "animism provides no satisfactory answer to the question of the meaning of life and the significance of history," that "the religious leaders—shamans, sorcerers, or mediums—are the 'lunatic fringe' of society," and that "a fourth liability in primitive beliefs is the undue emphasis upon the physiological and infantile in religious practice," which exposes animism's "inability . . . to deal effectively in so many instances with the needs of the social group."[5] For being so dysfunctional, such beliefs and practices have not gone away. This brings us to the insights provided by Paul Hiebert concerning "the excluded middle."[6]

In the old paradigm, animism (as the belief in souls, ghosts, spirits, and demons) might evolve into the worship of gods (polytheism), and finally into the worship of one God (monotheism). Or so the story goes.[7]

James G. Frazier (1854–1941) sought to divide magic, religion, and science, and put them, in that order, into an evolutionary scheme that implied that as humans got more rational they moved from a belief in spiritual forces, to a belief in gods or God, to a belief in the laws of science. Religion characterizes a period in history when people gave up and submitted to imagined higher powers. Then, to save the day, science led a return to the issue of causes, though this time with better observation of the relationships between events. This view of progress marks the modernist project, and is still strong in the Euro-American psyche today.

Frazier interpreted magic as a misguided attempt to get at causes. Sympathetic or contagious magic presumes a connection between the part and the whole. For example, some people believe that doing something to a person's hair or fingernail clippings will affect the person they came from. Homeopathic or imitative magic assumed that actions carried out on a surrogate will be replicated on the real thing, for example, that throwing darts at a picture of a politician will really end up hurting him.

5. Ibid., 57–58.

6. Hiebert, "Flaw of the Excluded Middle."

7. A missionary from the last century produced a volume about animism and Islam: Zwemer, *Influence of Animism on Islam*. Despite the deconstruction of the concept, it still tends to appear in missiological literature as well as in anthropological literature: Aragon, *Fields of the Lord*; Harvey, *Animism*.

This style of reasoning, sitting in an armchair and imagining what "primitive" people might have thought, though popular at the turn of the century, ultimately fails on several grounds. First, it is speculative, imagining what people might have done without proof that anyone ever did that. It has about the same status as Sigmund Freud's imaginings about the origin of the incest taboo. Second, it is full of Western assumptions about what is of interest and what is mysterious. Third, it is based on the assumption that a "primitive" person thinks like a child, a common assumption even in the social sciences up through the 1950s.

Anthropological Theory and Higher Criticism

Cross-disciplinary work often contributes to fresh insights, as when biblical studies draws on the findings of archaeology for insights into the social and cultural context of Bible times. Those who borrow from other disciplines, however, are under an obligation to try to keep up with developments in that discipline. It seems that scholars in biblical studies in the nineteenth century borrowed current anthropological theories, developed their own criticisms, and never checked again to see if the paradigm that was foundational to their studies had changed.

Julius Wellhausen (1844–1918), for example, following on the work of Baur and Semler, used the assumptions of the emerging discipline of anthropology to develop what now is called the Graf-Wellhausen Hypothesis, the foundation for *higher criticism*.[8] His *Prologue to the History of Israel* provided an extended critique of the development of the Jewish religion and an exploration of the origins of the Pentateuch. On the assumption of a movement from simple to complex, Wellhausen argued that the Israelites could not have begun with monotheism (an assumption vigorously attacked by Fr. Wilhelm Schmidt[9] beginning in 1912) and could not have exhibited certain features because of their stage of cultural evolution. Wellhausen dismissed Old Testament history and religion as a fabricated story and

8. The following account depends heavily on Arnold and Weisberg, "Centennial Review."

9. Fr. Wilhelm Schmidt (1868–1954), the founder of the journal *Anthropos* (1931), was an early Christian anthropologist who upheld the integrity of the discipline in the service of the church and mission. His opposition to simple cultural evolutionary theory generated a 12-volume work, *Der Ursprung der Gottesidee* ("The Origin of the Idea of God"), published over his academic lifetime.

not an appropriate foundation for Christianity. For this he was accused, even in his day, of anti-Semitism.

One of his contemporaries was Friedrich Delitzsch, whose series of lectures on "Babel und Bibel" systematically dismissed the Hebrew Bible as being full of superstitions and thus no longer "authoritative for modern German Christians."[10] Instead, Babylonian religion and culture were more reliable, but, in the end, he argued that the Hebrew Bible should be replaced with stories of Germany's heroes of the past.[11] Ultimately, Delitzsch introduced the idea that Aryan stock had infused Babylonia and Samaria, and that Jesus himself was Aryan, not Semitic. All this, he said, was "for Germany's honor and for Germany's science."[12]

Arnold and Weisberg conclude that an uncritical appropriation of an early anthropological theory actually served an underlying agenda of the biblical scholar.

> . . . among contemporaneous European scholars of the Hebrew Bible, Delitzsch stood in a long line of anti-Jewish predecessors. For a prime example, we need look no further than the celebrated Julius Wellhausen. . . . One of the fundamental assumptions pervading Wellhausen's rather imposing historical construction was the conviction that the postexilic, law-centered religion of Judaism was a decline from the higher prophetic insights of the earlier period.[13]

The irony is that the cultural evolution paradigm in anthropology was critiqued, overturned, and discarded by anthropologists in the decade between 1910 and 1920. However, the biblical scholars seem never to have heard the news of the fall of Babylon.

The Functions of Religion

Sigmund Freud might have been pleased with Tylor's method of explanation because it provided a psychological explanation of a social phenomenon, but Emile Durkheim (1858–1917) would not have bought it. In *The Elementary Forms of the Religious Life*, Durkheim argued that religion is to be explained not by speculation about how an individual

10. Arnold and Weisberg, "Centennial Review," 445.

11. Ibid., 446.

12. Ibid., 442. The authors reference pages 50–52 of Delitzsch's *Ein Vortrag.*

13. Ibid., 446–47.

might have reacted to the elements, but rather by the role that religion played in everyday life. However, he did believe that this might be easier to discover in "primitive" society, so he followed James Frazier's descriptions of the role that *totemism* served in Australian Aboriginal society. In Durkheim's interpretation, a totemic animal represents the clan and thus provides the link between this world and the "other" world. By establishing the sacred character of the rituals associated with propitiation and expiation, the rites associated with initiation, and the stories that account for the existence of objects in nature and rituals in society, religion functions to encourage social cohesion in a society that might otherwise fall apart. Thus, for Durkheim, religion is a means by which society worships itself.

Durkheim's work, though he was a sociologist who stayed in France rather than travel to Australia to actually live with and talk to Aborigines, influenced the next generation of anthropologists.[14] When cultural evolutionism failed, a paradigm shift occurred and functionalism dominated anthropological thinking in the mid-twentieth century.

Just how religion functioned in society was not a matter of common agreement. Max Weber, in his *The Protestant Ethic and the Spirit of Capitalism*, argued that religion was the depositum of values for society and thus affected other institutions, such as economics and politics. As a case study, he argued that the Protestant countries of Europe led the industrial revolution because their people embodied the ideology of self-discipline and accountability; in other words, the values of individualism, hard work, and saving money that he traced to the Protestant Reformation.

On the contrary, Karl Marx (1818–1883) perceived that religion is associated with class and power. In this reading, it is economic facts, such as the division of labor and the ownership of the means of production, that shape society. Religion, under the control of the upper classes, serves to justify class differences. Religious ideology, then, serves to maintain inequality and injustice by shifting workers' concerns to the afterlife so that they do not see the reality of this life. Thus, "religion is the opiate of the people."

14. I used this theory myself in my master's thesis (1968), arguing that the people on one reservation stopped dancing when they lost their land and, thus, their sense of community. If there is no community solidarity, then there is no need for a celebration of community. Rynkiewich, "Chippewa Powwows."

Bronislaw Malinowski (1884–1942), a Polish-born British social anthropologist, did his field research in the Trobriand Islands,[15] focusing primarily on the *Kula*, an exchange network that took an enormous amount of the time and attention of the men. His well-known article "Magic, Science, and Religion"[16] produces ethnographic evidence that all three kinds of thinking exist within the same society, and that the difference is the degree of uncertainty involved in a particular enterprise. Humans use scientific reasoning when the relationship between ends and means is clear, and when there is high probability of success. Humans add magic formulas and actions when the chances of failure increase when unknown and uncontrollable factors threaten to scuttle an enterprise. When the community organizes to face those events that cannot be avoided—primarily death—then religion is in the making. So, it is the function of the beliefs and actions that make a difference, not the nature of the beliefs themselves. This claim effectively dismantled Frazier's evolutionary explanation.

Religious Practitioners and Practices

There is a great variety of casual and formal, part-time and full-time, public and private religious practitioners. We are familiar with pastors, evangelists, priests, nuns, and chaplains, and read about monks, imams, prophets, witches, sorcerers, wizards, and shamans, not to mention seminary professors. The critical issue is not to be able to find a category in which to force the people you meet in a local context, but to discover how the people in the village or city where you live identify that person, how they function in society, and how God may or may not be working through them. The categories are not mutually exclusive, as more than one kind of practice might be carried out by the same person, and what seems like one practice might have different functions in different societies.

For example, the practice of offering up an animal killed by a religious practitioner, generically called a "sacrifice," engenders a wide range of interpretation. In *Primitive Culture*, Tylor argues that sacrifice is a gift made to a supernatural being to defuse its hostility.

15. The Kula Ring includes Misima Island, where I lived in 1997–98 and which is still involved in the Kula trade.

16. In Needham, *Science, Religion and Reality*. Reprinted and more widely circulated in Malinowski, *Magic, Science, and Religion*.

Frazier, in *The Golden Bough*, argues that sacrifice was a magical way of rejuvenating a god (through death comes rebirth). H. Hubert and Marcel Mauss, in *An Essay on the Nature and Function of Sacrifice*, argue that the sacrifice stands on the boundary of the profane to keep people from dangerous contact with the sacred. Edward Westermarck, in *The Origin and Development of Moral Ideas*, sees sacrifice as the fulfillment of an obligation to pay for a sin. W. Robertson Smith, in *Lectures on the Religion of the Semites*, argues that it was the sacrificial meal that represented and enhanced the communion of those who shared it with each other and with their god. All these arguments were in place just after the turn of the last century.

The category of *myth* also includes a variety of narratives, songs, and other kinds of performances, and is susceptible to a variety of interpretations. In Micronesia, myths are distinguished from folktales, and both from what we might call "history." Myths are "owned" by clan elders and/or trained specialists, who bring them into the conversation at appropriate times, e.g., community celebrations or disputes. On Chuuk (formerly called Truk) in the Carolines, there are schools that train specialists (*itang*) to memorize and manage sacred narratives.[17] On nearby Pohnpei (formerly called Ponape), myths shape the issues of origins, migrations, wars, and the struggles involved in dealing with the supernatural.[18]

To the east, in the Marshall Islands, storytellers are called *ribwebwenato* (*ri* = people; *bwe* = talk; *bwebwe* = a lot of talk; *nato* = a practice).[19]

> In the Marshall Islands parentless Lowa is said to have glanced down and murmured until a reef, islands, plants, and a white tern rose from the primeval sea. The tern then created the sky by flying back and forth as if weaving a spiderweb. Lowa's commands produced deities, each with specific duties. A couple born from a blood tumor on his leg had two children who tattooed nearly every living being. Because the sky rested on people's heads, two maternal nephews of Iroojrilik (god of the west and of reproduction), netted it and raised it by flying about in the same way as had the tern. His brother, Lomotal,

17. Goodenough, *Under Heaven's Brow*.
18. Petersen, *Lost in the Weed*.
19. Tobin, *Stories from the Marshall Islands*.

created the seas, lagoons, fish, and seabirds in the same way with his voice.[20]

In other places, like Melanesia, the stories pay little attention to origins and genealogies, but are concerned, instead, with current issues like sickness and death.

Missionaries have long been suspicious of local narratives, at first dismissing them, then identifying evil spirits as examples of comparable cases in the Bible, and then considering whether or not God, through the Holy Spirit, might have left a witness in this place. For example, in the Misiman New Testament, Wycliffe translators Bill and Sandra Callister, along with their advisory team of Misiman speakers, chose to represent Beelzebub/Beelzebul with the local name *Tamudalele*. Thus, "Nau tonlimi, he hi ba tage nau Tamudulele, inoke komiu no limi ana heniheni, nasi alan nanakil hot abwe nihi tunewa eliyamiu."[21]

Tamudalele is the spirit who is the master of *puripuri* ("sorcery"), who calls the *olal* ("sorcerers") to *Walaya* ("a secret place") to teach them their craft and to plan their attacks. Yet, the team also decided not to use the name of the high but distant god, *Yabowaine*, for the Old Testament YHWH, but instead transliterated *Yehoba*.

Paul Hiebert has helped missionaries by making a distinction between three levels of belief.[22] These range from concrete to abstract and from immanent (more involved in everyday life) to transcendent (more removed from everyday life). We have different ways of organizing the world around us. First, there are sensory perceptions. We observe and organize the world around us. This might be folk science and folk social science, or as is common around here, the academic disciplines of science and social science. Second, there is what might be called "folk religion." This is religion concerned with life in the here and now. Part-time practitioners are the religious specialists, but the community is just that, informally organized rather than specialized (such as meeting at a particular time and place). Most beliefs are found in myths and legends, and are expressed in dance, drama, and song. What is in focus is people's daily needs: healing from sickness, reconciliation for broken relationships, satisfaction of the need for

20. Luomala and Rynkiewich, "Micronesian Religions," 6009.

21. Matt 10:25b in *Bateli Vavaluna*, 23.

22. Hiebert, "Flaw of the Excluded Middle."

food, water, love, and power. The rituals people use have a magical quality about them: do this just right and the result is guaranteed. The third level is what might be called "high religion" or "highly organized religion." The questions concern the nature of the cosmos, eternal life, the ultimate meaning of life, right beliefs, and moral codes. This is the familiar realm of the well-known religions: Buddhism, Hinduism, Judaism, Christianity, Islam.

The problem is that seminary prepares church workers to deal with high religion: ultimate questions. Seminary does not prepare missionaries to speak to folk religion. Hiebert calls this "the excluded middle": the daily beliefs and practices of the people that are left out. Western missionaries are focused on the questions and beliefs that concern them. They tend to let science, medicine, and technology take care of their everyday concerns. This is why Christians in many societies return to magic and sorcery to deal with problems of sickness and health or issues concerning prosperity and power. The result is *split-level Christianity*, or Christianity that is "a mile wide and an inch deep."

In the face of this problem, it is often the Pentecostal approach of a *power encounter*, such as Peter had with Simon Magus, that is required for the people to see that this new religion has power over everyday problems, or, put another way, that God cares about scraped knees and sick children too. Western missionaries tend to depend too much on a *truth encounter*: "My beliefs are more rational and logically compelling than your beliefs." Western scientists, trying to bring technological changes like green revolution or some other form of economic development to other nations, depend on an *empirical encounter*. "We will show them that wheat that is planted by big expensive machinery, fertilized by costly potash and nitrogen, and sprayed with high-cost herbicides and pesticides will produce more bushels to the acre than their wheat." Of course, all of these have backfired for a number of reasons.

Adherents of the Western version of Christianity tend to concentrate on the concerns of high religion, the abstract level of cognitive domains. That is why it is often difficult to get a practical application out of a sermon. Western missionaries tend to dismiss the middle range of religion. For example, the German and English missionaries who first arrived in Papua New Guinea in the 1870s and 1880s

were children of the Enlightenment. When people asked for protection from the evil spirits that were causing sickness, the missionaries politely explained that there was no such thing as evil spirits. So, the people stuffed their concerns and, because the white men had power, came to church anyway and learned what they could. But at home, Christianity was of little use. Christianity answered questions that people were not asking. When disease or disaster struck, people tended to turn back to the beliefs and practices that did give answers. Or, they reinvented Christianity to create new meanings that would speak to the world they face.

For example, in 1999, a tsunami hit the northwest coast of Papua New Guinea. Three villages were devastated with a loss of over a thousand lives. The scientific explanation is that an undersea landslide promulgated a wave of energy that emerged as a wave of water when it came ashore. Papua New Guineans agree with this explanation, but find it limited, insufficient to speak to their questions. Why did it hit those villages and not others? Why did it happen at 7:00 in the evening when families were gathering in their houses for the evening meal? Why did some die and not others? The scientific explanation is that these things happen in nature, but the time and place cannot be predicted. That is, the disaster was a result of chance. However, in Melanesian thinking, there is always a cause and it must be found. Many suggestions were surfaced. One noted that this had been a Catholic area, but had recently been the "target" of Pentecostal "crusades."[23] Then, some young men, perhaps acting out old village rivalries, took a statue of Mary and threw it into the ocean. This treatment of his mother offended Jesus, and the payback was the tsunami.

Sorcery and Witchcraft

In Papua New Guinea, one of the reasons that coastal people first (1870s) accepted the gospel was the promise of release from the fear of warfare and sorcery. There are accounts of villages in the interior of New Britain, for example, sending shell money to the coast to "buy" a missionary so that the peace would come to their village. However, peace was short-lived unless reinforced by colonial power. Now, in the post-independence era, sorcery is again emerging as a problem.

23. I put these terms in quotes because our language can be misunderstood. See Rynkiewich, "Corporate Metaphors and Strategic Thinking."

The Melanesian Institute for Pastoral and Socio-Economic Care, where I served as a faculty member for five years, recently conducted a series of studies on sorcery, and a PNG student who recently took a doctoral degree from the E. Stanley Jones School of World Mission and Evangelism at Asbury Theological Seminary was a part of that project. William Longgar studied the Tolai of the Gazelle Peninsula on New Britain, an island on the north edge of Papua New Guinea. I cite his conclusions here at length.

1. We believe we have the knowledge of good and evil, the choice we make will always be able to go either way. Sorcery we believe is the result of those who make the choice to use evil to their advantage, to hurt and kill other people. But what should encourage us is that the proportion of those who choose this evil for their personal advantage is smaller than those who choose 'good' over evil. Human nature being as it is, there is always room for abuse, the evidence of which is the prevalence of the anti-social behaviour pattern shown through witchcraft and sorcery.

2. Sorcery is a means of survival, i.e., through sorcery a sorcerer acquires things for himself and others in close relationship with him, things he would normally not acquire through normal socially determined methods. Economic disparity is the reason for the increase in sorcery activities in New Guinea Islands. As long as these economic hard times are in place, and this involves scarcity of land, sorcery will increase. With the population increase in many parts of the Gazelle Peninsula, land will increasingly become a scarce entity; the process of elimination through sorcery for the purpose of having access to someone's land will gain momentum. This economic disparity will also see the upsurge of fake sorcerers and healers simply for the purpose of making a living.

3. One sees here an unethical assumption of power that already is creating a new social stratification opposing the powerful and the powerless. The sorcerers are the powerful group who will continue to hold society to ransom through people fearing being victims of the sorcerer's craft.

4. One witnesses here also a general departure from the social functions that sorcerers, witches, healers and shamans played in society through the practice of such crafts.

5. The young people who are practicing sorcery are the children of church members. They are the future of our communities and of the church itself. If we church people are serious about building the church on the shoulders of this generation, we must seriously consider helping the younger generation.

6. Addressing the issue of sorcery is the task of the whole church. Church members need to take ownership of church ministries in order to see the concept of the whole church carrying a holistic ministry to societies. Addressing the sorcery issue is not just the task of the clergy.[24]

This is just one of many studies of *sanguma* or *posin* in Papua New Guinea, where the beliefs and practices vary with each language group (835 languages). In the New Guinea Highlands, there are cases of old women being wrapped in a mat and burned because of witchcraft accusations.[25] Accusations and the practice itself are two different things. Those accused were often older women who had married into a village or clan but whose husband had died. Some women are marginalized and often demonized. There are many issues that the church must deal with in these matters.

Ritual Processes

All peoples concern themselves with major transitions in life: birth, puberty, marriage, family, career, death. Rites of passage mark a change in a person's or group's social position. This is a touchy and tricky time, so the transition is usually marked with symbol and ceremony. Notice that churches mark some of these transitions as well, for example in birth, catechism, marriage, and death.

The social problem is that the transition breaks some old networks of relationships and, at the same time, creates new relationships. Major changes are occurring. Arnold van Gennep (1873–1957), an early anthropologist, did the classic work on rites of passage.[26] He argued that all rites of passage have three distinct phases.

Separation: Breaking any links or reminders of the initiate's previous status. This may involve shaving the head (e.g., US Army, the

---

24. Longgar, "Sorcery and Christianity," 355–56.

25. Such a case occurred while I was in Papua New Guinea at a village just outside Goroka, where I was an occasional preacher.

26. Gennep, *Rites of Passage*.

Nuer, the Xhosa), may involve a change of clothes or even going naked, and may involve physical separation and seclusion. For example, until recently in the Goroka area, men would come and take a cohort of boys away, keeping them hidden in the bush while the rituals were performed.[27] Women were not allowed to view them, nor vice versa. The men considered the women to be too dangerous for boys trying to become men, so a boy was separated from his mother.

Transition: This is the stage in between the old status and the new status. It is an ambiguous, uncertain, and dangerous time. No one knows whether the process will work or not, that is, whether boys will become strong men and girls will become strong women. Just one mistake, and it might fail. This phase is often marked by tests of endurance and patience. The initiate may have to endure unpleasant food, may go hungry and thirsty, may experience circumcision or a clitorodectomy, may be cut in other places or tattooed, or may be the subject of homosexual behavior.[28]

Incorporation: This is the stage when the initiate emerges with a new status and identifies with a new reference group. This may involve a ceremony of returning to the community in a dramatic fashion: new dress or paraphernalia or regalia, a dance or song, a new place of residence, a new vocation, a new relationship with the family.

The anthropologist Victor Turner developed Gennep's work in his studies of Ndembu rituals.[29] Turner's work confirmed van Gennep's theory, but added to our understanding of the transition phase. He developed the concept of *limnality*. *Limn* is the Old English word for "threshold." The limnal state is in between, on the threshold between the already and the not yet. Turner's description of the state of society in the limnal phase involves the notion of *anti-structure*. This is a time when the social order is leveled, all initiates are equal, and all possibilities for social relations are open. Anything can happen and initiates are open to change. This is a time not of community, but of *communitas*, in some ways the opposite of community because there is no hierarchy and not even a formal social structure.

27. Read, *High Valley*.

28. Traditionally, across the Highlands, boys received semen to enhance their growth either anally, orally, or deposited on top of their heads. In addition, they were encouraged to cause vomiting and bleeding from the nose in order to rid themselves of the pollution of women.

29. Turner, *Ritual Process*. See also: Turner *Forest of Symbols*.

This is the state the disciples were in after the crucifixion and before Pentecost. As we frequently hear, "At the foot of the cross, we all stand on level ground." That is when change is possible. A clear example is the familiar story of the ten lepers.[30] Each had a life before leprosy struck. Some had been Jews, and at least one was a Samaritan ("Jesus was going through the region between Samaria and Galilee"), but now they were separated from society ("keeping their distance, they called out . . ."), living in *communitas* ("Jesus, Master, have mercy on us!"). Jesus asks them to perform a ritual ("Go and show your-selves to the priests") and on the way they are transformed. Only the Samaritan seems to recognize that reincorporation does not mean re-turning to society as the same person. That is not possible. The person who began the ritual process is dead, and the person who emerges is alive in a new way.

There are other rituals. Rites of solidarity, or rites of restoration, occur when a community celebrates itself, restates its own values and achievements, and holds those up for all to see and appreciate. In America, Memorial Day, Fourth of July, and Thanksgiving Day serve these purposes. People take these occasions to remind themselves of who they are as a family, a community, or a country. They restate their foundational myths and celebrate. Some just celebrate, but the feeling is there. Around the world the most common type of ritual of solidar-ity is probably the various forms of "ancestor cults." Here the com-munity is expanded beyond the living (as American celebrations do as well), to include the ancestors who are guardians of the moral order of society. The ancestors have supernatural powers to back up this duty, and the living conduct rituals in order to stay in good relationship with the ancestors.

There are also rituals of renewal. These involve notions of reviv-ing or renewing the environment or broken social relations. In the Christian liturgical year, both Easter and Pentecost serve this purpose.

There are even rituals of rebellion. These involve setting aside a time and place for the reversal of the social order; the day when the slave is king and the king is slave.

---

30. Luke 17:11–19.

Interpreting New Religious Movements[31]

A common aspect of all revitalization movements is their connection to the spiritual dimension of life. In fact, outside the West such movements often are responses to colonialism or to the paternalism sometimes associated with Christian missions. One of the themes of modernity in its present globalized form is the naming of the secular and its separation from the spiritual side of life. Resistance often takes the form of asserting the unity of life, including recovering local control of expressions of spirituality.

"New religious movements theory" arose in the 1970s from culture change studies in anthropology and an initiative for the study of primal religions in the discipline of religious studies. A parallel development called "new social movements theory" arose at the same time.

A benchmark for these theories is Ralph Linton's 1943 article, "Nativistic Movements." Linton organized current thinking about movements that reacted against the destructive effects of colonialism. However, he tended to focus only on movements that sought to restore a precolonial golden age. Anthony Wallace broadened the discussion, arguing that *all* revitalization movements follow a similar pattern.[32]

As Wallace described it, revitalization includes these stages:

    I.   Steady state

    II.   Period of increased individual stress

    III. Period of cultural distortion

    IV. Period of revitalization

        1. Mazeway reformulation

        2. Communication

        3. Organization

        4. Adaptation

        5. Cultural transformation

        6. Routinization

    V.   The new steady state

Wallace used what he called an "organismic analogy," something that was in vogue at the time as scientists in many fields were

---

31. This is a rewrite of an article I wrote for the newsletter of the Center for the Study of World Christian Revitalization Movements.

32. Wallace, "Revitalization Movements," 264.

doing interdisciplinary research where the "concepts of 'stress' and 'equilibrium' were being widely applied to unite biological, psychological, and social domains of inquiry under the rubric of 'systems theory.'"[33] Wallace admits that this is "rather abstract and perhaps fails to attend sufficiently to the unique texture of cultural and historical circumstances."[34] Wallace worked in the paradigm called "psychological anthropology" and admits that he depended too much on the notion of individual agency.

The study of "cargo cults" in Melanesia contributed to the growth of new religious movement theory. Earlier studies had fallen back on claims that the natives were "child-like" or "crazy" because they could not handle rapid culture change. However, Peter Lawrence argued that cargo movements (he dropped the pejorative "cult") were rational when analyzed from within the participants' worldview.[35] Vittorio Lanternari[36] maintained that these movements were attempts to escape oppression by positing a world turned upside down, while Peter Worsley[37] described them as early political organizations resisting colonialism.

The field of new religious movements however was established primarily by the work of Harold Turner in Africa. Formerly a pastor in New Zealand, Turner went to Nigeria, where he researched and wrote an ethnographic description of a significant new religious movement, the Church of the Lord (Aladura).[38] From this intensive study Turner developed a comparative framework for studying what he called NERMS (New Religious Movements in Primal Societies). His critical observation was that wherever Christian missionaries worked, a variety of indigenous movements emerged that combined Christian beliefs and practices with indigenous ones. Missionaries often dismissed such movements as syncretistic, but we have come to see that Western Christianity, and in fact all churches, are syncretistic to one degree or

33. Wallace, "Foreword," viii.

34. Ibid., viii.

35. Lawrence, *Road Belong Cargo*.

36. Lanternari, *Religions of the Oppressed*.

37. Worsley, *Trumpet Shall Sound*.

38. I am indebted to John Hitchen's eulogy for Turner for some of this information. "Celebrating a Fruitful Life: Harold W. Turner: 13 January 1911—5 May 2002." http://gospel-culture.org.uk/harold_turner.htm.

another. Where syncretism gives way to authentic contextualization (or vice versa) is, of course, the question of the day.

Turner established the religious studies department at the University of Leicester, England, and began collecting extensive information on new movements. Later he moved to the University of Aberdeen to work with Andrew Walls. Broadening his scope beyond Africa, Turner spent time in America collecting information on Native American movements and even traveled to Papua New Guinea to the Melanesian Institute to initiate its three-volume work on new religious movements in Melanesia. His paper in the first volume shows his emerging classification: "Neo-Primal, Synthetist, Hebraist, and Independent Churches." By the 1990s, new religious movements in primal societies were recognized alongside the standard categories of comparative religion, as seen in the new edition of the *Encyclopedia of Religion*.[39] Now numerous dissertations and research projects are devoted to the study of new religious movements.[40] Turner's phenomenological perspective has brought to light the diversity of religious beliefs and practices in today's world.

Missiological Implications of the Anthropology of Religion

What do we need to do?

- *Remember that the gospel is story, and stories speak to people. One example is the Jesus Film, now translated into many languages.*

- *Demonstrate how the Holy Spirit can meet the needs of daily life. Do not exclude the very area where people live and struggle the most.*

- *Give people medicine, but also pray with them. The spiritual forces are real, their fears are real, and the germs are real.*

- *Learn the symbols and stories of the people, and use them to reach people where they are in life.*

---

39. Jones, ed., *Encyclopedia of Religion*.

40. See, for example, Wilson and Cresswell, eds., *New Religious Movements*; Clarke, *Encyclopedia of New Religious Movements*.

My mother died in the fall of the year 2000. She had suffered from Alzheimer's disease for over five years. I had said my goodbyes when we left for Papua New Guinea. I got the call on a Saturday. I checked flight schedules and availability, and it was clear that it would take me until the next Thursday just to get home. It was always dangerous in the Highlands and I was reluctant to leave my family. I told my siblings that I would not be coming home.[41] The next day, Sunday, my wife went to church and I stayed home. She shared about my mother's death as a prayer request. That afternoon, someone called from one of the Provincial Groups at church.[42] They asked permission to come over Monday evening to grieve with me. A group of twenty to twenty-five people came. They asked me to tell them about my mother, they sang songs, they read Scripture, and they prayed with me. Teresa fixed tea and biscuits.[43] They stayed until about 10:30. Tuesday another group came, Wednesday night another group, Thursday night another group, and Friday night yet another. A Melanesian understanding of death, grief, and community dictates that the community cannot leave the bereaved person to be alone but must surround them with care. It was helpful to me. The last night, as people were leaving, a friend who was a professor at the University of Goroka shook my hand. He said, "Thank you for letting us minister to you in your grief." Then he pulled me closer and said, "We have never done this for a white man before."

41. Which puts me in the ironic position of not having attended either of my parents' funerals. I was on Arno Atoll in the Marshall Islands doing ethnographic research in 1970 when my father died, and I did not hear about it until two weeks after the funeral.

42. The church was composed primarily of migrants from other provinces in PNG, and so there was a Milne Bay group, a New Guinea Islands group, a Central Province group, etc.

43. Cookies, for American English speakers.

9

Caste, Class, and Ethnicity

WHILE ANTHROPOLOGISTS MAY TALK ABOUT "EGALITARIAN societies," the truth is that there is no society in which everyone is absolutely equal. All societies have rank, though societies may be more or less egalitarian. While status may be inherited by or conferred on particular individuals, even in more egalitarian societies most societies also are divided into categories or groups that possess differential privilege and/or power. The classic case of inherited rank applying to whole categories of people in society is the caste system in India.

Caste

In fact, there is not one caste system in India, but many. There are hundreds of castes across the subcontinent, but usually only a small number in any one village. There are dozens in trading centers and hundreds in cities. How the local fits into the regional caste system involves varied and contested narratives. One foundational narrative is part of the earliest written records in Sanskrit and explains the origins of four major *varna* (caste categories). "From his [the first man] mouth issued the Brahmins, who became priests and scholars. From his arms came the Kshatriyas, warriors and rulers; from his thighs came the Vaishyas, tradesmen, and from his feet rose the Shudras, cultivators."[1] Behind this myth is a theory of society: Brahmins should be concerned with the overall conservation of culture because of their purity and expertise in religion; Kshatriyas should organize and direct

1. Mandelbaum, *Society in India*, 22-23.

society from their positions of power; Vaishyas should use business, agriculture, and trade to supply the needs of various sections of society; and Shudras should do the manual labor to produce the goods and services.

While these castes are "pure," and the first three are even *dvija* ("twice-born"), there are others who are ranked beneath these four *varna*. These people carry out the tasks that put them into contact with impure things: sweepers touch trash, tanners touch dead animals, barbers deal with hair and nail clippings, potters touch the soil, blacksmiths touch metals, and night soil haulers handle . . . night soil. Association with impure things pollutes the person and will pollute anyone else who gets too close to them. These people, once called "Untouchables," then *Harijan* ("children of God") by Gandhi, and sometimes *Dalits* ("the crushed"), are now recorded as *scheduled castes and tribes*. They live servile and segregated lives. Especially in the past, they could not live near, eat with, nor marry among the *varna*. Although the Indian Constitution officially dissolved castes and divisions, tradition is difficult to overturn.

It is this dichotomy between pure and impure that Louis Dumont claims is at the heart of the caste system.[2] Dumont argues that the issue is status, and then status affects economics. Dumont accepts the traditional definition that castes are hierarchically arranged groups that people are born into, that are separated from each other by rules concerning marriage (they must marry within the group), table fellowship (they cannot eat with people from other groups), and social relationships (they cannot touch people from other groups), but are linked to each other in a larger network by certain practices (they exchange labor and resources, albeit in an unequal way). He claims that the pure/impure dichotomy gives meaning to this hierarchy, and, as with most societies, it is religion that provides the ideology that explains and justifies the inequality.[3] The debate continues about whether ideology drives behavior or behavior (economics) precedes (and thus is implicated as the cause of) ideology.

At the local level, the named castes are called *jati*. These named groups have a local history and a local genealogy as well as a place in the local system marked by restrictions with respect to food, social

2. Dumont, *Homo Hierarchicus*, 43.

3. Ibid., 66.

relations, worship, and work. In rural areas and villages, the *jatis* all stand in a particular relationship within a network of *jatis*. Most stand in a client relationship to a patron, a rich landlord, or a political leader.

Paul Hiebert describes the relationships in Konduru.[4] *Kamin* (clients) from the Shudras and Dalits stand in reciprocal relationships with patrons who are from various castes but are, as a category, *jajman* (rich landowners) in a system called *jajmani*. A rich landowner/farmer needs the services of many people throughout the year, and these services are "paid for" with gifts during the year and with a share of the harvest. The ironsmith maintains and sharpens metal tools such as plows. The carpenter makes and repairs the wooden parts of tools, furniture, and houses. The potter provides the household with the pots that are required throughout the year. He also receives a share for his priestly services as he makes offerings to the goddess of the fields. The washerman launders the patron's clothes as well as those of his family and guests. The washerman is especially important at births and deaths since clothes are defiled at those times. He also helps whitewash the patron's house in preparation for a wedding. Hiebert describes each as they come forward to receive their dues at harvest. This is the case of the barber.

> The Barber measures out a gift share, four to six fans of grain, for shaving the household males and a *poli cherta* [priest share] for ritual performances. He pulls aside his bonus (*addam dōsili*) "for showing the mirror" to his prosperous masters so they can have the privilege of observing their tonsure while it is taking place. Since the poor do not give a bonus at harvesttime, they are shaved without the benefits of soap or a mirror. The Barber does more than shaving, however; his knive is used at births to sever the umbilical cord while his wife assists in the delivery of the child. After funerals he shaves the clients at the time of their purification. But it is at weddings that he is most needed. He prepares the groom and is given small gifts of grain, liquor, coins, and the clothes that the young man had been wearing. He pares the nails of the couple during the ceremonies and claims the unhusked rice used in making the ritual designs. He arranges for a Barber band to play for the ceremony and also for the many processions that welcome the bridal party, that fetch the ceremonial pots and sacred earth, that accompany the wedding party to the temple, and that pa-

4. Hiebert, *Konduru*.

> rade the newlyweds through town. Finally, on an auspicious
> day fixed by the *purohit* [family priest], the Barber performs
> the ritual tonsure and receives the groom's turban as a symbol
> of his assumption of the jajmani rights over the new home.[5]

The leatherworker is not one of the Shudras but rather a Harijan. He repairs shoes, harnesses, and irrigation buckets, as well as works the irrigation system and sometimes sleeps in the fields to protect the crops. In addition to grain, he receives all the skins and meat of cattle that die during the year, but must return half the skins when they are tanned. His bonus is that he gets to sweep up the spilled grain after others have taken their shares.

The relations between *jajman* and *kamin*, patrons and clients, can take the form of father-son relations. The patron may give clients small plots of land on which to build their house and cultivate a small garden. For these benefits, the patron may call on the clients to take up arms on behalf of the patron in an armed struggle. On the other hand, tensions arise when the client does not perform services well, or the patron is slow to give gifts for services. Complaints may be referred to the client's caste leadership, who will admonish him to do the work and keep up the reputation of their *jati*.[6]

The system worked, even though, at every turn, people had to deal with someone of higher rank or someone of lower rank. After all, the system had been divinely arranged, according to the Brahmins, and it provided security, as patrons reminded clients that they would take care of them "like a father." Yet there was the yearning to move up as seen in the practice of *Sanskritization*, when lower castes emulate the beliefs and behaviors of the upper castes.

Culture and society have never been static, either in India or in the world at large. Ancient Indians were pushed south by invading Aryans (the people of the Sanskrit tradition). They, in turn, were over-run by Muslims (the Mogul era). They, in turn, were subjugated by the British.[7] Through the years, there have been many people who have found a way out of the caste system. For example, the Buddha taught that the caste system was of human and not divine origin, that caste was not the product of *karma*, and that purity or pollution was not

---

5. Ibid., 87.

6. This section follows Hiebert's chapter on networks in ibid., 81–100.

7. India has a rich and varied history that is not captured by these three events.

connected to the work people did. Thus, Buddhists do not follow the caste system.

The most famous case of Buddhism as a way out of the caste system was the conversion of B. R. Ambedkar (1891–1956). Ambedkar was born into an Untouchable caste, the Mahar *jati* in Maharrastra ("Land of the Mahars"). His careful and public conversion led nearly the entire caste into Buddhism. The historical narrative for the Mahar caste claimed that they were warriors who fought against the Aryan invasion, who, on their defeat, refused to enter the Vedic caste system. They were banished to become outcastes who lived on the outskirts of villages performing tasks that were polluting within the Hindu ideology. During the era of British colonialism, Mahars indeed served as colonial soldiers. Some of them converted to Christianity under the evangelism of British and American missionaries. Ambedkar was the first Mahar to receive a university education and went on to chair the Drafting Committee of the Constitution. During the 1950s, he converted to Buddhism, arguing that the original Mahars were Buddhists and so he was reverting. Most of the Mahar followed him in conversion thus escaping, in their minds, the Hindu caste system.

There have been Christians in India since the earliest centuries of the Christian era.[8] Neither the Syrian and Persian traders, nor the local converts, have followed the caste system. Yet, as Christians have lived under various rulers in India, they were assigned status and privileges that have tended to integrate them into the system as a caste-like group. More recent caste converts to Christianity have encountered two problems. First, their caste meant that they had a job, albeit in a patron-client relationship rather than an employer-employee relationship. Second, their newfound freedom in Christianity is not always welcomed by elder Christians, who have benefitted in their own way from caste-like distinctions (compare this with Luke 15).

The arrival of Muslims, though the conquest of states ruled by the higher castes, offered an opportunity to those most oppressed by the Hindu caste system to convert to Islam as a way of escape. There are, of course, other stories of kings and military commanders converting to Islam as a matter of survival. The conversion of the Pallar caste, agricultural laborers in Tamil Nadu, from Hinduism to Islam in

8. Moffett, *History of Christianity in Asia*. See also Neill, *History of Christian Missions*, 45, 122–26.

1981–1982[9] not only is a case that demonstrates an attempt to do an "end run" around the Hindu caste system, but also is one of the events that revitalized Hinduism in its conservative form. Like the Christian case, not all converts to Islam have found it to be a religion without caste-like qualities.

There are global forces at work, and they are not always compatible with each other. With increasing access to world news and views, to the Internet, and to transportation, some people are imagining that they do not have to remain in their low caste for the rest of their life. New opportunities for education and for local jobs in the global market (for example, work at I.T. centers has given people hope about an upwardly mobile India).

However, as indicated above, there are other forces that work against the dissolution of caste. *Hindutva* has operated as a revitalization movement for conservative Hinduism. In some ways, the revival and consolidation of Hinduism owes much to the dual forces of colonialism and mission. Some colonialists took an antiquarian interest in the language and context of the texts that Hindus revered: the Rig Veda, the Puranas, and others.[10] A new narrative of an early golden age began to be woven for what had been identified as a religion in the Western sense, even though *dharma* is better translated as "a way of life." On the other hand, Christian missionaries were preaching to convert people from their "religion" to the introduced Christian religion. Brahmins, in particular, began to take pride in their origins and to resent attempts to convert Hindus to a religion with a foreign origin. So, the push and pull began to revitalize Hinduism as a way of life/religion in India.

The driving force in *Hindutva* is the *Rashtriya Swayamsevak Sangh* ("National Patriotic Organization") and the associated *Bharatiya Janata Party* ("Indian People's Party"), which won major elections in the late 1990s. In a familiar nationalism strategy, the movement has defined India as a Hindu nation that needs to return to the beliefs and practices of its "founding fathers." This requires re-

9. Mujahid, *Conversion to Islam*. See also Sikkand, *Muslims in India*.

10. Notable here is Max Müller (1823–1900), a German philologist and expert in Sanskrit and the early texts of the Hindus. He promoted reform in Hinduism, supporting the *Brahmo Samaj* movement of Ram Mohan Roy. He is also one of the founders of the field of comparative religions.

sisting Westernization, but also demonizing Islam and Christianity.[11] In fact, India has the third largest Islamic population of any nation.[12] India also has a larger Christian population than Northern Europe.[13] Eriksen argues that the notion of Hindu-ness is a modern one, in part because traditions and texts are diverse and not unified as imagined, and in part because it is an oppositional movement that is now organizing and centralizing in order to meet perceived threats from the West, from Christianity, and from Islam. But, the threat is also from within. In a sense, the demise of caste has been accelerated by growing caste mobility in India,[14] and this has led to an increase in ethnicity with its identity politics.

Class

Many societies still rank groups of people without the rigidity of a caste system. Karl Marx (1818–1883) tied class to a group's relationship to the means of production. This is still an important question to ask: Who controls the extraction of resources, the production of goods, and the distribution of those goods in a society? However, Max Weber (1864–1920) pointed out that other cultural and social factors work together to constitute social classes. As F. Scott Fitzgerald dramatized, it is more than money that separates the rich from the poor.[15]

William Lloyd Warner (1898–1970), an anthropologist who originally studied Australian Aborigines, applied anthropological methods to the study of Newburyport, Massachusetts. He presented his work in 5-volume series called "Yankee City."[16] Later he conducted research in a Midwestern town he called "Jonesville." Warner used occupation, church, association membership, residence, and income as measures of class, even developing a scale to see what attributes tended to group together. For example, lower-class people in Yankee

11. For a discussion of *Hindutva* as a modern nationalist movement, see Eriksen, *Ethnicity and Nationalism*, 156–61. See also Hansen, *Saffron Wave*.

12. This includes the entire Middle East excluding Egypt and Iran; that is, there are more Muslims in India than in Baharain, Djibouti, Iraq, Israel, Kuwait, Oman, Palestine, Qatar, Saudi Arabia, Syria, and Yemen combined.

13. Iceland, Norway, Sweden, Denmark, Finland, Estonia, Latvia, and Lithuania.

14. See, for example, Giridharadas, *India Calling*.

15. Fitzgerald, *The Great Gatsby*.

16. See the first volume, Warner and Lunt, *Social Life of a Modern Community*.

City tended to be blue-collar workers or hourly-wage workers, attend Catholic and Pentecostal churches or city missions, read *Readers Digest* or *National Inquirer*, and belong to the Elks or Knights of Columbus. His interest in rank, inequality, and class followed the Chicago School of sociology.

Later, others have critiqued his model. He depicts classes as having sharp boundaries when in fact they do not—at least not as sharp as caste. His model tends to be static when there is evidence of class mobility. Still, he focused on class when most other anthropologists were still trying to find "tribes" to work with. Warner established the categories of upper, middle, and lower classes based on the attributes of income as well as education, occupation, residence, and networks of relationships.

John Kenneth Galbraith (1908–2006), an economist, added the notion that different areas of life are linked.[17] Thus, in cities, an upper class or elite develops that has connections and influence in industrial, governmental, educational, financial, and religious areas, among others. This follows the work of C. Wright Mills (1916–1962) who demonstrated the nearly caste-like character of the ruling class in America,[18] and echoes President Eisenhower's warning about the influence of the "military-industrial complex."[19]

Paul Hiebert argues that class is more about what people think it is (ideology).[20] That is, it gives people a mental picture of the social order. Class does this by ranking groups according to cultural, economic, and lifestyle factors. Thus, even the institutions of society can be ranked by class. Certain schools are upper class, others are middle class, and others are lower class. Certain neighborhoods are upper, middle, or lower class. With this mental map, people tend to join groups of roughly the same rank in the different sectors. Within this set of institutions, people often choose one to establish their main sense of identity. For example, they identify with a church that is compatible with their class. If people are mobile, they try to move up, not just in one area, but in all linked areas. Mobility in occupation often

17. Galbraith, *Affluent Society.*

18. Mills, *Power Elite.*

19. A phrase coined by Republican President Dwight D. Eisenhower in his "Farewell Address" on January 17, 1961.

20. Hiebert, *Cultural Anthropology,* 177–94.

facilitates, and sometimes even requires, mobility elsewhere because money and connections go together with symbols and style.

Ethnicity

America is a land of immigrants. Only the Native Americans have lived in the United States for more than five hundred years. The popular vision promised that as America made progress by industrialization and urbanization ethnic divisions would disappear. As applied to the nationality of European migrants, there was some evidence that this was happening. As immigrants moved from the East through the Midwest to the West, they seemed to lose their sense of national origin and become "American."

It was a popular American theme that there would emerge from these different immigrant groups a homogenized national society characterized by a single set of shared cultural values, expectations, and behavior. However, America has not become a "melting pot" for several reasons. First, if "melting pot" refers to a soup where everything is ground up fine and cooked together, then that has not happened. In every city, beginning with New York and going west through Chicago, St. Louis, Denver, Los Angeles, and on to Honolulu, people have tended to live, work, and worship with others like themselves. Some ethnic groups have refused to assimilate, and, lately, some have begun to valorize their ethnicity. Americans are more like a stew pot, with big chunks of meat and vegetables, than a melting pot.

Second, there has been an irregular flow of new immigrants, creating ethnic communities to replace any that might be assimilating. More often, there was competition between established immigrants and new immigrants. This has led to an increase in the power of ethnicity rather than the expected decrease. As Nathan Glazer and Daniel Moynihan demonstrated fifty years ago, the pot never melted.[21] Instead, the nature of American society has led people to continue to emphasize their origins as they search for jobs, houses, spouses, and places of worship.

Third, ethnic groups persist because, sometimes, the prejudice of others prohibits their assimilation. Contrary to the promise that "if you change you will become one of us," many people have found that no matter how much they change they will never be permitted

21. Glazer and Moynihan, *Beyond the Melting Pot.*

to "become one of us." Part of the African experience in American society has been to expose the fallacy, and then to create an alternative path. Thus, beginning in the 1920s and 1930s, thinkers and writers began to explore the positive values of the African heritage and the hybrid culture that had emerged.[22] This is reflected in the shift from "Negro" to "African-American" to "Black." Black consciousness led to Black power.

The resurgence of ethnicity, as a response to modernity, particularly the force of resilient nationalism confronting the fact of increasing migration, exposes one of the main issues of ethnicity theory. Is ethnicity linked to primordial (built-in and deep-seated) attributes of persons in groups, or is ethnicity continually constructed and reconstructed to meet political and economic challenges in society? Those who argue that ethnicity is primordial point to enduring attributes of some groups; things like language, customs, and beliefs. Those who argue that ethnicity is a construct point to the shifting set of attributes that define groups and to the continual emergence of new groups, each replete with a freshly minted tradition.

Others sidestep the issue, noting instead that it takes two to play the ethnicity game. That is, ethnicity is about a relationship negotiated with a dominant cultural group and shared with other "minorities" in a given society. Thus, ethnic identity is situational; it depends on to whom one is representing oneself. Ukranians living in the middle of Ukraine are not an ethnic group, but a neighborhood of Ukranians living in Chicago with their own restaurants and churches are an ethnic group.

Ethnic identity arises through experiences with other people that tend to highlight differences in culture, language, and customs. That means that ethnic identity does not derive entirely from within the ethnic group but in interaction with other groups. Groups can be different in many ways, but the issues that stand in marked contrast to the nearest neighbor or most powerful neighbor tend to be emphasized while other issues are downplayed because they do not make a difference in that context.

---

22. In the French colonies, the movement was about "Negritude"; in the Spanish colonies "Negrismo." These movements linked with the "Harlem Renaissance" in the United States, and all contributed to the intellectual base for the civil rights movement of the 1960s.

Fredrick Barth redirected the gaze of anthropologists from the center of ethnic groups, the concern for abstract attributes that define a group, to the periphery, the boundaries of ethnic groups.[23] The active issue, Barth argued, is boundary maintenance. Considering forces that would assimilate a group, and forces that would marginalize or disenfranchise a group, how is it that groups are able continually to negotiate their identity in society? Of course, how an ethnic group accomplishes this depends not just on its contemporary social setting, but also on the resources that it has to draw on, such as history, wisdom, and practices.

Michael Lolwerikoi has shown that the ability of the Lmaa (Maasai) to negotiate their way through local, national, and international challenges to their land and identity depends on the oral narratives, the elders who embody traditional wisdom, and the practices of negotiation and dispute settlement that have served the people well in the past.[24] At the same time, the Lmaa are searching for new answers to threats to their land and identity because they are experiencing unprecedented challenges ranging from raiding militias from other countries to NGOs pushing nature conservancy at the expense of the indigenous people.[25]

Thus, while a definition of ethnicity might be helpful to begin the discussion, it is not enough to generate all the questions that we would like to ask about ethnic groups. Abner Cohen initially defined an ethnic group as "a collectivity of people who (a) share some patterns of normative behavior and (b) form part of a larger population, interacting with people from other collectivities within the framework of a social system."[26] He distinguishes ethnicity as "the degree of conformity by members of the collectivity to these shared norms in the course of social interaction."[27] While "interacting" seems rather neutral or benign, Cohen goes on to link ethnicity to political and economic forces.[28]

23. Barth, *Ethnic Groups and Boundaries.*

24. Lolwerikoi, *Orality and the Land.*

25. Lolwerikoi, "My People"; Palmer, "When the Police are the Perpetrators"; Downie, "Conservation Refugees."

26. Cohen, "Introduction," ix.

27. Ibid.

28. Ibid., xv. Another standard text, Shibutani and Kwan, *Ethnic Stratification,* 57, defines ethnic groups by culture, communication, values, and symbols, and not

Insofar as competition for scarce resources is a driving factor in the creation and maintenance of ethnic groups, then language and customs function as symbols of ethnicity and not causes. Eriksen puts it this way: "the extremes in this debate are defined through, on the one hand, a position which holds that ethnic groups are simply culturally defined and determined groups; and on the other hand, a position which argues that culture enters ethnicity only in so far as it can be exploited politically."[29] Part of this debate revolves around the question of whether one emphasizes the insider's view of ethnicity (it is about our culture) or the outsider's view (it functions to enhance people's political and economic position in society).

Cohen argued for a sliding scale of ethnicity. If there is a high degree of conformity, for example, the Amish, then there is a high degree of ethnicity. If there is a low degree of conformity, for example, German-Americans, then there is a low degree of ethnicity. Again, one can imagine the cultural perspective (we are distinctive and proud of it) as well as the economic perspective (it pays to be distinctive). Ethnic groups maintain this distinctiveness through control of who people marry (think *West Side Story*), through identification with particular occupations (think *Gangs of New York*), through population growth, and through political leverage in small and large arenas.

Cohen, speaking about New York as well as the Hausa in Nigeria, claims:

> These ethnic groups are not a survival from the age of mass immigration, but new social forms. In many cases members who are third or more generation immigrants have lost their original language and many indigenous customs. But they have continuously re-created their distinctiveness in different ways, not because of conservativism, but because these ethnic groups are in fact interest groupings whose members share some common economic and political interest and who, therefore, stand together in the continuous competition for power with other groups.[30]

Why is it that some ethnic groups persist and others assimilate? Part of the answer depends on class structure. If an ethnic group includes

as much by economic and political factors.

29. Eriksen, *Ethnicity and Nationalism*, 56.

30. Cohen, *Custom and Politics*, 191–92.

all the classes, then there may be more cooperation across class than within the ethnic group. In other words, the rich look rich and the poor look poor. Their identity is by class. For example, as diverse as the British are, by the time of Queen Victoria, Benjamin Disraeli could call the country "two nations": the privileged and the underprivileged. Notice that he did not say a nation composed of Welsh, Irish, Scots, Angles, Saxons, and Normans.

However, if class differences correspond to ethnic differences, then the situation is different. The privileged will be identified with one ethnic group and the underprivileged with another. In this situation, cultural differences between the two groups will become entrenched because they serve to express a class struggle, which is economic and political as well as a struggle between cultures.

Cohen notes that old customs take on new meaning. However, if the researcher tries to study an ethnic group with just a cultural approach, the result will not be helpful or accurate. What is needed is a study of the social structure of society that will show the structural contradictions and oppositions. For example, in New York City immigrants from Scandanavia and Germany were assimilated into the main body of WASP society. However, Italians, Jews, Blacks, Hispanics, Irish, and Chinese remained distinct ethnic groups, primarily because they were associated with distinct classes and the subject of ethnic stereotyping.[31]

Missiological Implications

Caste, class, and ethnicity are only broad categories of the way in which human beings segregate and rank themselves and others in society. These processes vary in their strength, their relationship to power, and the ways in which they structure society. For example, ethnic groups can be important in urban settings, particularly in the case of new migrants. If groups serve political, economic, or identity functions, then they organize and persist. Churches tend to form within ethnic groups. For this religious-social function, ethnicity is often stronger than class. That is, upper-class African-Americans may still prefer to

31. Even after World War II, Jews were stereotyped and restricted in careers and housing. This is the subject of the 1947 movie *Gentleman's Agreement*. Though it won the Oscar for Best Picture, its actors were investigated by the House Un-American Activities Committee, and many were added to the Hollywood blacklist.

worship with other African-Americans of all classes, rather than attend a White church with people of upper class. Ethnic groups can be communities in which the gospel spreads by connection. However, where White Christians have been complicit in oppression, the result can be not only Black churches but also Black Muslims. Ethnic churches face two problems: maintaining identity over several generations, and the prospect of never moving into fellowship with other ethnic groups.

The sense of identity that people gain from belonging to different groups is variable, depending on the reference group. So, a person can be is a teacher at school, a Methodist at American Academy of Religion meetings, and a father at Girl Scout meetings. If all the identities are brought together in one place, in one context, then they may come into conflict with each other. Therefore, most people arrange their identity in a hierarchy. They may be a longstanding Methodist, but only recently have joined the Lion's Club in town. When push comes to shove, which identity is deeper within the person?

Christian conversion, then, must be seen in a context of caste, class, and ethnic identity. These can act as barriers to fellowship. People in America tend to join churches of their own class. Such homogeneous churches are socially stable, but that means that it is difficult for other people to break in. It also raises the theological question of how they are able to minister to the lower classes. When lower-class people are converted, they often do not feel at home in middle- or upper-class churches. This is especially true in many Protestant churches where the stress is on fellowship.

There is a lot of mobility in America, but the church seems to be one arena where people have difficulty making room for other classes. While people might prefer to be evangelized by people like themselves, the jury is still out on whether growth must also be homogenous, and whether or not discipleship and mission require something more of a congregation.

10

Colonialism, Neocolonialism, and Postcolonialism

Colonialism

ANTHROPOLOGY WAS BORN NEAR THE END OF THE AGE OF Colonialism (approximately 1492–1960) when European explorers sailed along the west coast of Africa, around the Cape of Good Hope, and into the Indian Ocean while others sailed across the Atlantic, down along the east coast of South America, around Cape Horn (or through the Straits of Magellan), and into the Pacific. Initially, they were looking for another route to the Spice Islands and India in order to recover the trade that had been lost by the Muslim closing of the Silk Road. However, it did not take long until the explorers were looking for gold, ivory, slaves, and other goods to acquire, ship, and trade. The trade diversified into furs, fish, whale oil, cotton, corn, wheat, copra, sandalwood, *beche de mer*, and a variety of other goods as Europe became the center of a worldwide trade network.

It was the encounter with the "other," with people who did not look, nor act, nor think like them, that raised questions among Europeans and Euro-Americans—questions that anthropologists rose up to answer. From the beginning, anthropology was a Western discipline, shaped by Western questions and attempting to find answers that made sense in Western categories. Anthropology is still a Western discipline, though there are subaltern practitioners and even

departments of anthropology in universities in former colonies. Now, anthropology has learned that not only its answers, but its overall perspective on the colonial encounter are being interrogated, and need to be critiqued. That process of self-criticism is what keeps anthropology fresh.

The missionary movement of the church, while not strong during the Reformation and Counter-Reformation, was revitalized as the Age of Colonialism matured. The discovery of "others" sparked a renewed interest in missions. The continuing conflict between Catholics and Protestants, overlaid with the national interests of Great Britain, Holland, Spain, Portugal, and France, was the driving force behind the religious, economic, and political competition in the colonies. Some historians would argue that most of the wars of the seventeenth through twentieth centuries were colonial wars. Indeed, the French and Indian War was fought on the North American continent for North American colonies and trade, but was also fought on the European continent. There it was called the Seven Years' War, as France and England fought for control of the world trade while Spain, Portugal, and Holland lost ground. Later, Belgium, Germany, Italy, Russia, and the United States joined the fray. Each sent missionaries to their own colonies, and sometimes to other country's colonies.

Table 21. Colonial Wars of the Seventeenth and Eighteenth Centuries

Years	Name in North American Colonies	Name in Europe	Fighting in Other Colonies
1689–97	King William's War	War of the Grand Alliance	none
1702–13	Queen Anne's War	War of the Spanish Succession	West Indies and South America
1744–48	King George's War	War of the Austrian Succession	West Indies & India
1754–63	French and Indian War	Seven Years' War	West Indies, West Africa, India, and Philippines
1803–15	War of 1812	Napoleonic Wars	Wars of Independence in South America

Colonialism and Missions

As the eighteenth- and nineteenth-century "colonial wars" settled out, and as established churches were slow to send missionaries, mission societies sprung up across Europe and America to work in the new

colonies. Depending on one's view, these may be attributed to revivals such as the Second Great Awakening (1820s–1830s) or they may be attributed to the conquest and colonization of new lands.

Table 22. New Mission Societies in the Nineteenth Century

YEAR	MISSION SOCIETY
1792	English Baptist
1795	London Missionary Society
1796	Scottish Missionary Society
1799	Church Missionary Society
1799	Rhenish Missionary Society
1804	British and Foreign Bible Society
1810	American Board of Commissioners for Foreign Missions
1813	Wesleyan Missionary Society
1814	American Baptist Mission Board
1815	Basel Mission
1817	General Baptist Missionary Society
1819	Methodist Episcopal Church Missionary Society
1823	Colonial and Continental Church Society
1825	Church of Scotland Mission Boards
1836	Colonial Mission Society
1837	Board of Foreign Mission of the Presbyterian Church
1840	Welsh Calvinistic Methodist Mission Society
1843	Free Church of Scotland Missions
1843	Primitive Methodist African and Colonial Missions
1844	South American Missionary Society
1865	China Inland Mission

Neill describes this moment in time:

> For this was the great age of societies. In many cases the Protestant Churches as such were unable or unwilling them-selves to take up the cause of missions. This was left to the voluntary societies, dependent on the initiative of consecrated individuals, and relying for financial support on the voluntary gifts of interested Christians. The first of the new missionary societies was that of the English Baptists (1792). This was followed by the London Missionary Society (1795), which started with the laudable aim of preaching the eternal Gospel to the heathen without being tied to any particular form of

> Church order or government, but in fact became before long
> the organ of the English Congregational body; and by the
> Anglican Evangelical Church Missionary Society (1799). In
> 1804 the British and Foreign Bible Society gave a notable ex-
> ample of inter-Church cooperation, having a committee which
> was made up half of Anglicans and half of Free Churchmen.
> America entered the lists in 1810 with the American Board of
> Commissioners for Foreign Missions, mainly Congregational,
> and in 1814 with the American Baptist Missionary Board.
> Germany had its first missionary society in 1824, the Berlin
> Society. Switzerland, with the Basel Mission (1815), was a little
> earlier. Denmark (1821), France (1822), Sweden (1835), and
> Norway (1842) followed in due course. And then the list be-
> comes so long.... By the end of the century every nominally
> Christian country and almost every denomination had begun
> to take its share in the support of the missionary cause.[1]

Unlike anthropologists, missionaries and mission scholars have
been slow to be self-reflective and to rethink what missionaries are
doing. Both anthropologists and missionaries have been entangled in
colonialism, but missionaries have resisted admitting the entanglement, and slower to do something about it.

Many forces and events worldwide have contributed to the rise
of modern colonialism. Yet, the question remains: Why were the
Europeans able to dominate most of the rest of the world in the period
between 1500 and 1900? Jared Diamond argues convincingly that it
has nothing to do with racial superiority, or with greater intelligence,
or with better political, economic, or social structures, or with having
better values and morals. What it comes down to is *Guns, Germs, and
Steel* (the title of his book). Ironically, the Europeans can take little
credit for these. The germs developed in the way Europeans lived with
their animals, in fact, until recently, in the same house. Europeans
developed immunities to these germs, at a great price of epidemics
that left survivors immune. Europeans carried these germs and they
spread to others, usually unknowingly, but at times the germs were
used in germ warfare to destroy native populations. The technology
for making steel and guns was developed elsewhere, but Europeans
were able to put the two together, and ended up with more firepower,
stronger steel, and more mobility (on horseback, early tanks) than

---

1. Neill, *History of Christian Mission*, 214–15.

most people they faced. Over 700 years of fighting the Moors (North African Muslims) in Spain and Portugal contributed to the military fervor and expertise of the Spanish. In 1492 the last battle was fought at Grenada. Thus, small, highly trained units of soldiers were prepared to be unleashed on a world where they had the technology to defeat whole armies (e.g., the Aztecs and the Inca).

This does not answer the question of why Europeans would want to conquer and plunder, migrate and confiscate, or settle and stay. That question cannot be answered by citing the accidents of history, but rather by searching the hearts and minds of Europeans. Of course, it is not only Europeans who fight wars, conquer territories, and displace local populations, but they have conducted the most recent sustained colonial project.

From Biblical Narratives to Colonial Myths

There are always those who confuse the message with the messenger; it is an occupational hazard of mission work. Sometimes the messenger is killed; sometimes the message itself takes the hit for a faulty messenger. When biblical texts are misinterpreted and misused in colonial situations, some call for a rejection of the text, others call for a revision of the text, and a few realize that we keep the text but we need a new hermeneutic to recover the meaning.

What is it that has gone wrong in Christian circles that so many biblical narratives have been used to support colonial, neocolonial, and globalizing projects? Why do Christians let others appropriate their texts? Why do Christians sometimes help in the colonialism project? How can Christians recover a prophetic edge to biblical narratives that will resist being co-opted for any purpose other than that the kingdom of God coming on earth and the will of God being done on earth as in heaven?

Paradise Lost and Paradise Found (and Lost Again)

This myth is based loosely on the story of creation. After some twists and turns, the myth appears in the minds of European explorers as the notion that somewhere the Garden of Eden exists, and within the garden there are human beings who are either untainted by the Fall, in their natural state (naked and innocent), or at least closer to the beginning than are civilized Europeans. This takes various forms as

explorers expected to find the "noble savage" or "man in a state of nature." With each disappointment at not finding their ideal, Europeans moved toward categorizing new people as "brute savages" after all.

Dominion Means Domination, and Domination Includes Exploitation

This myth depends on a particular translation of God's instructions to Adam and Eve concerning the earth, the plants, and the animals. The King James Version says:

> And God said, Let us make man in our image, after our likeness: and let them have dominion over the fish of the sea, and over the fowl of the air, and over the cattle, and over all the earth, and over every creeping thing that creepeth upon the earth. So God created man in his own image, in the image of God created he him; male and female created he them. And God blessed them, and God said unto them, Be fruitful, and multiply, and replenish the earth, and subdue it: and have dominion over the fish of the sea, and over the fowl of the air, and over every living thing that moveth upon the earth.[2]

According to this myth, there is nothing in the text that might hint of stewardship, or responsibility for the earth, plants, and animals. However, the text does say that humankind is made in the image of God who is a creator and sustainer, not a destroyer and exploiter. Further, God gave the command to replenish the earth, not to diminish it.

At any rate, "dominion" has been interpreted to mean "dominate" and "exploit as you will." Through the last four hundred years the abuse of this passage has expanded from a justification for colonialism to a justification for industrial exploitation: logging, mining, fishing, etc. Finally, dispensational theology obviated the need to care for creation since, in that view, it is all going to disappear anyway.

The Curse of Ham and the Three Races of Humankind

The Bible my parents gave me in 1960 is a King James Version with Scofield reference material. In the back, there is a map of the old world with three colors on it; one for Asia, one for Africa, and one for Europe. The map purports to show where the descendants of Shem, Ham, and Japeth settled. Years later I took some time to map out the

2. Gen 1:26–28 KJV.

names listed in Genesis for the children of Shem, Ham, and Japeth, and found out, insofar as names could be identified with territories, that it was not like that at all. The people were mixed in amongst each other, not clearly divided, and thus the text provides little support for the myth of the Caucasian, Mongoloid, and Negroid races. Later I learned in anthropology that race is a socially constructed category but it no longer has any scientific standing in human biology or anthropology. In short, race, though at one time supported by a particular biblical interpretation, actually does not exist; though it remains powerful as a social construct.

Still, for Americans who held slaves, the myth provided another justification. If Ham was cursed with the destiny of serving his brother, then surely Africans, the descendants of Ham—or so they thought—could be owned, treated, and traded as slaves. One would think that even if the curse of Ham applied to Africans, which it clearly does not, then Christ's death on the cross would remove this curse. Thus, as the slavers recounted it, there is no good news in this myth for the black man.

The Promised Land and the Conquest

Literature, art, and songs about the settling of the territory that became the United States are full of allusions to America being the "promised land," with European refugees analogous to Israelites entering Canaan-land. That myth cast the Native Americans as Canaanites who could justifiably be conquered and destroyed. Stories circulated about how evil they were, the more so to justify genocide. Christian ministers often paved or led the way, as noted above in the case of the Sand Creek Massacre (1862). Interestingly, African slaves tended to identify with the Israelites coming out of slavery in Egypt in the first place. On the other hand, Native Americans tended to identify with the owners of the land, the Canaanites who were begin pushed out.[3]

What was the relationship between the mission of the church, the strategies of the state, and the business plans of corporations? This is a tangled and complex story that mission historians are beginning to tackle.[4]

3. Warrior, "Native American Perspective."

4. See, for example, Stanley, *Bible and the Flag*; idem, *Christian Missions and the Enlightenment*; and idem, *Missions, Nationalism, and the End of Empire*.

The London Missionary Society sent the first missionaries to Papua in 1871.[5] They had begun their work in the Pacific in 1797 when missionaries arrived in the Marquesas and Society Islands on the good ship Duff. The church there ended up with an oppositional stance toward the colonizing power, because eventually the area became French Polynesia, so there was a Catholic colonizer with a Protestant church.

The LMS moved on to the Cook Islands (1820s), Samoa (1830s), and Fiji (1840s). At the same time, the Australian Methodists were evangelizing and discipling parts of Samoa, Tonga, and Fiji, making converts and establishing schools. By the time that the British LMS and the Australian Methodists moved on to Papua New Guinea (1874 for the Methodists), they had inspired many Polynesians to go in mission with them. Both of these groups arrived before the flag, that is, before any European nation claimed a colony or declared a protectorate (another name for a colony). But, they did not arrive before the traders and planters.

One major early planter was Emma Forsythe, later called "Queen Emma."[6] She had come from Samoa, with a Samoan mother and an English father. She was ambitious and was able to acquire land and build up coconut plantations for the burgeoning copra[7] trade. Bags of copra were shipped to Lever Brothers and other manufacturers to be made into coconut oil, a base for soap and cosmetics. The planters and traders did not look kindly on the arrival of the missionaries, whom they saw as do-gooders who would interfere with their exploitative relationship with the local people. Problems had arisen, and these served as an excuse for European governments to intervene.

The Congress of Berlin in 1885 was called in order to consider claims to colonial territories, and ended up establishing boundaries on the map over the last unclaimed places on earth, or at least unclaimed by Europe. Germany, who came into the nation-state game late (1870), was able to make claim to German Eastern Africa, German Southwest

5. Papua was not a colony then. In 1884, Germany declared Northeast New Guinea as their territory and England responded by declaring Papua (southeast New Guinea) as their territory.

6. Robson, *Queen Emma*.

7. Copra is dried coconut meat. It was a basic ingredient in soap, shampoo, and even cooking oil. It is still used for these purposes, though other vegetable oils have overtaken it.

Africa, German Cameroon, Ruanda-Urundi, and Togoland in Africa. In the Pacific, Germany claimed Micronesia from Spain, two thirds of Samoa, and Northeast New Guinea. When Germany claimed northwestern New Guinea, England responded by claiming Papua. All of this was about 13 years after the first missionaries arrived.

Soon Lutherans and Catholics came from Germany to do missionary work in northeastern New Guinea. They carried with them their animosities, particularly intense because of the recent *kulturkampf* or "culture wars."[8] And thus, denominationalism took hold in Papua New Guinea as it was inherited from European missionaries.

The missionaries who came—LMS from England, Methodist from Australia, Lutheran and Catholic from Germany—were in some ways little different from other colonists from their own country. For example, both missionary and trader had an ideology of property that permitted individual ownership of land, buying and selling full title to land, and negotiating hard to strike the best bargain. In fact, missionaries bought land under the same colonial land regime as did merchants, traders, and plantation owners. The missionaries, no less than the plantation owners, sought to buy the best land for the least amount of money, because they believed that a mission should be self-sustaining and therefore should run plantations to pay for the school, the clinic, and the house of worship. The reasons were understandable: supplies took a long time to come by ship from the home country, and sometimes supply lines were interrupted for many months and even years.

Then, throughout the German empire there came a major interruption from which many missionaries and agencies did not recover. As World War I began (1914), battles and skirmishes occurred in the colonies as well as in Europe. For example, the Australian military quickly took control of administrative centers and missionary stations in German New Guinea and interred the missionaries until they could send them home. (Is World War I another Colonial War?) At the same time, to the north, the Japanese entered the war on the side of the British and sent their navy through the islands of Micronesia, capturing German settlers, traders, and missionaries. In Africa as well, the

---

8. Bismarck solidified Prussian politics by suppressing the Catholic Church. For a while, Catholic seminaries were closed and Lutheranism prevailed. From this base, Bismarck forged modern Germany.

German missionaries were captured, held until the end of the war, and then repatriated to Germany. Nationalism had trumped the missionary movement, while British and Australian missionaries inherited new mission fields.[9]

Land and Missions

In the summers of 1966 and 1967, I conducted research in northern Minnesota. At times I stayed on a Chippewa/Ojibwa reservation to the northwest, and at other times I stayed at another Chippewa reservation to the east of Bemidji. The project I was working on involved, among other things, attending community celebrations in the area. I attended the Fourth of July powwow at the northern reservation, and later attended the *Mi-gwitch-Mah-nomen* ("Wild Rice Thanksgiving") celebration on the eastern reservation. I observed and participated in these celebrations both summers. I made observations of a quantitative nature (counting cars, counting dancers at different times during the day) and observations of a qualitative nature (lull times, attempts to get things going again, drummers stopping others from drumming). I also conducted a number of interviews with dancers, particularly older people who could tell me the history of dancing on either reservation.

One surprising observation differentiated the two cases. The Fourth of July powwow on the northern reservation had a continuous history going back into the nineteenth century, when it emerged as a mid-summer celebration brought by a Dakota prophet. By contrast, the *Mi-gwitch-Mah-nomen* celebration went back only to 1963, when it was initiated as a result of the reorganization of the Local Indian Council which was stimulated by Federal grant money through the application of the federal government's Community Action Program to reservations. The people planned to build a community center and a baseball diamond, develop a housing program, and encourage tourist trade on the reservation. Central to these concerns was the development of a powwow ring. The powwow would bring money in terms of admissions and concessions, including bingo games and dinners.

9. For example, the Australian administration invited the Missouri Synod Lutherans from America to supplement the Australian Lutherans in expanding the former German Lutheran mission enterprise in New Guinea. For more on this topic, see Stanley, *Missions, Nationalism.*

The more I questioned older dancers, the more it became clear that this was a revival or reinvention of dancing on this particular reservation. Dancers were skilled because they had traveled in previous years to other celebrations, including the Fourth of July celebration. However, a picture began to emerge of dance halls falling into disuse in the 1930s, and of powwows being absent from this reservation during the 1940s and 50s. What had happened? Why was there such a difference between the robust history of dancing on the northern reservation and the demise of dancing on the eastern reservation?

The answer lies somewhere in the interplay between land, community, and identity. Emile Durkheim, and others following him, argued that religious ceremony was essentially the community celebrating itself; that is, taking an occasion to lift up the values and ideals of the people for all to see, appreciate, and learn. If that is the case, then the demise of dancing on the eastern reservation implies a loss of community there. How did that happen?

All land in the United States belonged at one time to Native Americans. As European colonialists settled along the east coast, the colonists appropriated or alienated the land in many ways: purchase, trade, claim, conquest, subterfuge, and others. At first, it did not seem to be a big problem, but more and more European settlers arrived demanding more and more land. In the years between the Revolutionary War and the Civil War, eastern tribes were destroyed, fenced in, or relocated. Before he became president, Andrew Jackson was known for participating in relocating the Cherokee from North Carolina and Tennessee to west of the Mississippi.

After the Civil War, more and more settlers moved west, confronted Native Americans, and continued to take large chunks of territory. The church, including missionaries, was complicit in this process. For example, the notorious Sand Creek Massacre (1862) was perpetrated by an irregular force led by a Methodist minister, Colonel John Chivington. The force made a dawn attack against an encampment of Cheyenne and Arapaho who had come to make peace, and had been told to camp near Sand Creek under the protection of the US government. Approximated 135 were killed, two thirds of those women and children.

By 1880, nearly every tribe or band had been reduced to living on a small reservation. The "Indian problem" was the subject of wide-

spread debate in governmental and public circles. The options under consideration were: break the treaties and eradicate the Indians; fulfill the obligations of the treaties and protect the Indians against white oppression (perhaps by paying off miners and farmers who wanted the land); break the tribes up by dividing up reservation land among individuals; or force the people off of the reservations and make them assimilate into mainstream life.

A variety of organizations had been formed in the East to foreground concerns with the plight of the American Indian: for example, the Boston Indian Citizenship Association, Women's National Indian Association of Philadelphia, and the Indian Rights Association (Philadelphia). What was happening in the East was quite contrary to what was happening in the West.

In 1879, President Hayes got word of a plot to invade the Indian Territory, part of what is now Oklahoma, and seize all the land by force. Most of the routes for cattle drives out of Texas ran through Oklahoma and both farmers and ranchers were eager to get their hands on the land. A new proposal came before Congress: to allot land in "severalty"; that is, to assign to each individual adult male Indian a fee simple title to a fixed number of acres of land (ideally 160 acres). This land had been held by bands or tribes in communal ownership. The Board of Indian Commissioners, the Secretary of the Interior, and the Commissioner of Indian Affairs were all in favor of this option.

In 1880, Secretary of the Interior Carl Schurz promoted the idea, claiming that Indians were asking for that option. Helen Hunt Jackson, a poet and leader of the Boston Indian Citizenship Association, wrote to Henry Wadsworth Longfellow that that claim was a "fair specimen of his (Schurz') hypocrisies." She also wrote to Oliver Wendell Holmes that:

> ... the famous Severalty Bill which he framed, and introduced, was, as he framed it, an infamous bill. It, as White Eagle said, "plucked the Indian like a bird." And the minute that Bill was ... so amended, that it could have been passed without danger to the Indian, and without profit to the land speculators originally afforded in it—that minute, the men in charge of the Bill, and Schurz being back of them—ceased to push it—refused to bring it up! This I know, for I was in Washington and watched it all.[10]

10. Washburn, *Assault of Indian Tribalism*, 7. Note that Jackson later wrote *A*

Most Native Americans seemed to be opposed to the bill, but their voices are buried in reports and thus were not heard, not heeded, or were falsely reported. As a result, the record has to be read through the statements of sympathetic Whites.

Senator Nathaniel Hill of Colorado recorded that the statement that the Indians favored severalty "certainly is strangely in conflict with the statements made by my colleague and others, that the Indians are almost unanimously opposed to it, and that they can never be brought to submit to it."[11]

The editor of *The Council Fire*, A. B. Meacham, reported that there were very few of Indian blood that favored severalty. Through him the voices of the Cherokee, Chickasaw, Choctaw, Creek, and Seminole (known as the "five civilized tribes" because they lived in villages and farmed across the Southeast) were heard, and they were excluded from the act when it was passed (although later acts, the Curtis Act of 1898 and the Burke Act of 1906, forced severalty on all the Indians in Indian Territory).

Lewis Henry Morgan, early American amateur anthropologist, argued that the bill should "never be adopted by any National Administration, as it is fraught with nothing but mischief to the Indian tribes." The inevitable result "would unquestionably be, that in a very short time he would divest himself of every foot of land and fall into poverty."[12] Morgan thought it would be better to train them as herdsmen on common ground rather than try to force them to become individual farmers.

John Wesley Powell, the one-armed (he lost the other one in the Civil War) head of the Smithsonian Institute's Bureau of Ethnology, said, "the occupation of lands in severalty is opposed to the customary laws, traditions, and religion of primitive tribal society."[13] However, he later sided with the senators who were pushing severalty. It is not clear whether from political pressure or from belief that the Indians had to change.

Century of Dishonor, which severely criticized government policy concerning Indians.

11. Washburn, *Assault of Indian Tribalism*, 8.

12. Ibid., 9.

13. Ibid., 10.

Alice Fletcher, an anthropologist, reported on the experience of the Omaha of Nebraska. Their situation was that they had been resettled on land that belonged to the Ponca, who had been resettled elsewhere. When the Ponca tried to return, the Omaha had to defend their title to the land. They did so by allotting the land in plots of five to fifty acres, building houses, and then having Fletcher report to the Senate that they now required titles. Indian voices were often hushed, distorted, or smothered in humanitarianism.

In 1885, a debate was held at Lake Mohonk, New York. No actual Indians were invited or attended, but the people who eventually made policy were there. The leading voice was the Reverend Dr. Lyman Abbott,[14] coeditor of the *Christian Union* with Henry Ward Beecher. In an article entitled "The Reservation Must Go," he advocated an end to the tribal system, asserting that "barbarism has no rights that civilization is bound to respect." When others objected to beginning with breaking the treaties, he responded, "Our first duty to the Indians is to give them the benefit of that civilization which we enjoy. They are in fact part of our commonwealth, subject to our authority, amenable to our law . . . such treaty obligations themselves violate the superior law of civilization, that a treaty which devotes a land to idleness and a people to barbarism cannot stand."[15]

At the time, Senator Henry L. Dawes of Massachusetts opposed the forcible allotment of lands to Indians, but two years later he introduced just such a bill in Congress. At about the same time, the Board of Indian Commissioners sent a questionnaire to their 49 Indian agents. Not one thought that their group was ready for allotment.

Between 1885 and 1888, President Grover Cleveland received a letter from his Secretary of the Interior, Lucius Quintus Cincinnatus Lamar of Mississippi, who wrote that the solutions proposed to the Indian problem were "dictated less by a regard for the interests of the Indian than for those of the white people who want his lands."

In February of 1886, Senator Dawes introduced a bill into Congress that would allot reservation land to individuals, and that permitted the Secretary of the Interior to buy up any land not needed for allotment. Ironically, Dawes came to this new conclusion because

14. A Congregational minister who served churches in Maine, Indiana, and Brooklyn, New York.

15. Washburn, *Assault on Indian Tribalism*, 16.

he could see that Westerners were going to take Indian lands one way or the other, and that the best way to save something was to give secure title to less land to individual Indians. So he bowed to the "inevitable."

Dawes insisted on including a citizenship clause because a few years before a man named John Elk had been prohibited from registering to vote on the basis that he was not a US citizen. In addition, there was a new emphasis on schools in the act, in order to train the Indian in citizenship. Finally, the bill authorized the allotment of 40–160 acres of reservation land to each adult male. The balance of the reservation land reverted to the federal government, and would eventually be opened to White settlement. Although there was, temporarily, an amendment that prohibited the breakup of a reservation without a majority vote of the adult males, in the end the measure was passed without that amendment on January 21, 1887.

What were the results of the passage of the Dawes Act?

1. Native Americans lost reservation land that was not needed for the allotments.

2. Even Native Americans who received allotments soon lost their last 160 acres to corrupt land dealers.

3. Several land rushes occurred, including the 1889 land rush into Oklahoma to claim Native American land.

4. What had been Native American reservation land ended up in the hands of ranchers, miners, railroaders, and timber companies.

5. The Indian Reorganization Act of 1934, led by Commissioner of Indian Affairs John Collier under President Franklin D. Roosevelt, was an admission that the Dawes Act had been a mistake, and that the Reorganization Act was an attempt to repair the damage, but with much less land available.[16]

In Minnesota, there are seven Chippewa reservations. Six of them complied with the Dawes Act, including the eastern reservation that I was studying where land ended up in timber company hands.[17]

---

16. This story comes from my own master's research, published now as "Chippewa Powwows," in Paredes, *Anishinabe*; and from Washburn, *Assault of Indian Tribalism*.

17. Thus, "heroes" Paul Bunyan and Babe the Blue Ox cut and hauled timber on Indian land.

One reservation, the one to the northwest that I was also studying, refused to divest land from communal ownership in the band.
Community remained strong on that reservation, and the community
celebration, the mid-summer powwow in particular, thrived. On the
eastern reservation, without land the community fell apart, and the
community celebration faded and died. Only the Community Action
Program and federal money associated with it brought the powwow
back. There are a million stories like this one in colonized countries
around the globe.

The Critique of Colonialism

The modern era of colonialism has involved the expansion of Europe
and Japan through trade (state or private corporations), military
conquest, forced eviction, resettlement, cultural imperialism, and
economic exploitation of local populations, lands, and resources.
Neocolonialism, as defined by Kwame Nkrumah, follows colonialism. "The essence of neo-colonialism is that the State which is subject
to it is, in theory, independent and has all the outward trappings of
international sovereignty. In reality its economic system and thus its
political policy is directed from outside."[18]

Neocolonialism emerged when the colonized became "independent" nations (late 1950s and 60s), and were entangled with the
new development programs that the West was pursuing. This kind of
"cloaked colonialism," Nkrumah argued, meant that the colonizer was
no longer accountable, nor the colonized clear about how to resist.
Development programs, themselves, imbued with faulty assumptions,
often carried the seeds of their own destruction. The "free" nations of
the 1960s became the debt-bound nations of the 90s.

It is not clear whether globalization is the next transformation
in the persist strategy of economic exploitation of the "other" or an
engine of equality and prosperity. A neutral read is that "Globalization
is both the reality and the consciousness that the context of life has
stretched from one's own city or nation to include the whole Earth."[19]
Some see the triumph of economic pragmatism; others see more sinis-
ter forces at work. Some regions have elevated their business exposure,

18. Nkrumah, *Neo-Colonialism*, ix.

19. Snyder, *EarthCurrents*, 24–25.

but the world is not flat. Other regions show almost no impact of the global market at all.

The impact of colonialism, neocolonialism, and globalization has long been contested, most often by the colonized critiquing the ideology of the colonizers, but also by voices among the colonizers as well. Karl Marx (1818–1883) first claimed that, in terms of the economic dialectic, imperialism was the last stage of capitalism. Vladimir Lenin (1870–1924) followed Marx in declaring that monopoly (not free trade) capitalism expanded into the world as imperialism. However, even Communist Russia held on to its colonies in Asia, including Siberia.

Out of England there arose minority opinions such as a book by E. D. Morel (1873–1924), *The Black Man's Burden*, originally published in 1920.[20] Morel had experience in business and politics and noted that the shipments in and out of Brussels included raw materials coming from the Congo but arms and munitions shipped to the Congo. The Black man's burden was to be reduced to a provider of raw materials for European industry, held in check only by superior arms.

> For three centuries the white man seized and enslaved millions of Africans and transported them, with every circumstance of ferocious cruelty, across the seas. Still the African survived and, in his land of exile, multiplied exceedingly. But what the partial occupation of his soil by the white man has failed to do; what the mapping out of European political 'spheres of influence' has failed to do; what the maxim and the rifle, the slave gang, labour in the bowels of the earth and the lash, have failed to do; what imported measles, smallpox and syphilis have failed to do, the power of modern capitalistic exploitation, assisted by modern engines of destruction, may yet succeed in accomplishing.[21]

Walter Rodney (1972) followed this theme in *How Europe Underdeveloped Africa*. His main argument is that Africa was developing before the colonial era (kingdoms, empires, large-scale production, and trade economies), but during the colonial era the White colonists relegated Africa and Africans to the production of resources, raw materials that were exported and refined elsewhere in order to produce finished products to trade on the world market, making

20. Morel, *Black Man's Burden*.

21. Ibid., 7.

profits for non-African companies. He argues, along with Nkrumah, that this condition continued into postcolonial times. And, he argues, along with Andre Gundar Frank, that underdevelopment is a result of Western colonial and neocolonial practices.

> African economies are integrated into the very structure of the developed capitalist economies; and they are integrated in a manner that is unfavorable to Africa and insures that Africa is dependent on the big capitalist countries. Indeed, structural dependence is one of the characteristics of underdevelopment.[22]

The psychological impact of colonialism was explored by Frantz Fanon (1925–1961). Born in Martinique (French West Indies), he was taught by Aime Cesaire (1913–2008), a founder, with Leopold Senghor, of the Negritude movement that turned the tables on racism, proclaiming Black to be good, African culture to be rich and good, and thus African people to be worth something. When Martinique was occupied by the Petanists, Fanon escaped to join the Free French. But, he was disappointed to find racism with the French in North Africa as well. After the war, he studied at Lyon, moving from medicine to psychiatry. He was influenced there by the left-wing school of Sartre, as well as by Alioune Diop and his journal *Presence Africane*. From 1953 to 1957, Fanon worked at a psychiatric hospital in Algeria. The Algerians were waging a war of independence against France, and Fanon was influenced by the divided loyalties of Algerians and the problems they had with a colonial identity. He was expelled from that hospital, caught up in the politics of the war, and transferred to Tunisia.

Fanon wrote *Black Skins, White Masks* to explore the colonized's dilemma: they were expected to imitate the European colonizer, but forever were prevented from achieving that goal by the racism of colonial society. Near the end of his life, Fanon wrote *Wretched of the Earth*, in which he concluded that nothing but a clear break would solve the psychological as well as social, political, and economic problems brought by the colonizer to the colonized. Since "it is the settler who has brought the native into existence and who perpetuates his existence," so "this narrow world, strewn with prohibitions, can only be called into question by absolute violence."[23] From a psychological

22. Rodney, *How Europe Underdeveloped Africa*, 25.
23. Fanon, *Wretched of the Earth*, 36.

point of view (catharsis) and from a social point of view (revolution), Fanon came to advocate violence as the only way out for the colonized. It was clear where he thought the church was in this struggle.

> The Church in the colonies is the white people's Church, the foreigner's Church. She does not call the native to God's ways but to the ways of the white man, of the master, of the oppressor. And as we know, in this matter many are called but few are chosen. . . . The violence with which the supremacy of white values is affirmed and the aggressiveness which permeated the victory of these values over the ways of life and of thought of the native mean that, in revenge, the native laughs in mockery when Western values are mentioned in front of him.[24]

Albert Memmi (1920–) is a Tunisian Jew who migrated to France. There he associated with Albert Camus and Jean Paul Sartre, among others. Memmi faced a similar dilemma. He supported Tunisia's struggle for independence, but since he was Jewish, he was marginalized in the Muslim state that emerged. He was French in language and culture, but was doubly marginalized in France, for being Tunisian and for being Jewish. In *The Colonizer and the Colonized*, he argued that they have created each other, and thus the colonizer is as much caught in a trap as the colonized.

> The bond between colonizer and colonized is thus destructive and creative. It destroys and re-creates the two partners of colonization into colonizer and colonized. One is disfigured into an oppressor, a partial, unpatriotic and treacherous being, worrying only about his privileges and their defense; the other, into an oppressed creature, whose development is broken and who compromises by his defeat. Just as the colonizer is tempted to accept his part, the colonized is forced to accept being colonized.[25]

The only solution for the colonizer is to convert and join the colonized in the struggle for independence. He argued that "all Europeans in the colonies are privileged,"[26] and that includes missionaries. Thus, the missionary never arrives in a colony or former colony with a clean slate. The missionary identity is not of his or her own making, but is a

---

24. Ibid., 42–43.
25. Memmi, *Colonizer and the Colonized*, 89.
26. Ibid., 10.

creation of the colonized, the privileged community, and the missionary. For expatriates, their presence is often justified by the creation of
myths about the laziness of the colonized that makes them destitute,
and the industriousness of the colonizer that makes him rich.[27] The
myth assumes that: "The colonized is a weakling, he suggests thereby
that this deficiency requires protection"; "The colonized is a wicked,
backward person with evil, thievish, somewhat sadistic instincts, he
thus justifies his police and his legitimate severity"; and because of
"the colonized's notorious ingratitude; the colonizer's acts of char-
ity are wasted, the improvements the colonizer has made are not
appreciated."[28]

Christian mission is not exempt from this critique.

> The same goes for the indisputable hold of a deep-rooted and
> formal religion. Complacently, missionaries depict this for-
> mality as an essential feature of non-Christian religions. Thus
> they suggest that the only way to escape from one would be to
> pass over to the next closest one. Actually, all religions have
> moments of coercive formality and moments of indulgent
> flexibility. It remains to be explained why a given group, at a
> given period in its history, goes through a certain stage. Why
> such hollow rigidity in the religions of the colonized?[29]

Memmi's solution was not the violent revolution proposed by Fanon;
rather he called for a change of heart (repentance) on the part of the
colonizer when he realized that he was caught in a trap that made him
a brute at the same time as it made the native a victim. This was not
unlike the position of Mahatma Gandhi, who, when asked whether
he expected the British to just pack up and go home, responded: "Yes,
that is exactly what I expect." And, that is exactly what the British
did. Gandhi expected this because he saw that the British still had a
conscience.

Octave Mannoni (1899–1989) was a French writer who spent 20
years in the French colony of Madagascar. He was part of a movement
that questioned theories of modernization that underlay neocolonialism and development projects. The critique was called "dependency
theory." In *Prospero and Caliban: The Psychology of Colonization*, he

27. Ibid., 79.
28. Ibid., 81–82.
29. Ibid., 100.

argued that generations of colonialism produced in the colonized the character traits, and that this would be a barrier to both independence (they would not know how to take care of themselves) and development (they will not be used to working toward their own economic and political goals). This argument developed in some circles, including anthropological circles, into theories of neocolonial people as *Victims of Progress*[30] and the notion of *The Culture of Poverty.*[31] A number of anthropologists have been critical of dependency theory because it undermines the agency of the colonized, that is, it blames the victim.

Kwame Nkrumah (1909–1972) was born in a British colony called the Gold Coast, but traveled to the United States in 1935 where he earned a BA, a Bachelor of Sacred Theology, and two master's degrees, in science education and in philosophy. He was influenced in the US by the Negro civil rights struggle. He spent time in London as well, but returned to the Gold Coast to lead a political movement for freedom. In 1947, veterans who had served the British Empire during World War II protested because they were not being paid what they had been promised, and some were shot. The colonial government arrested party leaders, including Nkrumah, thinking that they were behind it. Nkrumah began to push even harder for independence. In 1957, the Gold Coast became the first African colony to achieve independence, and Nkrumah led the new country of Ghana. In the 1960s, most African colonies followed this path. Southern Rhodesia, Angola, Mozambique, and South Africa were exceptions where White minorities tried to hang on to colonial power.

Nkrumah soon found out that political independence did not guarantee economic independence. In fact, his nation, rich in diamonds, gold, and other products, was completely tied up by European companies with interlocking directorates. This Nkrumah exposed in *Neocolonialism: The Last Stage of Imperialism.* Nkrumah developed a vision of a United States of Africa and struggled all his life toward pan-African unity. But, the Cold War was hot at the time, and when Nkrumah, as well as Seke Toure of Guinea, could not find support in the West, they turned to the USSR. The West began to undermine the economies of Guinea and Ghana. Nkrumah was ousted in a military coup in 1966 while he was visiting the USSR and China. He died in exile.

30. Bodley, *Victims of Progress.*
31. Lewis, *La Vida.*

Andre Gunder Frank (1929–2005) was a German-born Swiss citizen with a PhD in economics from the University of Chicago (1957). He moved from *laissez-faire* economics (his advisor was Milton Friedman), to dependency theory, to being one of the founders of "world systems theory." In a series of articles, particularly "The Development of Underdevelopment" and "The Sociology of Underdevelopment and the Underdevelopment of Sociology,"[32] he argued that underdevelopment was not the original condition of peoples and cultures in Latin America or other former colonies, but instead was a product of centuries of colonialism.

Finally, Immanuel Wallerstein (1930–) has devoted his life's work to developing "systems theory" of economic development. He has been working to demonstrate that the current programs of development, when the sources and outcomes are mapped out, is really an effort to maintain the colonial system of exploitation. Wallerstein argues that one of the effects of so-called economic development is the commodification of land, labor, and resources, all things that have a different value in other cultures with traditional, indigenous, and pre-modern understandings.[33]

While there are other critics of colonialism and neocolonialism, these capture the range of approaches. By 1960, on one side were those who thought that there could be a smooth transition from colonized to nation-state, if only all sides would cooperate and move slowly. On the other end of the argument were those who thought that only violent revolution would bring about the psychological, social, economic, and political liberation that was required for a people to move from having been colonized and oppressed to being liberated and free. The irony is that no critique was forthcoming by the longest-standing radical group in the West, the church.

Postcolonialism

The term "postcolonial" has meaning in several areas: literature, literary criticism, biblical studies, and the social sciences. Sugirtharajah, for example, revisits the Colonial Commentaries in India and finds that the examples tend to stereotype Indians and the interpretations support the empire, e.g., the commentary notes that even Jesus

32. Frank, *Latin America.*

33. Wallerstein, *Essential Wallerstein.*

supports the empire because he said "Render unto Caesar what is Caesar's . . ."[34]

The Postcolonial critique has alerted us to the colonization of the body, not just society. This is seen in the extreme in the case of slavery. The body is commodified, packaged, sold, and used for labor, sex, prestige, and a variety of other reasons. The point is that control over the colonized person's body has been lost to the colonizer.

The postcolonial critique moves beyond the land and resource exploitation, and beyond the body and its commodification, to the colonization of the mind. The notion came to prominence with the publication of *Decolonising the Mind* by Ngũgĩ wa Thiong'o.[35] If it is not clear from the previous discussion why people in the majority world might be suspicious of traders, soldiers, and missionaries, if not downright hostile to people from the West, this account should clarify the great divide that exists between colonizer and colonized.

In order for a small group (the colonizers) to conquer and control large areas of land, they must enlist the people (or at least most of them) in their project. What the colonials needed was to colonize not just the land and the bodies, but the minds of the people. That is, colonizers succeed if they convince the colonized to accept the worldview, values, motives, goals, and outcomes that they desire. One step in the process is to teach local people to suspect, resist, and reject their own worldview, values, motives, goals, and outcomes. How is this possible? That is the subject of the lifelong project of Jean and John Comaroff.

The Comaroffs have conducted extensive fieldwork among the Southern Tswana on the northern border of South Africa.[36] They call the colonization of the mind a "long conversation" between the local people and colonial agents.[37] The timeline below shows how long.

---

34. Sugirtharajah, *Asian Biblical Hermeneutics*, 65–70.

35. Thiong'o, *Decolonizing the Mind.*

36. As a demonstration of the dedication of anthropologists to their task, consider the following account of fieldwork: 1969–70 (19 months), 1972–73 (15 months), 1977–78 (3 months), 1990, 1991, 1992, 1993, 1994, 1995, 1996, 1997, 1998 (summer each year), 1999–2001 (15 months). A total of 79 months or over six and a half years of field research.

37. This account depends heavily on vols. 1 and 2 of Comaroff and Commaroff, *Of Revelation and Revolution.*

Table 23. A Timeline of South African History

1815	British acquire Cape Colony from Dutch, including Dutch settlers or Boers.
1834	Abolition of slavery in British Empire. Adoption of English language in colony.
1835–37	The Great Trek; Boers travel north to grazing lands, establish Transvaal and Orange Free State.
1840s	Establishment of British colony in the east called Natal.
1852	Sand River Convention: British acknowledge independence of Boer 'republics'
1877	British annex Transvaal
1880	First Anglo-Boer War; Pretoria Treaty frees Transvaal
1880s	Discoveries of diamonds and gold brings in prospectors and settlers whom the Boers call 'Uitlanders' and try to dominate.
1895	Jameson Raid: With support of Cecil Rhodes, Dr. Jameson leads militia into Transvaal expecting an uprising of Uitlanders; however President Paul Kruger defeats the raiders and is sent a congratulatory note by Kaiser Wilhelm.
1899	Boer War. Not well fought nor popular back home, but Boers surrender.
1910	Creation of the Union of South Africa from Cape Colony, Transvaal, Orange Free State, and Natal.
1948	Establishment of apartheid as official state policy by newly elected Reunited National Party (HNP).

The "colonization of the mind" is the answer to the question, "How come relatively small group of people—class fractions, ethnic minorities, or whatever—often succeed in gaining and sustaining control over large populations and in drawing them into a consensus with dominant values?"[38] Some missionaries, such as the non-conformist English missionaries (London Missionary Society, Methodist missions) who went in the 1800s to South Africa, were interested in recreating in Africa what they felt they had lost in England. That is, they had a romantic vision of a countryside where every man owned a small plot of land and could make a living farming and gardening. They looked down on the Batswana because they were cattle herders, and rejoiced when a rinderpest epidemic killed most of the herds. It is ironic that missionaries were offering prayers of thanksgiving to God because people's cattle were dying. They tended to assume that the

38. Ibid., 1:17.

Batswana had no history, so they would begin giving them a history. They tended to equate the Batswana with the lower classes at home who had given up on country life and traveled to the city where evil was dragging them down. Both at home and in South Africa, they thought that education and reformation would bring salvation.

Missionaries' relationship with other colonialists was ambivalent. They looked down on the Dutch Boers, who tended to enslave the Batswana, so they encouraged the British to take control. They opposed traditional chiefs because they saw them as having a despotic hold on the people, but they misunderstood the traditional system (which was not despotic) and thus undermined local authority. Through their schools, their language classes, and their practices, they ended up colonizing the Batswana mind, and thus paved the way for British takeover and, eventually, the apartheid state of South Africa.

One step in the colonization of the mind is illustrated in a formal letter from Chief Montshiwa to the Queen.

> I give to the Queen to rule in my country over white men and black men. I give her to publish laws and to change them when necessary, and to make known the modes of procedure of the courts, to appoint judges and magistrates, and police, and other officers of government as may be necessary, and to regulate their duties and authority . . . to collect money . . . which will go to defray the expenses of the work done in this country by the Queen; and to levy court-fees, to impose fines, and to employ the money thus obtained according to the laws of the Queen.[39]

The Comaroffs distinguish between hegemony and ideology. Ideology is a public narrative, full of symbols, values, and claims about power. For example, "We have come to educate and civilize these poor, ignorant people." The claim is that colonialism is a good thing that will help the colonized peoples who are in grave need.

Hegemony is the fait accompli that lies behind this quote from Chief Montshiwa. First, the language is English. Second, the worldview is that of the colonizers; not just the concepts, but also the unwritten assumptions behind the concepts. The chief recognizes a queen, a country, a distinction among people based on skin color, publishing, laws, courts, judges, magistrates, police, government as a separate institution, money, fees, fines, etc. Fifty years previous, no chief would

39. Ibid., 1:307.

have spoken like this. The Southern Tswana had a language, a culture, a society, a way of being in the world that was not like this. The truth is, once the chief agreed to have this conversation in terms that acknowledged the reality of the colonial world, he had already lost the war. Hegemony snuck up on him and infiltrated his mind.

What part did Christian mission play in establishing hegemony? This question is still being debated, as the Comaroffs say:

> While this unjoined debate foreshadowed later theoretical disputes over the relative weight of human agency and structural forces in African social change, both arguments were cast with reference to the same tacit question: "Whose side were the Christians really on?"[40]

The gains in converting people's worldview were solidified by the colonial practice of education. They observe that

> . . . perhaps the domain in which the encounter with the mission made its deepest inroads into Tswana consciousness was that of literacy and learning. . . . It is little wonder that the Tlhaping and Rolong [local groups of Tswana] became ever more self-conscious about their own culture as a distinct system of signs and practices; that setswana [Tswana culture] came to stand in opposition to sekgoa [British culture] as, among other things, tradition to modernity.[41]

The London Missionary Society and the Wesleyan Methodist Missionary Society, in the view of the Comaroffs, were part of the process of colonizing the minds of the Tswana, sometimes in a contest with the Dutch Boers, sometimes championing indigenous causes, and sometimes inadvertently serving the interests of the larger colonial project with their narrative of conversion and education.

> However, the individualistic moral and material Weltanshauung of the age, and of modern Protestantism in particular, was especially transparent in Methodists—which is not surprising, since the latter had grown up in response to the radical social reconstruction of contemporary Britain. . . . The Methodist position in this regard was expressed in John Wesley's well-known theological axiom: that "the labor relationship [is] an ethical one" in which employee and master

40. Ibid., 1:7.
41. Ibid., 1:311.

have different functions by virtue of divine calling. . . . At a stroke the alienating experience of wage labor became the necessary cost of salvation, and inequality—measured, in large part, in monetary terms—was elevated into a sacred instrument of moral sanction.[42]

Finally, the Comaroffs make the argument that English non-conformist missionaries were trying to recreate on the mission field what they sensed that they were losing back home in a changing England.

As we shall see from the writings of Wesley, the rising evangelical movement was somewhat ambivalent about such imagery. Ignorance of salvation clearly tainted the primitive paradise. But the critique of European worldliness appealed to Puritan sensibilities, and missionaries were hopeful that the savage wilderness might be made to yield a new Christian Arcadia.[43]

There is much more to the "colonization of the mind." The conception and construction of society differs. In the West we have tended to think of the parts of society as separate entities, and have even formed academic disciplines around them: economics, politics, religion. Indeed, all of science and social science in the West tends toward reductionism. Those in particle physics tend to think that the answer to all things will be told in the behavior of quarks and leptons through the action of the strong force, the weak force and electromagnetism. Yet, every level up from there through the atomic level, the molecular level, the chemical perspective, the biological perspective, the geological perspective, and the cosmological perspective, has its own manner of talking about cause and effect. The same is true from the neurological through the psychological, social, and the cultural levels of explanation for behavior. Those studying at the next level up always say, "Yes, but . . ."

This search for ultimate causes, the separation of levels of nature and culture, and the dissection of life in order to understand it is not the only way of looking at the world, or looking at society. Yet, the Western Enlightenment project has become for much of the world the way to develop/progress/become "civilized." Evangelists and missionaries are frequently seduced into participating in this "civilizing project."

42. Ibid., 1:66–68.
43. Ibid., 1:112.

> But the capacity of the evangelists to act on the indigenous
> world, to impose upon it new ways of seeing and being, lay
> primarily in the diffuse processes of the civilizing mission, in
> the inculcation, among Tswana, of the values and conventions
> of modern European culture. Processes of this sort—which we
> began to trace in the last chapter—rarely entail the overt exer-
> cise of power or coercion. . . . Indeed, there was to be a yawn-
> ing gap between the power of the missionaries to transform
> Tswana cultural life and their powerlessness to deliver the new
> society promised in their evangelical message: a contradic-
> tion, that is, between their worldview and the world created
> by colonialism.[44]

In effect, missionaries have been used by colonialist interests,
and then discarded when the hegemony is in place.

Now, without a doubt, Jesus worked hard to help the disciples
and the crowds see that there was an alternative world, the kingdom of
God, in which people could live by submission to the will of God, by
accepting the forgiveness of God and the reconciliation that only God
can provide. Two worlds, two choices, a new way of seeing. However,
was this "civilizing project" what Jesus was talking about?

Think here of how the South Africa described by the Comaroffs
turned into the South Africa that practiced apartheid aided and abet-
ted by the theology and practices of the Dutch Reformed Church
(remember the Stanley book). Even though the London Missionary
Society and Methodist missionaries showed some resistance to the
later developments within the Dutch Reformed Church and the
apartheid policies of the South African government, were they in part
responsible for the revolution in the thinking of the people as well as
the habits of the people that laid the groundwork in the nineteenth
century for a new economic, political, and religious order in the twentieth century? Elphick leads off an article considering the connection
with this quote from the (Reunited) National Party:

> The National Party, anxious to stimulate active Christianising
> enterprise among the non-Whites, will gladly support the ef-
> forts of mission churches. Churches and missions, however,
> which frustrate the policy of apartheid or which propagate
> foreign doctrines, will not be tolerated.[45]

44. Ibid., 1:254–55.
45. Elphick, "Missions and Afrikaner Nationalism," 54.

Postcolonial people who have been on the receiving end of this process are suspicious of Christian mission and ministry, and rightly so. What will it take to be in mission with Postcolonial people?

1. **Kenosis.** Empty yourself. Do not grasp your own ideology, privilege, or authority. Identify with the other.

2. **Guest.** Receive hospitality. You are the guest; the other is the host. Learn what that means in Scripture and in the cultural setting.

3. **Forgiveness.** Seek the forgiveness of the other for the privileges you and yours have received from unequal colonial, neocolonial, or globalizing oppression.

4. **Good news.** News is good when the recipient thinks it is good. Identify with the poor and oppressed. Discover what good news would mean to them. Speak of God's great love in Jesus Christ, and follow with practices that are good news.

5. **Reconciliation.** Learn where people have been hurt and are hurting. Seek to mediate God's reconciliation in those situations. We have a message of reconciliation, and we have a ministry of reconciliation.

6. **Justice.** Study the structures and behaviors that give rise to injustice, then become an advocate for the poor and oppressed.

7. **Settle down.** The poor and the oppressed have had a succession of do-gooders pass through their neighborhood, and most have kept going. Stay in the place that God has sent you, pray for "the good of the hood," and work for the community.

8. **Relate.** The poor have heard "good news," but there was little good in it. Develop relationships that honor the other.

9. **Submit.** Submit yourselves one to the other. The other has a vision, a goal, a plan. Discover what it is and what your place in it can be.

10. **Give.** The measure of a religion is not what it does for its own adherents, but what it does for those who are not adherents. Be clear that what you do, you do because of Christ and for the other, and not for yourself. Give yourself.

11

Migration, Diaspora, and Transnationalism

Migration

SOME PEOPLE STAY PUT, OTHER PEOPLE LEAVE HOME AND GO to another place. That has been a constant in human history. In the recent past, laborers were pushed off the farms when mechanization occurred and small-plot owners were pushed out when large land-owners took the land. These are called "push" factors. However, there are also "pull" factors. People are seeking a way out of poverty, a better life, or a better-paying job. So, both empire and desire play a part in the movement of people. Another country, or the big city, may represent a refuge, a better job, a chance for an education, the hope of medical care, the lure of entertainment, or the anticipation of excitement.

The biblical narrative is replete with migration stories, some up front and some hidden in the text: Adam and Eve were pushed out of the Garden of Eden, the builders of the Tower of Babel feared being scattered but the Lord scattered them anyway, Abraham was pulled out of Ur, the Israelites were reminded that their "ancestor was a wandering Aramean,"[1] the northern kingdom was scattered by an empire, the southern kingdom was pushed into exile by another empire, some people of Judah returned by the generosity of an emperor, Samaria developed a hybrid population, the Greeks migrated primarily for trade, the Romans migrated for conquest and colonies, and the Jews

1. Deut 26:5.

were already in diaspora so the early church also spread in diaspora.[2] Jesus began life as a subject of empire, then as a refugee from political oppression, and then as a return migrant to his father's home. What has changed, perhaps, is the intensity of migration in the twentieth and twenty-first centuries, and the increasing ease of communication and transportation.

The age of conquest and colonialism, the historical setting for today's social processes, began with the forced migration of slaves out of Africa. Eleven million Africans were transported to South America, the Caribbean, and North America between 1500 and the early 1800s (called the "Atlantic Slave Trade"). Another five million Africans were transported to the Middle East (primarily to a destination in the Ottoman Empire) at this same time. Colonial enterprises were only successful if they had cheap labor. Thus, after the abolition of the slave trade, a system of "indentured labor" continued. In the South Pacific, this trade was called "blackbirding" and was not much different than slaving. The migration of labor out of India and China in the nineteenth and twentieth centuries, both for push and pull factors, exceeded the number of slaves taken from Africa.

Of course, Europeans were also on the move during the period of conquest and colonialism. People left Spain, Portugal, France, England, Sweden, and the German principalities looking for opportunities, hoping to find new land, rich resources, and to realize unrealistic dreams. The number of territories named "New [something]" attests to the twin power of homeland and colony.[3] The millions of Europeans who left home to settle in North America, South America, Australia, North Africa, East Africa, or South Africa equaled the number of slaves and servants on the move.

For all the movement in the past, migration has continued at about the same pace since World War II. The war itself created a tremendous number of refugees in Europe and Asia, perhaps as many as had been displaced by the slave trade out of Africa centuries earlier. Not all could be repatriated for fear of political persecution or, in the case of some children, for lack of knowledge about where their parents and families were. Since that time, the wars of independence, civil

---

2. John 7:35, Jas 1:1; 1 Pet 1:1.

3. New Sweden, New Amsterdam, New Britain, Newfoundland, New South Wales, New Jersey, New York, New Holland, to name a few.

wars, colonial wars, and political strife have not reduced the number of refugees per year.

Who migrates? In the past, it was often men who migrated, looking for work or captured for work. The model of migration assumed that if a man migrated with his wife and children, the family was dependent on him. This might be called the "androcentric" model of migration. However, newer studies pay more attention to other issues. Sometimes it is women who migrate, and their situation is different from that of men. Sometimes, when a man migrates, he leaves at home a wife, or a wife and children. There are dynamics involved here as well: such as the nature of social life for the man in the city or new country, the expectations and demands for money from home, the problems of raising a family without a man in the village. Yet, today women or families migrate as often as single men.

For example, "in 2006, 59 percent of land-based Filipino workers given new contracts to work overseas were female, while additional women travelled as spouses of workers, or as international marriage migrants."[4] In 2004, I was with a group of missions professors as we sat in St. John's Church (Catholic) in Kuala Lumpur, Malaysia. Three groups of migrant laborers spoke. The Filipinos arrived with full families—husband, wife, and children—and they were accompanied by a representative of the Filipino embassy. The government is very interested in the happiness of migrant laborers because Filipinos send so much money home (remittances) that they have an impact on the Filipino economy.[5] The Indonesian group was composed primarily of men without wives or children. They were Christians from Flores and surrounding islands, small communities in the largest Muslim nation in the world. Their embassy did not show an interest in them. Their stories involved more exploitation by local employees. Finally, the Myanmar group had the most tenuous situation of all; for the most part these Burmese laborers could not go home again. Because they had left the country, and because they were Christians from a Buddhist country, they were out of sight and out of mind. Every group of immigrants is different.

4. King et al., *People on the Move*, 78.

5. It is estimated that, in 2007, migrant workers sent over $250 billion dollars home. Recipients of the largest amounts include China, India, Mexico, the Philippines, Poland, France, and Spain. Ibid., 98–99.

What happens when people migrate? In the past, one model assumed that laborers often moved to the city, whether in their own country or another, and there encountered obstacles difficult to overcome: challenges to language and culture, particularly values and ethics. They often failed to establish primary relationships, and thus failed to enter into strong communities. So, life fell apart and they experienced disillusionment and depression, the feeling of anomie. This is the "disintegration" model.

However, more recent studies show that migrants are very adaptable; they have strategies for entering into urban life. New life can be constructed, primary relationships can be developed, and the sense of community can be found. These may not look the same as back home: single-strand relations instead of multiplex relations, networks instead of groups, and friends instead of families. This can be called the "adaptation" or "social construction" model, where migrants are not victims but agents in their own right.

What is the nature of the migration process? In the old model, it was assumed that people moved to the city, found a niche, and stayed there until they died. They got "hooked" or "trapped" in the life of the city, and they could not find a way to leave again. They gained a family, kept their low-paying job, and could not get away. This is the "one-way street" model.

However, there is evidence now that migration is a process that works itself out in individual lives in response to the community and the times. People move to a new country or to the city, but they have plans and desires. Sometimes this includes a desire to return to their own country, and that happens. Sometimes this includes a desire to keep moving, to migrate someplace better yet, and that happens. This might be called the "two-way street" or "continuous migration" model.

What are the missiological implications? The Christian community in the city or other sites of migration may be a revolving door of people moving back and forth, or moving up and down, or moving out altogether. It may be that first-century churches, such as the one at Corinth, were no different. This raises a number of questions for missions and the church. How can ministry be done "on the fly"? What is the church's obligation to short-timers? How can a community be built that is constantly changing? How is faith maintained as people shift environments? How can the church help people operate in city

and village, or between one country and another? For example, in the city people are expected to be self-reliant, but they are also expected to send money back to the home country. In addition, they are expected to take care of people who come from the village to the city or from the home country to the migrant community.

How does the migrant cope with the change? Anthropological studies in the 1960s called the process "detribalization." This is the notion that a migrant to the city or to another country shed his or her tradition life and beliefs, and became a new person, a city person, instead. However, Max Gluckman, in his study of migrants in African cities, made the point that migrant laborers usually alternate between the city and the village. They spend time in each, and make their adjustments to each. For example, young men migrate to the city for work, but come home for family or village occasions. The question arises as to whether people are able successfully to make these adaptations; that is, whether they are able to move between these two identities with ease. Chinua Achebe, in his second book, *The Arrow of God*, tells of a young man who could not handle it, and, like the protagonist in his first book, the young man "falls apart."

Current theorists have argued that migrants have a core culture of the village, and then add an urban cultural overlay that enables them to survive in the city. The result may be an integration or tension between the two. The second generation learns a combination or mixture of values and strategies, a hybrid culture. The third generation becomes more fully identified with the new setting, but they often return, in story or in fact, to the old setting to recapture the cultural symbols for their identity. Another part of the process is that some aspects change, mix, or are replaced quicker than other aspects. So, technology and economy might change quickly, politics and social relations slower, and religion and worldview slowest. The question of integration is up for grabs. This might be called the "multiple identities" model.

The situation is more complex than any of these models. The experiences of want, violence, and rejection are also formative of the person. How can people gain more control over their situation? An older theory posited this scene: People move to the city, fail to find a good paying job, subsist on a low-paying job that is perhaps even intermittent labor. They marry, have children, then begin to depend

on neighbors, relatives and on whatever welfare the city may provide. Their children grow up in a different culture than the parents, a culture that features dependency. After a few generations, this could develop into a "culture of poverty," as Oscar Lewis phrased it.[6] That is, a self-perpetuating set of beliefs and practices about life that keeps people captive to poverty.

However, there is now evidence that people are much more mobile and open to change than this model would suggest. People who have adjusted to poverty are not trapped in irrationality, but in fact are acting rationally, given their options. When an economic opportunity arises, they will take it as an expression of that same rationality. This might be called the "culture of hope" model.

Any model that denies human agency moves away from the possibility of personal forgiveness and redemption. Structural reasons for poverty there are; John Wesley called them "complicated wickedness." There are always structural issues and personal issues, forces that limit choices and forces that preserve choices. Persons in mission must be aware of the setting, forces that are out of control of the individual, and at the same time not imagine so tight a web of economic, social, cultural, and personal forces that people have no choices and no hope.

Refugees

During the 1990s, over 186,000,000 people lost their houses/homes because of disaster.[7] Most of these became homeless because of collateral damage in armed conflicts. Natural disasters forced 88,000,000 of the total into the roads and streets. The impact is differential: the main producer of refugees in Africa was armed conflict, but in Asia it was natural disaster. Africa suffered 394 displaced persons per 10,000 of the total population, while Asia suffered 169 displaced persons per 10,000.

Armed conflict, revolution, genocide, and war are major drivers in producing refugees. In addition to the loss of millions of lives, World War I produced over 6,000,000 refugees. As the Austro-Hungarian Empire collapsed, the Ottoman Empire disintegrated, the Russian Empire crumbled in the dust of the Communist Revolution, and new nations were formed in the Middle East and

6. Lewis, "Culture of Poverty." See critique by Leacock, *Culture of Poverty.*

7. United Nations Centre for Human Settlements, *Cities in a Globalizing World.*

Eastern Europe, the end of the war found 6,000,000 people who were displaced. Boundary disputes, national conflicts, and attempts to expand and recolonize territories continued for the next two decades and led to World War II. Consequently, the twentieth century may have seen more refugees than any other century, but who can tell for sure what the expansion of the Mongols in the thirteenth century with the resultant collapse of the Sung Dynasty in China, or the collapse of the Roman Empire in the sixth century and its effect on Europe, meant for the production of refugees?

The most recent events of genocide the Hutu against the Tutsi in Rwanda or the Bosnian Serbs against the Croats and Bosnian Muslims—remind us that ethnic violence has not been eliminated by religion, nor by education, nor by politics. The scope and impact of these conflicts, as well as the conflicts of the decade of the 2000s, reveal that today the trouble is not confined to one country. This is another area where nation-states are becoming less important in postmodernity.

Second, the trouble has deep roots. For example, there was a precolonial class difference between the Tutsi and the Hutu. Those differences were exacerbated during the colonial period when the British colonial administration favored the Tutsi in terms of education and employment.

Third, the trouble works both ways. In the 1970s and 80s, in Burundi it was the Hutu who became refugees. Lewellen describes the variety of lifestyles of refugees, from living in camps to following networks of kin and friend to living in the city where they had to live an invisible existence on the run.[8] But in 1994, in Rwanda, it was the Tutsi who were killed and who became refugees within their own country and without.

Continuing cases of armed conflict, economic inequality (the world is *not* flat), the weakening of nation-states, and more open access to the flow of information, goods, and persons across the globe ensure that refugees and other migrants will change the complexion and character of the world's societies for a long time to come.

At the end of the first decade of this millennium, the United Nations High Commissioner on Refugees listed a total "population of

---

8. Lewellen, *Anthropology of Globalization*, 171–84.

concern" in the world at 36,460,306.[9] This includes 10.4 million who are clearly refugees or are living in "refugee-like situations," 15.6 million internally displaced persons being assisted by UNHCR, and 6.6 million stateless persons, as well as other smaller categories. These are unevenly distributed in the world: 10.5 million in Africa, 18.6 million in Asia, 3 million in Europe, 3.7 million in Latin America and the Caribbean, 0.6 million in North America, and 0.04 million in Oceania.

Some of those refugees are becoming permanent settlers in "displaced persons" camps. King et al. call it "refugee warehousing," noting, on a caption to a picture, "Around 14,000 Karen refugees from Burma live in this camp in Thailand. Many have been housed in similar camps for 30 years."[10] There are many similar cases around the world, and the "refugee problem" does not seem to be going away.

Diaspora

I was in Evansville, Indiana, and had dropped off my son, Jacob, at tennis practice. His twin brother, Michael, and I were walking out of a store when he said to me, "Dad, that van says 'Assemblies of God Marshallese Church' on the side." "Not bloody likely," I thought, as I assumed that there were no Marshallese people any closer than Arkansas. Then, I looked at the van and saw that he was right.

Aware that it could mean something else, I walked straight to the van, which was just backing out of a parking space, stopped the driver and said, *Ej mol ke, kwoj armij in Majol?* ("Is it true, are you from the Marshall Islands?"). He replied, "Yes, I am Marshallese." I exercised a few Marshallese explicatives: *Wujij, aiya, bokah!* I had no idea that any Marshallese lived in Evansville.

Since the United States took the Marshall Islands from Japan during World War II, fighting a huge naval battle at Midway (which the Marshallese government claims), and smaller actions on Majuro and Kwajalein, the Marshallese became wards of the US government (at first, the Marshall Islands were a UN Trust Territory administered by the United States). Beginning in 1946, the United States government relocated the population on two Marshallese atolls, Bikini and Enewetak, in order to test atomic and hydrogen bombs there, thus

9. UNHCR Statistical Online Population Database, Global Trends, Table 1. http://www.unhcr.org/pages/49c3646c4d6.html. Accessed December 28, 2010.

10. King et al., *People on the Move*, 65.

obligating the US government even more. Now the Marshall Islands are independent but tied to the US for security purposes.

When I went to do doctoral research on land tenure (1969–1970), there were 35,000 Marshallese, most of whom lived somewhere on the atolls that make up the Marshall Islands. Now there are over 70,000 Marshallese, and a significant number live outside the Marshall Islands. There is a large community on the Big Island (Hawai'i), a community in Southern California, a community in Enid, Oklahoma, and a community in Springdale, Arkansas (just north of Fayetteville), as well as one in Florida. Initial migrants came for school or jobs, and those paved the way for others to follow.

I asked if he was there alone or with others. He told me that there were 60 Marshallese living in Evansville, and added, "More are coming." I asked him where he was from, and he said, "Enid, Oklahoma." This alone is significant, because I asked the question in Marshallese and expected him to tell me what atoll he was from. I asked where they were working, because the Marshallese in Enid work in the food packaging industry and the Marshallese in Springdale tend to work in warehousing. He answered that they were working for a large chicken processor.

For a researcher, this raises questions about identity, about the shifting center of diaspora, the relationships between various diaspora communities, and between those communities and the home community.

Their church, the Assemblies of God, meets in a rented building vacated by a large store. The Marshallese were evangelized by missionaries of the American Board of Commissioners for Foreign Mission, who went to Hawai'i in 1820 and were made infamous in Mitchner's book *Hawaii*. Mitchner had a vivid imagination. The true story is strange enough. While Hawaiians had had contact with the outside world since Captain Cook's fateful visit in 1779, their contacts had been with explorers, military personnel, whalers, and traders— no missionaries. A high chief, Kamehameha, had, with the help of European cannons, become King Kamehameha I of all the Hawaiian Islands by 1810. He died in 1819, and his son Liholiho became King Kamehameha II.

Liholiho, influenced by his mother and aunties, decided that the time had come to break with the past and move into the future as rep-

resented by British and American examples he had seen. He moved against the traditional *kapu*, symbolizing his break by sitting down on a mat to eat with his female relatives. Then he ordered the destruction of all carved images of the traditional gods: Ku, Lono, Kane, and Kanaloa. Thus, he overthrew the traditional religion six months before the first missionary arrived on shore.

The Hawaiians took to Christianity, and, in the period from 1850 to 1880, when the ABCFM was moving west in the Pacific, newly converted Hawaiians joined up as missionaries. Thus, most of the missionaries who worked in the Marshall Islands were Hawaiians and the dominant church for a long time was the Congregational church. However, as part of the new wave of Pentecostal mission efforts, new American missionaries arrived in the Marshall Islands in the 1960s. Though the Marshallese were already Christians, the Assemblies of God thought that they were nominal and, at any rate, did not have sufficient evidence of the Holy Spirit.

Through work as missionaries, sailors, and whalers, Hawaiians ended up spreading across the globe, but particularly in the Pacific Northwest and in California. In the globalizing world beginning in the 1970s, Marshallese too began to migrate to America. And now, here they were in my hometown.

One of the newest areas in anthropology and related disciplines is *diaspora studies*. There is now a journal by that name, and a growing list of books and articles about diaspora. Diaspora is a hot topic in anthropology, and that means that the concept is applied loosely to a number of phenomena.[11] Not all migration ends in diaspora. The current consensus is that a diaspora community is composed of people who (1) have migrated from a homeland and settled in a new place, (2) have taken the time and trouble to form a separate community there, and (3) still maintain connections with the homeland.

The processes of migration and diaspora formation are not new. Sidney Mintz implies that not just the Caribbean,[12] his region of interest, but the whole world has been in motion, at least from the nineteenth century on. What has changed now is that people can maintain relationships, even exchanging goods, ideas, and persons, between the home community and the diaspora community. But, the two are not

11. A helpful review is Dufoix, *Diasporas*.
12. Mintz, "Localization of Anthropological Practice."

mirror images of each other. James Clifford argues that "diaspora . . . bends roots and routes to construct forms of community conscious- ness and solidarity that maintain identity outside the national time and space in order to live inside, with a difference."[13] The difference is that the diaspora community is neither at home nor fully abroad.

The sending community provides cultural and social resources for those who are migrating, but the selection of which concepts and institutions to use will shift as new challenges arise. The family in diaspora now has to deal with two languages. The home language helps develop identity and camaraderie, while the language of the host country opens up avenues for work and integration. The concept of family may be important at home, and continue to sustain people in migration, but in diaspora the meaning of family may change. Of course, indigenous concepts and institutions will not have host coun- try names, so the problem of the interface between the culture of the home and host arises.

Indians have spread across the world in several waves of dispersal: indentured servants, contract labor, in the company of empire (e.g., clerks in Uganda, shopkeepers in Kenya), refugees from the collapsed empire, and workers in search of a job. Dufoix notes that after the surge in nationalization of the oil business in the Middle East, Indians in diaspora there rose from very few to three million by 2001.[14]

This raises the question: Does caste travel? That is, do the institu- tions of a people travel from home to diaspora, or do they stay behind? There is evidence that caste persists,[15] and that it even takes on new functions. What was waning at home may move to center stage in the struggle to establish identity and build community in a new setting. For example, a dance that was peripheral at home may become the defining feature of a community in the context of other communities that have their own ethnic dance.

In diaspora, customs and institutions may be deployed with added functions. The church was important at home as a site of rein- forcement of the hierarchy of the village, but the church may become important in diaspora as a site of identity formation vis-à-vis the

13. Clifford, Routes, 251.

14. Dufoix, Diasporas, 75,77.

15. Vertovec, Indian Diaspora.

dominant cultural setting. In other words, the church supports the dominant culture at home, but is countercultural in a diaspora setting.

The church has provided the refuge and stability that people need to adapt to a new land. Armenians, like the Jews, had been without a state for many years (1045–1991).[16] In this period, many had scattered, sometimes as refugees and sometimes as traders. While they were under the Ottoman Empire, "the Armenian Apostolic Church was the cement that held the dispersed population together until the idea of Armenian nationalism very gradually began to spread in the eighteenth century."[17] Between the Armenian diaspora and the Soviet Socialist Republic of Armenia, "the Apostolic Church and the Armenian language played a crucial role in maintaining national unity, as did the growth of local Armenian neighborhoods (as in Issy-les-Moulineaux, southwest of Paris) . . ."[18] This case also shows the entanglement of diaspora, church, and nationalism.

Dufoix claims that "diaspora studies have long neglected the religious factor in favor of ethnicity and nationalism. . . . The reworking and transformation of rituals and practices in the migratory context"[19] changes religion as religion changes the community. The church building is often a primary site for the enactment of identity, but there have not been enough studies to explain how that happens, whether or not the role of the church is changing, and what might be replacing it. However, the area begs analysis because "of two seemingly contradictory developments over the last two decades: economic and political globalization that is taken generally to point to unprecedented global integration, and the resurgence of religions or, more broadly, traditionalisms, that create new political and cultural fractures, or reopen old ones."[20]

New institutions such as clubs and associations may form. Ethnic neighborhoods in Pittsburgh are anchored by ethnic churches as well as social clubs such as the "Polish Falcons" or the "Lithuanian Citizens Society." These voluntary associations sometimes united people

16. That is, in their homeland. Armenians in diaspora did found the Armenian Kingdom of Cilicia (1199–1375) on the fringes of the Ottoman Empire.

17. Dufoix, *Diasporas*, 51.

18. Ibid., 52.

19. Ibid., 75,77.

20. Dirlik, "Modernity in Question?," 147.

without a country, as Poles had been after the German, Russian, and Austrian divisions of what had been Poland.[21] In other cases, peoples who had become a country in Europe remained separate in Pittsburgh; for example, Serbs and Slovenes.

Mintz argues that, in the nineteenth century at least, people, things, and ideas flowed through very specific channels. Thus, there were only certain origins, specific transfer spots, and particular destinations that were possible or permitted. The speed, direction, scale, and distance of movement were regulated by gatekeepers. There were even reversals of flows, oscillations of flows, bottlenecks, and blockages of flows.

This led to some interesting combinations. For example, Mintz reports that, in the nineteenth century, "nearly 250,000 migrants . . . sailed from India out to British Guiana, (but) more than 75,000, or nearly a third, actually returned home." Mintz then adds, "We know next to nothing of what became of them."[22] There is a lot we do not know about diaspora. What of the new Chinese in Britain[23] or the Japanese in Brazil?[24] What of the African diaspora in Peru?[25]

Anthropologists and missiologists are searching for language to talk about the cultural processes that shape migration and diaspora. There is a tendency to talk about assimilation, acculturation, culture loss, culture mixing, and creolization as if they were all negative things. Mintz argues that the process is not destruction or loss, but culture-building. Further, he argues that the processes are different in different regions:

> But the term "creolization," which is thought to embody these processes, had been historically and geographically specific. It stood for centuries of *culture-building*, rather than culture mixing or culture blending, by those who became Caribbean people. They were not becoming transnational; they were creating forms by which to live, even while they were being cruelly tested physically and mentally. They had to devise new

21. Poland was partitioned in 1795 and did not exist as an independent country again until 1918.

22. Mintz, "Localization of Anthropological Practice," 125.

23. Kuah-Pearce and Davidson, eds., *At Home in the Chinese Diaspora*.

24. Lesser, *Discontented Diaspora*.

25. Aguirre, *Breve Historia de la Esclavitud*. See also a book review that surveys the field: Garofalo, "Quinto Suyo."

forms of communication, new norms of interaction, new ways to maintain life's meaning, and to do so using the materials in their hearts, heads and hands—as well as those materials they found lying around them. They were no longer going anywhere—they had, as it were, arrived. Resistance, both symbolic and real, figured importantly in the way such culture-building happened, because people in chains must deal with living meaningfully in one place, *and* with their chains, *at the same time.* Those five centuries of embattled creativity have to do with "global cultural history" most of all because global capitalism was battening its military and political power, seizing land, moving people, creating markets. Creolization was both geographically and historically specific.[26]

Mintz's model is standard anthropology because it assumes that cultural processes and cultural production is specific to the local regions of the world. Within the diaspora community, the processes of selection, discernment, resistance, acceptance, modification, construction, and adaptation are all going on at the same time.

There are a number of identity issues in diaspora. The very fact of the existence of a diaspora community means that its members do not intend to assimilate and disappear into the dominant society. That does not mean that they oppose the society of the host country, or that they unequivocally support the society of the home country. After all, they left the home country for a reason, and they came to the host country for a reason.

Sites of identity formation include the family, the neighborhood, a church, a social club, or more abstract things such as songs, dances, foods, dress, arts, crafts, and even fragrances. Memory, as shaped by storytelling, public speaking, and preaching, serves the first generation well, but begins to fade for later generations.

As in the opening story of this text, it takes two to create identity. The question is never: What is a person's identity? Rather: What is a person's identity vis-à-vis a specific other? A person presents an identity, but others confer an identity. The two may not be compatible.

Identification with a community, as well as incorporation within a community, is a constantly constructed and contested process. In some contexts, people want to present a local identity, but others will contest that identity. People may want to identify with their home

26. Mintz, "Localization of Anthropological Practice," 119.

community, but also not be too incorporated. Helen Morton tells the story of some Tongan women in Seattle who wanted to maintain relations with others in the diaspora community, but on their own terms.[27]

Transnationalism

As a separate category, transnationalism refers not to the diaspora community itself, but rather to the constant flow back and forth of goods, ideas, and persons that occurs in some diaspora communities. "A transnational migrant is one who maintains active, ongoing interconnections in both the home and host countries and perhaps with communities in other countries as well."[28]

What kinds of connections do people have with their home community and with other diasporic communities in the host country or countries? What are the channels and what kinds of flows are established? For example, some children are sent from home to the diasporic community for schooling, but then some children are sent back home to care for aged parents and to secure inheritances. Sometimes money flows from diaspora toward home as remittance, but sometimes money flows from home to diaspora as support or as investment. How do people, things, and ideas flow from one part of the network to another? What is the emerging nature of new communication channels?

William Udotong is studying the movement of goods, ideas, and persons between Nigerian Pentecostal churches around Atlanta, Georgia, and the home denominations and churches in Lagos and Abuja, Nigeria.[29] Recently, Delta Airlines has put a larger passenger plane on the daily route between Atlanta and these cities because of the increased flow of persons and goods. Udotong has travelled the route and surveyed the passengers. He interviewed pastors and church members in Atlanta, as well as denomination officials in Nigeria. This kind of anthropology fieldwork requires the researcher to move with the people. Udotong is focused particularly on the neo-Pentecostal notion of "reverse mission," as it drives relationships between the Nigerian churches and the Atlanta churches, and how the flow of goods, ideas, and persons affects their sense of mission. Udotong finds

27. Morton, "Creating Their Own Culture."
28. Lewellen, *Anthropology of Globalization*, 151.
29. Udotong, *Transnational Migration*.

that ideas, that is, teaching and preaching materials, plans for ministry and mission, and instructions for evangelism and discipleship, flow primarily from Nigeria to America. The flow of persons involves top-level administrators from Nigeria as well as pastors and leaders from America. The flow of goods, both formal and informal, seems more balanced. On the whole, Udotong finds that the Nigerian-founded churches in Atlanta have yet to discover how to be in mission to the American-born population.

Missiological Implications

There is much work yet to be done in the areas of migration, diaspora, and transnationalism. In some ways, this is the frontier of mission because it involves populations that are difficult to identify, difficult to settle among, and difficult to minister among.

Christians must hold in check tendencies to condemn migrants and their desire to relocate. "Aliens" or "strangers" are referenced constantly in the Old Testament, and diaspora communities played a significant role in the spread of the early church. Migrants are neither helpless victims nor calculating opportunists. These models are part of the Western intellectual tradition, but not a part of the Christian tradition. Christians in mission will spend time listening to the stories of migrants, refugees, and people in diaspora, discovering where God has been at work and where they themselves might contribute to that work.

Diaspora can be a context in which Christians become missionaries. Diaspora can also be a context where non-Christians come into contact with the Christian narrative and Christian behavior. Filipinos have shaped a labor diaspora in service industries into a vehicle for mission.[30] African diaspora communities in Europe have been the source of revitalization for established churches.

If being in mission means social justice as well as evangelism in one seamless action, then the Christian community, in diaspora or hosting diaspora, would be interested in the migrant's story, would develop special ministries for women, children, and men without families, and would minister to those struggling to adapt to a new setting. After all, are we not all "resident aliens"?[31]

30. Pantoja et al., *Scattered.*

31. See Exod 22:21, 23:9; Lev 25:23; Deut 24:17-18; 1 Pet 2:11; but compare Eph 2:19.

12

Urbanization
and Globalization

Introduction

SOMETIME IN THE MID-2000S, THE WORLD PASSED A SIGNIFI-
cant milestone, and probably will never turn back.[1] For the first time
in history, more than 50 percent of the world's population lives in
urban areas. With the world's population over 7 billion people, over
3,600,000,000 people now live in urban areas. Where is the frontier for
mission? The frontier is where the people are.

While urbanization has been going on for thousands of years,
the number of people living in cities has suddenly gone exponen-
tial. In the past, urbanization was tied to regionalization: Rome and
the Roman Empire, Tenochtitlan and the Aztec Empire, the British
Empire and great port cities of England as well as the entrepôt cities of India, Southeast Asia, and Africa. In the past 25 years, cities
have become entangled with globalization. Cities provide the setting
where global forces operate because they provide the infrastructure,
labor, stability, and services to support the spread of neoliberal capitalism, representative democracy, and modern culture; the hallmarks
of globalization.[2] Never has the world seemed more interconnected,

---

1. Even at the end, since the book of Revelation itself ends in a city.

2. United Nations Centre for Human Settlements, *Cities in a Globalizing World*,
xxx–xxxi.

at some levels, and yet even globalization continues to produce diversity at the local level.

Urbanization

There are now 483 urban agglomerations[3] that have a population of one million persons or more in the world.[4] In fact, among these, there are 9 cities with a population of 20 million or more; 26 cities with more than 10 million; 64 cities with more than 5 million; and 219 cities with more than 2 million. While everyone recognizes the names of Tokyo, Guangzhou (Canton), Seoul, New Delhi, Mumbai (Bombay), Mexico City, New York, Sao Paulo, Manila, and Shanghai (the ten largest cities in the world), who is prepared to be in mission with (or even would recognize) Shenyang, Belo Horizonte, Sūrat, Kano, or Surabaya?—all cities with more than 3 million people. At a much smaller scale than this, God already had asked Jonah, "And should I not be concerned about Nineveh, that great city, in which there are more than a hundred and twenty thousand persons . . . ?"[5] The question remains.

The urbanization of human life has been going on for thousands of years. The ancient cities of Ur and Uruk, Harappa and Mohojendaro, Teotihucan and Tenochtitlan, Seleucia and Alexandria, Honan and Changan, each were in the top ten cities of the world in their time. Not until 1700 did European cities (London and Paris) emerge as world-class cities, and not until 1900 did European and American cities dominate the category. Today, as noted in the previous paragraph, Asian cities once again dominate the list of the largest in the world. Overall, Asia has 122 cities with a population larger than one million, Latin America has 63 such cities, and Africa has 45.

---

3. There are three common ways to measure city population: (1) count the people within the city limits; (2) count the people within a metropolitan area, that is, the city and its suburbs; and (3) continue to count people as long as the population density is above 50,000 persons per square mile. The latter produces an urban agglomeration. The largest urban agglomeration in the world is Tokyo-Yokohama-Kawasaki-Saitama, which provides a continuous landscape of 50,000 persons per square mile or more.

4. There are many websites with city and/or urban population figures. The data here come from http://www.citypopulation.de. A site with a narrower definition is http://www.citymayors.com.

5. Jonah 4:11.

Urbanization has reached a "take off" point. Even in 1800, only 3 percent of the world's population lived in cities and towns of 5 thousand persons or more. By 1900, approximately 13 percent of the world's population lived in cities or towns. By 1950, the percentage had risen to 29 percent, and by 1975 it was 39 percent. For all the migration routes of the 1900s, and there were a lot, the biggest migration was from rural to urban places. Not only do we live in a post-modern, post-colonial world, we live in a post-rural world. It is a world marked by globalization, which includes not only the movement of goods and ideas, but the incredible movement, and continual foment, of people. People in motion, living on the run, provide challenges both for anthropologists and sociologists who want to describe and explain human behavior, and for evangelists and missionaries who can no longer set up shop in an established place and expect people to come to them.

In anthropology, we no longer construe the world as composed of villages where people are related to each other, where everyone speaks the same language, everyone makes their living in the same way, and everyone shares the same culture. In missiology, we need to engage the world as it is, full of cities that are all products of urbanization and globalization. These cities share some characteristics, but also each one is unique, every one different enough to require a missionary to go beyond general knowledge to understand the local ward or local business.

What country has the largest area of remaining rainforest, wild rivers, and hidden groups of people? Brazil? Now, what country is the most urbanized in the world, excepting city-states like Singapore? That is, in what country does the largest percentage of the population lives in cities? The answer again is Brazil, where 87 percent of the people live in cities.[6] In the region, Latin America, over 75 percent of the population lives in cities, about the same as Europe.

Who is a Brazilian? Approximately half the population is descended from immigrants from Portugal, though with a significant number of people with mixed heritage. The largest ethnic minority is Italian (nearly 15 percent of the population), then Spanish (nearly 8 percent), German (over 6 percent), Lebanese (4 percent), Syrian (1.6 percent), Polish (0.7 percent), and Japanese (0.7 percent). The Italian

---

6. Central Intelligence Agency, *World Factbook*, s.v. Brazil. Brazil was 87 percent urban in 2010.

and Japanese populations are the largest clusters outside of their home countries. The population of Lebanese descent (8 million) is twice as large as the population of the country of Lebanon itself (4 million). Overall, Brazil has more women than men, is young (average age 29), is Roman Catholic (74 percent), literate, working, and expecting to live to age 72. Many live in Sao Paulo (20 million), Rio de Janeiro (12 million), Belo Horizonte (6 million), Porto Allegre (4 million), and Brasilia (4 million), but Brazil has 15 other cities with a population of over one million people.[7]

While most of the people who live in Chinese cities may be Chinese,[8] the most common case elsewhere in the world is that cities are cosmopolitan. Yet, the understanding of *cosmopolitan* and *local* is itself a contested arena, a structured opposition that shifts depending on the location of the person making the judgment.[9] As with other social science concepts, *cosmopolitan* and *local* are not fixed categories but rather are deployed in discussions, for example in the *medina* "market" in Tunis, where salesmen present themselves as cosmopolitan for their knowledge of the cultural and linguistic differences among tourists, and tourists present themselves as cosmopolitan when they attempt to haggle for souvenirs.[10] Life in the city is a contested issue.

Negative Stereotypes of the City

Anthropologists, like missionaries, have tended to avoid the city, and both have their own negative narrative to tell. Only in the 1970s did anthropologists begin to turn their attention to Western societies and to cities. One of the reasons was that formerly colonized people were withdrawing the welcome mat. Another is that anthropologists realized that they were missing the massive urbanization going on around the world. Previously, anthropologists thought they knew about cities because that is what they were fleeing, the places that were too complex and too compromised by "civilization." Missionaries, likewise, have tended to avoid cities because they wanted to "preach where no

---

7. http://www.citypopulation.de/Brazil-Cities.html.

8. The official ethnic minorities, 55 named groups, compose less than 10 percent of the population, which, otherwise, is Han Chinese.

9. Hawkins, "Cosmopolitan Hagglers."

10. Ibid., 9–12.

other man had preached," and, perhaps, because the challenge was too great.

If not, then where did our rural bias come from? Is it from American culture? Do popular narratives of fleeing Europe, and then fleeing the cities of the East to settle the Midwest and West as farmers and ranchers predispose Americans toward the rural? Has Christianity and a particular interpretation of the Bible also contributed to the negative stereotype of the city?

This narrative, a cultural construct, usually begins in the Garden of Eden and moves to the sin of pride in the cities. Abraham left the city and civilization, lived in tents, and herded sheep. Lot preferred the city of Sodom. The Israelites were pastoral people who conquered cities. Their enemies came from Nineveh, that great evil city, and then from Babylon, another great evil city. Babylon fell in disgrace, as prophesied by Isaiah,[11] but rose again as a metaphor for the epitome of sin in a city.[12] The same words are used for both to show God's judgment of the city: "Fallen, fallen is Babylon."[13]

The city that Cain builds seeking a name for his son, Enoch,[14] as Harvey Conn points out, does stand in contrast to the children of Seth, who instead "call upon the name of the Lord;"[15] however, this is not a contrast between country and city as much as it is a contrast between those who seek a name for themselves and those who call upon the name of the Lord.[16] Out of the same city that Cain builds comes the flowering of civilization: art, music, and technology. These things can be in the service of the Lord or in the service of evil. Even the Genesis story supports mission to the city.

> And, against this pattern, the people of God were called to display their faith in covenant through "doing what is right and just" (Gen. 18:19). Establishing justice and peace for the cities of the earth was to be their mission (Ezek. 18:5–9; 2 Pet. 2:4–10). Their prayer was for righteousness (Gen. 4:26; 18:22–33).

11. Isa 13:1—14:32.

12. Rev 17:5.

13. Isa 21:9; Rev 17:5.

14. Gen 4:12–24.

15. Gen 4:26.

16. Conn, *Planting and Growing Urban Churches.*

> As we, like the Genesis saints, await the final consummation,
> the same calling makes its demands of us.[17]

Yet, the bias against the city by American Protestants is so strong that urban ministry had to be pioneered in the late 1800s by women; the founders of Holiness and Baptist bible schools alike chose the rural areas for their colleges, and the Protestant mission ideal has been to do mission as far away from the city as possible.

The Modern Study of *the* City

Early work in sociology laid the foundations for the anthropological excursion into the study of the city. The Chicago School of the sociology of the city emerged from the synergy of Robert E. Park (1864–1944), Ernest Burgess (1886–1966), and Louis A. Wirth (1897–1952). This school emphasized the study of real cities, not the "ideal types" approach that had been used by Durkheim and Weber. Yet, their "real city" was Chicago, which became "the city" in their studies. In a landmark book, Park and Burgess developed a research program for the city.[18] They popularized the model of the city as a series of concentric rings, with industrial, commercial (retail and wholesale), and various types of residential zones. Growth of the city involved the succession of zones rippling out from the center. McKenzie, in his chapter, introduced the idea of "ecology" as a model for exploring relationships between different sectors in the city. The articles focus on institutions and issues within the city, for example, the function of the newspaper in the city, the problems of juvenile delinquency, and the life of the "hobo" in the city. Louis Wirth contributed the bibliography.

Wirth later published "Urbanism as a Way of Life." The biases of the Chicago School are clear. "The contacts of the city may indeed be face to face, but they are nevertheless impersonal, superficial, transitory, and segmental. The reserve, the indifference, and the blasé outlook which urbanites manifest in their relationships may thus be regarded as devices for immunizing themselves against the personal claims and expectations of others."[19] From the perspective of the Chicago School, the nature of the city was to reduce the importance of the family, of

---

17. Conn, "Genesis as Urban Prologue," 32.
18. Park, Burgess, and McKenzie, *The City.*
19. Wirth, "Urbanism," 12.

kinship ties, and of a sense of community (or neighborhood). Yet, at the same time, the school thought that the city could represent the best achievements of humanity: progress, freedom, toleration, enterprise, and rationality. This perspective reflects the American narrative that immigrants find freedom and opportunity in the city even though they may have to endure pain and suffering temporarily.

From an ecological perspective, the Chicago School noted the importance of technology and infrastructure. How goods move around depends on the modes of transportation available. Where markets are and what they sell depends on routes and what people can carry with them. Where people live depends not only on what they can afford, but also on how close they have to be to their worksite, to markets, and to other sites of social services. The density of a sector of the city depends, in part, on the compatibility of the infrastructure: water, sewers, roads, high-rise buildings, elevators, electricity, gas, mail delivery, and location in relation to jobs and markets. On the other hand, the school considered the degree to which density or crowding causes stress and deviant behavior.

The critique of the Chicago School argues that other cities are not like Chicago. For example, some cities, like Pittsburgh, had, before the 1970s, more heavy industry than Chicago and thus had different dynamics. In addition, the impact of the automobile has continued to change the way cities are organized in ways the Chicago School did not anticipate. No one walks anymore. Cultural preferences play a larger part in neighborhood loyalty and longevity than imagined. Finally, the place of city planning and development has increased considerably in the evolution of a city.

Over time, other researchers noted that some cities have sectors rather than rings, and some cities have multiple growth centers rather than a single center. The assumption no longer holds that there is a single model for *the* city. In all this, some truths about the church also emerged. The older churches are usually in the first ring downtown, but largely have been abandoned by their congregations, who have moved to the suburbs.

In *The Suburban Captivity of the Churches*, Winter reveals the perspective of the Chicago School in his assumptions about the city.

> The central concern of this book is the creation of a human environment in the metropolis. Can the metropolitan area be-

come a suitable environment for human life? Are we to resign ourselves to a vicious circle of demolition, redevelopment, and spreading blight? Urban blight signifies the breakdown of human community before it becomes a physical problem; when men and women no longer *care,* no longer feel that they *belong,* their properties and neighborhoods disintegrate.[20]

He argued that the churches were not fulfilling the mission of God in the city. "The churches could play a significant role in metropolitan planning, and yet, for the most part, they have failed to participate responsibly in the metropolis."[21] He developed the theme that the church was God's gift for the city, and that the church in mission and in ministry is the real church. However, insofar as Winter's work was based on the Chicago School, new approaches to urban research were already under way.

New Models of Urban Research

Beginning in the 1950s and on through the 1980s, some new research programs in urban studies departed from the notion of ideal types of cities and began to recognize how unique cities were. Robert Redfield, following the Chicago School, had established a distinction between folk or peasant societies and urban societies.[22] In an attempt to maintain a holistic understanding of culture, anthropologists imagined that they could characterize whole urban societies by examining parts of a city. The result was a bias toward rural society, in part because anthropologists could wrap their heads around such societies while urban society seemed too complex and disjointed either to study or to live in.

The first critique of this position came from Oscar Lewis, who studied the same Mexican village that Redfield had studied,[23] but reported that life did not run as smoothly as Redfield had claimed.[24] This undermined the ideal types that Redfield and others had established as a paradigm for studying the city, as well as raised the problem of *representation* in anthropology. That is, who is in a position to report on a culture and what biases does that person have?

20. Winter, *Suburban Captivity*, 9.
21. Ibid.
22. Redfield, *Little Community.*
23. Redfield, *Tepoztlán.*
24. Lewis, *Life in a Mexican Village.*

Another critique came from a sociological study that looked like anthropology. Michael Young and Peter Willmott studied a category of people who moved from a London inner-city neighborhood, Bethnal Green, to a new housing subdivision, Greenleigh.[25] They approached the problem of scale, that is the size of the research site, by restricting themselves to a section of London and to a category of people who moved out of that section. Young and Willmott described a cityscape where family and kinship ties were strong, where community persisted, and where people identified with their district of the city. They note that "very few people wish to leave the East End" and "they are attached to Mum and Dad, to the markets, to the pubs and settlements, to Club Row and the London Hospital."[26] But it is their "lasting attachment to their families" that fosters such a "deep . . . sense of belonging."[27]

Another study in England about the same time emphasized the place of social networks in urban life. Elizabeth Bott countered the proposal that urban life was lonely and without meaning by claiming that a lively network of relationships overcame tendencies toward anomie.[28] The connections between culture and society are still dynamic in the city.

> In my view a culture is specific to a particular social situation. In this book I have tried to show how certain sub-cultural variations in familial organization are associated with variations in patterns of social relationship with and among persons outside the family. The norms—or the culture, if one prefers that term—of conjugal segregation are appropriate to families in close-knit networks. If the family moves, or if for any other reason their network becomes loose-knit, a new culture becomes appropriate. I do not assert, however, that culture can be reduced to social relationships, or that it changes automatically when social relationships change. Some of the transitional families of the research set were finding it very difficult and painful to give up their old beliefs and practices and to develop new ones more appropriate to their changed situation.[29]

25. Young and Willmott, *Family and Kinship in East London.*

26. Ibid., 186.

27. Ibid., 187.

28. Bott, *Family and Social Networks.*

29. Ibid., 219.

The small-scale study of a slice of urban life became the dominant method for anthropologists studying cities.[30] These studies emphasized the persistence of subcultures in urban society, examples of a diversity of cultures that were not "melting" or assimilating into mainstream society. These exhibited some standard features of societies that anthropologists had studied as well as a vitality that implied that they would be around for a while. The church, therefore, would have to deal with the diversity as a given rather than as a problem to be solved.

Outside the West, social anthropologists were discovering that the Chicago model did not apply to the emerging cities of Africa, Asia, and Latin America. Philip Mayer raised the question of how much cultural baggage migrants to the city brought with them.[31] David Jacobson revisited this question for Uganda.[32] Both discovered that people brought to the city cultural and social strategies for adaptation, and that those strategies produced networks and associations peculiar to their city.

In addition to family and kinship, people brought their skills for constructing "associations," groups that are based on some common interest, a shared personal attribute, or shared purpose. These are, more or less, voluntary, in that one must choose to join the group. They often involve application and acceptance of membership, initiation and instruction into the ways of members, and rights and duties as members. Associations may have criteria for membership that includes age, gender, religion, political interest, or economic interest. These were once more common in the United States, as seen in the persistence of service organizations, country clubs, and even urban gangs. At one time, in Pittsburgh, every migrant group that settled in a neighborhood established something like a Sons of Poland club. Some associations are secret societies, thus enhancing the sense, importance of belonging.

Formal associations of recent migrants in cities have been reported from all over the world. Immigrants in the Chinese diaspora tend to construct formal associations wherever they settle, often based on province of origin and language. In West Africa, associations are

30. For example, Liebow, *Talley's Corner*; and Hannerz, *Soulside*.

31. Mayer, *Townsmen or Tribesmen*.

32. Jacobson, *Itinerant Townsmen: Friendship and Social Order in Urban Uganda*.

based on tribe of origin. Kenneth Little argues that, in West Africa, when a market economy is substituted for a subsistence economy and when people move from the village to the city, a whole new set of roles and relationships are formed.[33] People now interact on the basis of a common interest in things like wages, education, religion, and politics rather than in terms of genealogical origin, descent, kinship, and concern for the weather (rain-making cults). Voluntary associations provide a bridge for the person moving from the village to the city, offering a new set of roles and relationships, yet in terms that are understandable because they build on village culture. Little argues that the immigrant

> has been used to a highly personal set of relationships. He knows of no other way of communal living than this and so to organize similar practices of mutuality is for him a spontaneous adjustment to his environment. Nor in view of the strangeness of his surroundings is it surprising that the migrant often prefers to remain as far as possible in the company of previous associates. The result is that instead of weakening tribal consciousness, life in the new urban environment tends in some respects to make it stronger.[34]

One function of associations is to construct identity by employing dialect, narratives, and songs about the group. Migrants recognize the environment, feel at home, and do not have to be defensive about who they are. At the same time, shared knowledge of the city helps the migrant make his way in this new world.

Another kind of association in the city is the syncretistic cults that tend to form. People are attracted to these because they deal with the "excluded middle," that area of everyday living with sickness and failure that promises to cure, protect, and empower the migrant against both natural and supernatural forces. Some are a carryover from village life. Others are neo-Christian prophetic or messianic movements.[35] Others are straightforward Christian groups or churches, but these are often based on ethnicity.

33. Little, *West African Urbanization*. See also Little, *Urbanization as a Social Process*.

34. Little, *West African Urbanization*, 24.

35. Barrett, *Schism and Renewal in Africa*.

Another kind of association is the mutual aid society. The migrant discovers that all the areas of life that were functions of groups in the village have become his personal responsibility in the city. Mutual aid societies may offer help in the face of sickness or death in the family, problems with the law, the need for unsecured loans, or the desire for recreation.

Voluntary associations fill a need in the life of immigrants in the city. They may be a way to spread the gospel, or an impediment to the gospel if their loyalties override loyalty to the church. Churches themselves can serve the functions of an association for new immigrants, but not when other identities tend to exclude newcomers.

There is another way of organizing relationships in the city. A social network is not a group, but rather a series of links between people that a person may use to mobilize small groups, gather information, or obtain resources. For example, J. A. Barnes (1954) used network analysis in his study of a Norwegian island parish.[36] Elizabeth Bott, as noted above, used network analysis in her study of kinship and family in East London, as did J. Clyde Mitchell.[37] Network analysis was formalized in anthropology with the founding of the journal *Social Networks: An International Journal of Structural Analysis* in 1978, with Linton Freeman as editor and J. Clyde Mitchell as subeditor.

The main idea is that individuals in complex societies are faced with a large range of potential relationships, so the individual selects from among the possibilities those with whom he or she will establish social ties. The result is a network of relationships that is centered on the individual. Thus, no two persons have exactly the same network.

Networks can be close knit (people in the network tend to know each other) or loose knit (people in the network do not know each other). Links vary in density (how often) and intensity (how important) of relationship. Barnes labels the close or tight networks "effective," and the looser networks "extended." The point is that different social networks have different meanings and potential for action. Some of the early assumptions about urban life being shallow and instrumental failed to recognize the difference between a group and a network.

---

36. Barnes, "Class and Committees."
37. Mitchell, ed., *Social Networks in Urban Situations.*

Network analysis is important for the study of how new ideas and items are adopted and adapted by users.[38] Insofar as Christianity is an innovation, network analysis can be both a method of study and a strategy. Ray Bakke calls it "networking into the community."[39] Bakke describes his networking in stages. First, meet all the other pastors. Second, meet the leaders of public and voluntary agencies working in the community. Third, introduce yourself to all the businesses in the neighborhood. Bakke concludes:

> I place a high priority on networking and suggest that pastors spend about a fifth of their time on it, regarding this as invest-ment time. . . . The church must discover, and relate to, all the other churches, agencies and businesses in its community and know how they function, or it will always be marginal to ur-ban life; the pastors will always be reduced to rushing in with ill-thought-out programs which consume both personal and congregational energy.[40]

In addition to approaching the city through the study of family, neighborhoods, associations, and networks, the social problem at the center of the modern study of the city was poverty. The paradox is that people move to the city in order to better their life, to make some kind of economic gain. However, the city is characterized by the growth of mass poverty, so much so that the majority of poor people in the world live in cities.

> In 2001, 924 million people, or 31.6 per cent of the world's urban population, lived in slums. The majority of them were in the developing regions, accounting for 43 per cent of the urban population, in contrast to 6 per cent in more developed regions. Within the developing regions, sub-Saharan Africa had the largest proportion of the urban population resident in slums in 2001 (71.9 per cent) and Oceania had the lowest (24.1 per cent). In between these were South-central Asia (58 per cent), Eastern Asia (36.4 per cent), Western Asia (33.1 per cent), Latin American and the Caribbean (31.0 per cent) and Southeast Asia (28 per cent).[41]

---

38. Rogers, *Diffusion of Innovations*.

39. Bakke, *Urban Christian*, 110–11.

40. Ibid., 111–17.

41. United Nations Centre for Human Settlements, *Challenge of Slums*, xxv.

In the United States, there has been a long conversation about what to do about poverty, or what to do with poor people, or what to do for poor people in the city. In the early twentieth century, the dominant explanation for poverty was that it was a result of who poor people were to begin with. That is, the explanation singled out race or class as the cause. Biologically, people were destined to be poor because their intelligence or their character was substandard. This view was challenged by Franz Boas and his students. It was tested by the hard lessons of the Great Depression: even white, middle-class people became poor then. The search was on for the economic or structural reasons for poverty.

After World War II pulled the United States out of the depression, the great American Dream rose again to change how we looked at the poor. The soldiers who went off to war and the workers who stayed behind had accomplished a great task, as the narrative develops, by their dedication, strength, and sacrifice. Now the world was free. They returned home and began building "the good life." There were opportunities for education, for home owning, and for employment that anyone who had paid their dues could access, if they just tried. The dominant view in the 1950s and into the 1960s was that poverty was the result of individuals' character flaws. If people did not get a job and move up the ladder, it was their fault because there was plenty of opportunity to do so.

Yet, as the 1960s moved along, this narrative came under question. There were still poor people; there were even ghettos. In Europe, Jews had been restricted to ghettos by government rules. What structural arrangements put blacks, Hispanics, and poor whites in ghettos? Was it race, or was it individual failure, or were there other reasons? The questions would not go away. What causes poverty? What can be done to eliminate poverty?

Oscar Lewis was an anthropologist who worked among the poor. From his extensive ethnographic work, Lewis concluded that poverty is one thing, but there emerges also a "culture of poverty."[42] First, the poor develop a whole set of strategies for living based on the realities of life as it is for them. Second, when they can, the poor improve their situation, become upwardly mobile, and enter mainstream society. Their core values are the same, so they strive for this. However, when

42. Lewis, "Culture of Poverty."

one generation of poor is unable to make the transition, they then pass their temporary strategies on to their children. Their children learn the temporary and conditional strategies as a culture.

Lewis wanted to explain why, when opportunities come to a community, poverty often remains. That is, even if jobs, housing, water, and sewage come to the community; it seemed that people do not keep their jobs, do not fix up their houses, the water is left on, and the sewage backs up. The poor do not save, do not invest in property, do not keep up their own neighborhood.

Lewis argued that the reason for the persistence of these behaviors is that, although they were adaptive at one time, they have now been passed on to the next generation and become the tradition of the community. What are the implications of this? First, the culture of poverty is self-generating. It continues even when there is a change in the economic conditions that cause poverty. People are trapped. Lewis concluded that, by the time a child born into such a culture is seven years old, she is locked into a culture of poverty. The implication is that an individual raised in a culture of poverty is unable to take advantage of changing circumstances. In this view, culture is more like tradition, one that cannot be resisted. The poor disengage from society, live in dysfunctional families, and become chronically dependent on welfare.

While Lewis developed a sympathetic program for addressing poverty, his findings also contributed to the policy that became the "War on Poverty."[43] Assuming that the people's culture was at fault, the war became, in part, a war against people's beliefs and practices. In the end, the ideas led to a "blame the victim" mentality. For this reason, a serious critique of Lewis's work developed within anthropology.

Beginning with Charles Valentine[44] and on through Carol Stack[45] and Judith Goode,[46] solid ethnographic fieldwork has deconstructed the notions of the culture of poverty and of the underclass. These approaches ignore the structural conditions that lead to and perpetuate poverty. The primary cause is industrial capitalism, with its boom and bust cycles, uneven growth in different regions and sectors of society,

---

43. Along with the work of Daniel Moynihan, *Negro Family*.

44. Valentine, *Culture and Poverty*.

45. Stack, *All Our Kin*.

46. Goode, "How Urban Ethnography Counters."

and tendency toward obsolescence as technology develops.[47] The second cause is the organization of modern society along lines of racial discrimination, class privilege, and differential access to power. In short, poverty is produced by the structure of society.

Instead of stereotyping the poor as trapped in a cage of their own making, ethnographies have tended to illustrate the adaptability, resourcefulness, and determination of poor people. Goode reviews the work:

> Rather than illustrating laziness and work avoidance, ethnographers have discovered that making ends meet involves hard work and management skills. . . . Ethnographers have provided many insights about alternative (informal or underground) forms of production and consumption that poor people use. For example, self-built, makeshift housing; second-hand markets for clothing; home-based production of cooked food and other commodities; and unlicensed transportation systems emerge and flourish in poor communities.[48]

Yet the dominant narrative is powerful, and the poor continue to be blamed for their own condition, even as welfare programs also serve them poorly.

John Gulick has taken an applied anthropology approach to the study of urban societies.[49] He recognizes the inhumanity of cities that was one of the themes of the Chicago School, but argues, along with more modern studies, that cities also exhibit a great deal of humanity and hope. The question he addresses, in great detail, is: How can the study of anthropology contribute to the reduction of inhumanity and the increase of humanity in the cities?[50] That question is not unlike the missionary concern for the city.

Mission in Cities

The lack of a theology of the city today speaks as loudly as the presence of a theology. Some Christians even avoid their responsibilities by abusing Jesus' words, "The poor you have with you always,"[51] not

47. Ibid., 186–87.
48. Ibid., 188–89.
49. Gulick, *Humanity of Cities*.
50. Ibid., 218–19.
51. Matt 26:11

realizing that Jesus is using the common practice of quoting the first few words to reference a passage of Scripture,[52] as this was before there were chapters or verses.[53] The full verse says: "Since there will never cease to be some in need on the earth, I therefore command you, 'Open your hand to the poor and needy neighbor in your land.'"[54] Neither Jesus nor Paul were as wary of cities or as dismissive of the poor as modern Christians seem to be.

Wayne Meeks recovered for us the urban nature of the early church and mission.[55] The free cities of Greece were organized and directed to the mission of empire by Alexander the Great. Alexander spread his version of civilization by urbanization and trade. Roman armies followed Roman merchants to the cities of Greece, Asia Minor, Palestine, and Egypt. After a brief period of civil wars, the victory of Octavian brought a period of peace and prosperity for the cities that lasted a century. Cities provided an outlet for pride (naming the city after oneself, e.g., Alexandria, Caesaria), for trade to supply the homeland with needed goods and grain, and for security as a place for soldiers and civil servants to retire. Cities were the centers of colonies, providing another common name: Colonia.

Jesus' stories and metaphors frequently were set in the country, about planting and growing crops, but there were also some about cities, about masters and traders and kings. Paul's stories and metaphors are about cities: tent makers, silversmiths, dealers in purple dye. Paul himself was "a citizen of no mean city."[56] Christianity had success in the cities. Remember that before his conversion Paul was on his way to Damascus in order to stop the spread of the Way there.

After having preached in the cities, Paul could say, "From Jerusalem and as far round as Illyricum, . . . I have fully preached the gospel of Christ. I no longer have any room for work in these regions."[57] What about the rural areas? In Paul's mind, when the urban mission was complete, the mission, as far as he was concerned, was complete. Urban churches could take up the mission.

52. That is, our Old Testament.

53. Chapters were introduced circa AD 1220, verse in AD 1551.

54. Deut 15:11.

55. Meeks, *First Urban Christians.*

56. Acts 21:39.

57. Rom 15:19a, 23a.

Paul spent much formative time in Antioch. Antioch was a regional center of political, military, and commercial communication between Rome and the Persian frontier, and between Palestine and Asia Minor. It was one of the four most important cities in the empire. That was where Paul developed the kind of Christianity we see in his New Testament letters. The church there was multicultural and multiracial; it was the place where the controversy between Jews and Gentiles broke out in an argument between Paul and Peter, and the site of the first official church-supported mission.

Major cities usually had a native population, others who were refugees, migrants, exiles, and entrepreneurs, as well as Roman settlers of various types. Jews plied certain trades and nearly always lived in their own neighborhoods. While Greek and then Latin were the common languages, there was a variety of other languages in use, as Paul and Barnabas discovered in Lystra where the people spoke Lycaonian. Typically, the language and culture was Greek, and the politics and economics were Roman. There were differences, but the effects of Mediterraneanization were also felt (the local case of globalization). Each city likely had a central temple, government buildings, a marketplace, a school (gymnasium), a theater, public baths, inns, taverns, and small shops. Where they put these things differed from city to city.

Roman military power was everywhere, and was responsible for peace in the city and security in travel. Roman engineers worked wonders in building roads to all the major cities of the empire. It is clear that Paul and others used the main trade routes to go to major cities in the empire to spread Christianity. Paul was networking when he went outside the city walls where he supposed there was a place of prayer. Each city had similarities and differences. As his long-term strategy, Paul wanted to go to Rome, *the* city.

As a site of economic and political activity, as a multicultural and multilingual society, as a center that influences a periphery, as a religious marketplace, as a refuge for migrants as well as a den of thieves, the city is a prime location for mission. Christianity was birthed in the city, spread from city to city, and grew to maturity in the city. That is where the people are, and the people are in need of a Savior and a friend.

The Postmodern Study of Postcolonial Cities

Anthropologists tended to do small community studies in the city, but the problem remains of how the microcosm relates to the macrocosm. That is, how does life in Little Italy in New York relate to New York City as a whole? The study of ethnic neighborhoods will tell us some of what we want to know, but with globalization has come a dual concern in anthropology: an intense interest in the local combined with an imagination for the global. That is, anthropologists no longer search for an "ideal type" of a city, nor even a "paradigmatic" city, especially one based on US or European exemplars.[58] Each city has its own history and culture, and each city constitutes a different node in a network of cities engaged in global production, distribution, and consumption of information, raw materials, and finished products.

The perception of cities as "nodes' in social and economic processes on a global scale"[59] means that cities are no longer simply subordinate to the state, but rather engage in competition and cooperation with a global network of cities and corporations. When places become commodities to be packaged and marketed in a global marketplace, then the concerns of the state, on the one hand, and the concerns of the poor, on the other, become secondary to the concerns of the market.[60] By playing the economic globalization game, so to speak, cities create a "new set of urban inequalities,"[61] and it is not the goal or perceived responsibility of global capitalism to address social justice.

Since the assumption no longer holds that African, Asian, and Latin American cities are just late in following the European model, a new spate of ethnographies has emerged exploring the uniqueness of cities in the global network through dynamics as diverse as tourism, terrorism, vampire culture, gay culture, and postcolonial architecture.[62]

In all this, the presence of Christians in the city has not been studied adequately. For example, given the colonial emergence and neocolonial growth of Christianity in Singapore, what happens when the state belatedly requests religious positions on casino gambling of

58. Bunnell, Drummond, and Ho, "Critical Reflections."

59. Ibid., 3.

60. Ibid., 6.

61. Ibid., 7.

62. Bishop, Phillips, and Yeo, eds., *Postcolonial Urbanism*.

a church that is not used to doing public theology?[63] In some ways, Christianity has been a "good citizen" in Singaporean terms, and that means that Christianity contributes to Singapore's business goals. As Goh notes, "Evangelical cultural production is thus inextricably bound with such cultural influences and mechanisms as English as a global language; the values, images, and productions of foreign Anglophone (especially American) film and network companies; the Internet; the business of education, and of course the actual machinery directly concerned with Christianity as a global enterprise."[64] What are the economic and political connections of the church in the global city?

These are the issues that are being contested and constructed in the emerging cities of the Global South. The postcolonial city is the site where the colonial past meets the neocolonial present, where migrants refashion their village, tribal, and religious roots, where the meaning of person, family, leader, and provider all change. The communities that are emerging in the city may look back at the village, but they also link in unexpected ways through electronic technologies to international businesses as well as religious and political movements with a presence on the Internet.[65]

Viv Grigg has examined the nature of mission in the postmodern postcolonial city of Auckland.[66] His conclusion reminds us of the importance of what anthropologists would call "doing ethnography in the city," with its method of participant (presence) observation (empathy).

> At a missiological level, the most powerful way I have found to move people to this understanding has been through action involving Kingdom incarnation. For Jesus' first step of discipleship, his incarnation, is a historically central socio-economic-political subversive act, not simply a spiritual act. Luke 2, in its description of the incarnation, reflects the Jewish understanding of the prophets in their denunciation of social sins. The Magnificat tells us how the incarnation places the locus of economic theory at the point of uplift of the poor. The incarnation was a profoundly social act, making identification

---

63. Kwa, *Towards a Model of Engagemen.*

64. Goh, "Deus ex Machina," 308.

65. See, for example, Demissie, ed., *Postcolonial African Cities*. See also, Varma, *Postcolonial City*.

66. Grigg, *Spirit of Christ and the Postmodern City*.

or solidarity with the poor central to social action and placing the locus of Christian mission among the poor. The incarnation was a profoundly political act, defining godly politics as politics that serve the least important of society.[67]

Globalization

Globalization is the widespread engagement of people with an expanding worldwide system of communication, commerce, and culture that is producing broad uniformities across selected sectors of many societies as well as generating multiple hybrid cultures in various stages of reception, rejection, and reinvention of innovations.

The history of the world is marked by expanding boundaries. In a world where God reigns, this would mean the expansion of the circle of those called "family" followed by appropriate behavior toward them. However, instead, expansion has been accompanied by, and even driven by, political power and economic motive. There has been regionalization, frequently impelled by the rise of empire. The first century AD was such a time when Greek culture and Roman polity spread across the whole Mediterranean, that is, south Europe, the Middle East, and North Africa, and even out into the Atlantic Ocean and up to the Baltic Sea. At roughly the same time, the rise of Chinese culture and the empire of the Middle Kingdom spread their customs and practices over much of East Asia. The adoption of Christianity by the Roman Empire and the subsequent spread of Christianity resulted in a selected uniformity during the Middle Ages in Europe, known as Christendom. The spread of Islam across North Africa and into Spain, and across the Middle East and into Central Asia and India, brought another kind of uniformity, but still with the familiar mix of language, culture, society, and technology. What began as regionalization finally gained a worldwide reach in the era of Colonialism (1492–1960).

This means that it has been a long time since the world was populated by isolated groups speaking separate languages and making a living in a traditional way (hunting and gathering, gardening, herding, agriculture). In fact, it is doubtful that the world was ever that way.

There is evidence of the interaction of different societies, the movement of particular groups of people, and long-distance trade

---

67. Ibid., 107.

routes, no matter how far back you go. For, example, at about 1000 BC, there is evidence that obsidian (volcanic glass) was being traded from New Britain, at the north edge of Papua New Guinea, as far east as Fiji and as far west as central Indonesia. Copper forged in Indonesia is found at archaeological sites in Papua New Guinea. In China, centralization of power had already produced an empire with an emperor. In the Near East, there was trade from one end of the Mediterranean to the other. By this time, Aryans from the Eurasian steppes had migrated down into northern India, Siberian groups had completely populated the Americas, and Africans were diversifying into a variety of economies.

However, since 1492, to pick a particular date, the amount of interaction among cultures, the size of economic networks, and the reach of political power has expanded at an ever-increasing rate. Today, corporations, firms, NGOs, non-profits, missions, governments, universities, churches, banks, markets, armies, smugglers, and drug dealers all interact daily in an unimaginable myriad of ways. This is globalization: the movement of goods, persons, and ideas through networks that make it seem like every place and every time is immediately present to every person.

The primary vector for these practices is *neoliberalism*, or competitive capitalism, based on an assumption that a billion rational choices in a marketplace unfettered by rules and regulations produces the greatest good for the greatest number of people. Globalization makes all markets act like commodity markets, and globalization commodifies everything.

Is the World Flat?

In 1999, Thomas Friedman wrote a best-selling book about globalization called *The Lexus and the Olive Tree*, in order to explore the growing spread of neoliberalism (unregulated capitalism, free-market trade), which was leading to prosperity in some quarters (the Lexus) as well as being the impetus for repressed minorities, including religious minorities who were emerging from Cold War dichotomies to try to regain their identities through the reclamation of tradition (the Olive Tree). He wrote, in part, to counter the pessimism of Barber's *Jihad vs. McWorld*.

Friedman followed this with the thesis that *The World Is Flat*, in which he visited sites in India and China (among others) and declared that a number of trends were coming together to flatten out the world economically. As with the previous book, these trends were ignited by the fall of the USSR and the rise of the Internet, with its impact on business and trade. Friedman makes a convincing argument that new technology and a new business environment have created business networks that pay little regard to national boundaries.

However, the world is not flat. If anything, the world is punctuated by plateaus and plains. Not as catchy a phrase, but closer to the truth. While certain sections of Bangalore might resemble certain sections of the Silicon Valley in California, at least in terms of business connections and practices, the miles in between are filled with great stretches where people have no access to a computer or even a telephone, where production, distribution, and consumption (the economy) is local, and where family, clan, and religious community concerns are prioritized over global business or political concerns. Friedman is only the latest in a long line of Western apologists who think that tradition and religion (and that includes local Christianities as well as local Muslim or Hindu communities) stand in the way of progress and prosperity.

Globalization is widespread, but neither total nor totalizing. Some people are benefitting from globalization, some people are unaware of globalization, and some people are suffering from globalization. Globalization is an "engagement," not a done deal. The forces of globalization are resistible. People are operating as agents in their own right, picking and choosing, negotiating their relationship with the streams of technology that run through nearly every city.

Christians may look to their theology for resources for resisting the worst of globalization. Cynthia Moe-Lobeda, for example, finds in Luther's liturgy reason to question the extremes of capitalism. "Hear Luther speaking about the sacrament . . . : 'by means of this sacrament, all self-seeking love is rooted out and gives place to that which seeks the common good.'"[68] On the other hand, Muslims also draw on their theology to resist globalization. As Amer Al-Roubie notes:

> The great Muslim scholar Imam Al-Ghazali sums up Islam "as equally striving for earning on the one hand and striving in

68. Moe-Lobeda, "Offering Resistance to Globalization."

the cause of God on the other." Thus the purpose of allocation of resources in Islam is to enhance the welfare of all and not to be limited to serving the few as in the case of globalization.[69]

Some in both religions have not thought the issues through, have not developed a theology of globalization, and have little organized sense of how the community of the faithful might resist the power of the secular.

Globalization is an expanding worldwide system, but is seen as a threat by some.[70] Globalization is global, though uneven. Coca-Cola and McDonald's are nearly everywhere—nearly, but not quite everywhere.[71] The systemic qualities of globalization refer to the connections that link together seemingly every part of the globe. Whether or not there is a control center in the system is debatable.

The transition from neocolonialism to globalization is revealed in the failed economic development policies and practices of the 1960s through 1980s. This includes the work of the International Monetary Fund and the World Bank. Joseph E. Stiglitz, former president of the World Bank, exposes many of the practices of the IMF, particularly the "structural adjustment" programs that worked in favor of Western banks and to the detriment of developing countries.[72] For the even more conspiracy-theory minded reader, John Perkins admits to working as an economist to pump up the projected economic return of development projects so that developing countries would take loans, then fail to repay because the projections were bogus, resulting in a country obligated to Western capitalist interests.[73]

---

69. Al-Roubaie, *Globalization and the Muslim World*, 93.

70. Ibid., 28: "The Americanization of the global societies via Hollywood, McDonalds, Coca Cola, music, CNN, and internet websites has made the American lifestyle and personalities a model to follow for young people all over the world. On the other hand, interactions among cultures could have both negative and positive changes by influencing the main determinants of the socio-cultural elements, which characterize the distinctiveness of groups across human society."

71. There are many local cases of resistance. For example, in Peru, *Inca Kola* is the most popular soft drink, *Bembos* the most popular fast food restaurant, and *Wong* the most popular mass merchandiser.

72. Stiglitz, *Globalization and Its Discontents*.

73. Perkins, *Confessions of an Economic Hit Man*.

"The Land" Again

While the colonial era involved some of the greatest land grabs in history, that part continues in neocolonial times as well as in the current period of Globalization. Considering land ownership in 1492, several continents have been turned upside down in the last five hundred years. In North America, Native Americans now own about one percent of the land, with the other 99 percent owned by Euro-Americans or Asian-Americans. In Central and South America, the native people fell under the obligation of *economendia* as their land was claimed for *haciendas*, and even the Catholic Church assumed the role of landlord over a number of these plantations. The majority of the land was claimed by Euro-Americans. In Australia, until several recent High Court rulings,[74] Australian Aborigines were not considered to be people but a part of the landscape, as far as land rights were concerned. As described earlier, this colonial policy is called *Terra Nullius*, a legal term meaning "empty land," despite the fact that native people live there. Thus, until 1992, 100 percent of land rights in Australia were held by Euro-Australians or Asian-Australians, and none by indigenous Australians.

Some people may think that what happened is regrettable, but its now part of the past and so it is time to move on. However, recent reports of violence between national governments and developers, on the one hand, and indigenous populations, on the other, make the abuse of traditional land rights a continuing problem of globalization. For example, in Peru, as oil developers move into the Amazon, there is trouble. Consider the following news item:

> At least nine Peruvian police officers were killed Saturday as soldiers stormed an oil pumping station in the Amazon where Indian protesters were holding police hostage, the country's defense minister said. The deaths brought to 20 the number of police killed—some with spears—since security forces moved early Friday to break up a road-block by indigenous Peruvians who oppose government moves to exploit oil and gas and other resources on their lands.[75]

---

74. 1992, Mabo vs. Queensland (no. 2); 1996, Wik Peoples vs. the State of Queensland.

75. *Evansville Courier and Press,* "More Police Killed in Land Rights Dispute," A8.

This sounds like the issues that have arisen over the last few centuries between colonizers and the colonized. But, in globalization, something new is happening as well. Rich countries like Saudi Arabia, China, Kuwait, Djibouti, Qatar, Bahrain, the United Arab Emirates, and South Korea are looking to secure their food production against any future shortfall by acquiring land in poor countries. Consider this report:

> The Saudi programme is an example of a powerful but contentious trend sweeping the poor world: countries that export capital but import food are outsourcing farm production to countries that need capital but have land to spare. Instead of buying food on world markets, governments and politically influential companies buy or lease farmland abroad, grow the crops there and ship them back.[76]

One key phrase here is "land to spare." I have been doing research on the anthropology of land since the 1960s. There is no such thing anywhere as unclaimed land, or land where no one possesses rights. Rights differ significantly in their shape and distribution in different cultures, but all land is claimed. Hunters and gatherers (there are few if any left) need huge tracts of land in order to be able to access vegetables, fruits, and meat resources in different places when the time is right. Herders (there are a number left) need huge tracts of land as a hedge against drought in one area. Some gardeners (huge numbers, at least part-time) need large tracts of land in order to keep moving their gardens each year, leaving the former area fallow for up to ten years (slash-and-burn agriculture). The day that colonizers arrive, or that government officials show up to access land use, it may look like there is a lot of unused land, but long-term study shows that that is not true.

Second, this new form of colonialism within globalization is different in scale: "In Sudan alone, South Korea has signed deals for 690,000 hectares, the United Arab Emirates (UAE) for 400,000 hectares and Egypt has secured a similar deal to grow wheat."[77] The second difference is the lack of benefits for the local people who, in the past, at least were able to sign on as laborers on large plantations. Consider the way that China operates in Africa:

---

76. *Economist*, "Buying Farmland Abroad: Outsourcing's Third Wave," 61–63.

77. Ibid., 61.

China secured the right to grow palm oil for biofuel on 2.8m hectares of Congo, which would be the world's largest palm-oil plantation. It is negotiating to grow biofuels on 2m hectares in Zambia, a country where Chinese farms are said to produce a quarter of the eggs sold in the capital, Lusaka. According to one estimate, 1m Chinese farm labourers will be working in Africa this year, a number one African leader called "catastrophic."[78]

Here, agriculture is expanding in a country, but the work is being done by laborers brought from another country that has bought or leased the land. The system is a sealed one: from land ownership, to production, to shipping, to distribution and consumption; all the work is being done by the colonizer. In addition, it is not just private companies that are behind this new departure in business, it is the national government itself. Finally, it is not just an issue of the most arable land being bought up by outsiders, it is also an issue of water, which may be the new oil (that is, the most expensive yet widely necessary resource out there).

As in any deal, there are winners and there are losers, short-term gains and losses and long-term gains and losses. So far, the rich countries and the national governments of poor countries stand to gain, but, as usual, the local and indigenous peoples stand to lose. Where do the interests of churches and missionaries lie?

Mission in an Urbanizing Globalizing World

First, churches and missionaries should become knowledgeable and realistic about the world. Not everyone is happy with the spread of neoliberal capitalism, as evidenced by a review of the IMF and World Bank by a leading capitalist.[79] Yet, a Christian theology including a critique of economic systems is not common. "There are many contemporary systems and structures that facilitate injustice, and as Christians we need to be clear what these are and be concerned to break them."[80]

Around the edges of the formal economic system there are a million and one instances of an informal economy based on global flows

78. Ibid.

79. Stiglitz, *Globalization and Its Discontents.*

80. Schluter, "Risk, Reward and Responsibility," 66. See also Wallis, *Justice for the Poor.*

of illegal goods and persons, of unregulated commodities, and of legal goods transported and sold in illegal ways. There are few studies to inform us about what to expect, yet "the sum total of all extra-legal activities represents a significant part of the world's economy and politics."[81] How these practices entice, trap, hurt, or even help people is our business to know. Otherwise, as usual, missionaries run the risk of blaming the victim, then asking the individual to repent from his/her sin, without understanding the structural conditions conducive to sin.

Second, churches and missionaries should put themselves in a position to enter the global marketplace with a reasonable chance of doing well. One's lifestyle should reflect an understanding of what economic practices help poor people and what practices hurt poor people. For example, the rise of the Fair Trade label and its variants exposes a tangled network of production, distribution, and consumption. "Fair trade fosters empowerment and improved quality of life for artisan producers through an integrated and sustained system of trade partnerships among producers, retailers, and consumers."[82]

Third, considering the colonial past and the globalizing present, we are forced to ask some questions. First, who is in charge? North American and European mission leaders continue to spin out mission plans, and they have the means to support these projects, whether or not they make sense to the local people in other countries.

> This domination inevitably affects mission thinking and practice. A South African friend living and working in a township told me of the frustrations he had with the AD 2000 and Beyond Movement. He saw the push from Northern mission centres as being of a globalising order, carrying the implication that the rest of the world had to accept the priority of AD 2000 missiology. The economics of the situation made it difficult to resist or ignore, and countries in the South tended to lose the theological space to frame their own questions and make their own contribution to global mission. My friend spoke of contending against the hegemony of AD 2000.[83]

81. Nordstrom, *Global Outlaws*, xvi.

82. Littrell and Dickson, *Social Responsibility in the Global Marketplace: Fair Trade of Cultural Products*, 5.

83. Valerio, "Globalisation and Economics," 19.

Elsewhere, I have made a sustained critique of the "10/40 Window" movement and the impact that it has had on mission.[84]

The second question is: Who goes in mission? The illusion that mission is from the North to the South is rapidly fading. Some of the greatest missionary movements of our age are cross-cultural but internal to certain countries, especially India, China, and Nigeria. Other movements spread from the South: Brazil, Korea, Singapore. And, some of these go to the North, e.g., West African missionaries in Europe and the United States.

The third question is: How are these missions supported? Many postmodern mission movements are self-supporting, as people migrating for jobs see themselves as missionaries as well. This is the case of Nigerians moving to Atlanta, or Filipinos moving to the Middle East. The Global South churches are making contributions to evangelism, mission, church growth, and theology with some support from their home churches, self-support from their jobs, and some support from receiving churches.

The belated calls for "partnerships" may, in fact, be the swan song of Western missions attempting to maintain some semblance of initiative and control in mission.

84. Rynkiewich, "Corporate Metaphors and Strategic Thinking."

13

The Anthropology
of Christianity

ONE DAY I STOOD ON THE STREET IN THE CENTER OF BWAGAOIA
on Misima Island, Milne Bay Province, Papua New Guinea, watching
people and preparing to finish a bit of grocery shopping before walking the three kilometers back to Loaga, the United Church mission
station where we lived. People I knew greeted me and I returned their
greetings as I leaned up against the wall, as did others who considered
a trip to town to be a social occasion. A young man whom I did not
recognize came up and slipped me a 20 Kina bill. "What is this for?"
I asked. "I think you know," he replied, and then disappeared in the
crowd. In fact, I didn't know, but I tucked it away to probe its meaning
later. After a few minutes, another young man, whom I did recognize
but only vaguely, came up and began a conversation. He shifted back
and forth between English, Pidgin English, and Misiman. I understood very little Misiman, but also had trouble understanding where
he was going when he was speaking English or Pidgin English. My
frustration turned to comic relief when someone came up behind me
and whispered in my ear, "Don't worry, he's crazy." No wonder I didn't
understand him; no one else did either!

For a missionary, there is no substitute for living in a place with
your eyes open to the complexities of life. Some things have a deep
and hidden meaning. The gift of 20 Kina was linked at a number of
levels with the long history of "cargo cults" on Misima. These messianic and apocalyptic movements are non-falsifiable. When one

gambit fails, people search for another one rather than question the reasoning behind it.

In 1999, in Goroka, I gave one of the presentations in a day-long seminar that the Lutheran Church had organized to defuse hysteria about the turn of the millennium: the dreaded Y2K. I went about explaining that it was the wrong year, the millennium would turn at the end of 2000, not at the beginning; that the date was off by four or five years since the calendar had been recalibrated and the death of Herod the Great was now in 4 BC; and that, at any rate, they should not worry because no one knew the date of Christ's return anyway. I should have known better. Afterwards, a young man came up and thanked me for clearly these things up. Since he still had a rather quizzical look on his face, I asked what was wrong. "Oh," he said, "I was just trying to think what great thing happened in 1996!" Non-falsifiable.

Some things remain fuzzy or do not have a recognizable meaning. The young man speaking gibberish to me in Bwagaoia was a good soccer player who had been recruited from the islands to a Highlands team. Once there he got involved in drugs and smoked so much marijuana that he came back with his mind messed up. He tended to be overly aggressive and scary, particularly for children. When he got into trouble in town, the local police would lock him up and send word to his family. They would come and collect him, take him home, and keep him safe in the village, until he wandered into town again. I was trying to make sense out of what he was saying, but it turned out that not even Misimans could decipher his speech.

It is precisely here that postmodernity affects both anthropology and mission: not everything will make sense, not everything can be explained with certainty and finality, and not every problem can be solved nor ever issue resolved. The anthropologist Pierre Bourdieu gives voice to the methodological conundrum:

> The anthropologist's particular relation to the object of his study contains the makings of a theoretical distortion inasmuch as his situation as an observer, excluded from the real play of social activities by the fact that he has no place (except by choice or by way of a game) in the system observed and has no need to make a place for himself there, inclines him to a hermeneutic representation of practices, leading him to re-

duce all social relations to communicative relations and, more precisely, to decoding operations.[1]

The point is: without participation, observation deceives us; without observation, participation is meaningless. There is no way out, no objective place on which to stand disconnected and hope to understand. So, the anthropologist and the missiologist make an epistemological choice: to participate while observing, and to observe while participating in order to have the best chance of understanding the meaning, feeling the emotions, and discerning the values of an event.

This is a far remove from the modern generation of anthropologists who tended to dismiss Christianity as the fly in the ointment. In recent years, a less biased approach has arisen among younger anthropologists who, even when Christian mission has preceded their arrival at a research site, find that Christianity is important enough to the people that they have adapted its teachings and practices to local life, and thus conclude that they will study the existing Christianity. Previous generations tended to try to get underneath a "veneer" of Christianity to the "authentic" tradition, and thus tended to write Christianity out of their ethnographies, as if the missionaries never came and the people never converted. Joel Robbins at the University of California at San Diego is one of the founders of this movement with his seminal ethnography, *Becoming Sinners: Christianity and Moral Torment in a Papua New Guinea Society*. Bialecki, Haynes, and Robbins explain the rise of the anthropology of Christianity.

> To say that the anthropology of Christianity has only emerged in the last decade is also to say that until that time anthropologists had, despite the few kinds of exceptions noted above, largely neglected the study of this world religion. The reasons for the original anthropological rejection of Christianity as an object of research are numerous, and many of them are related to fundamental tendencies.[2]

The authors list a number of reasons why modernist anthropologists shied away from studying Christianity. First, European and American anthropologists tended to think that they already knew what Christianity was about. Second, most anthropologists tend to

1. Bourdieu, *Outline of a Theory of Practice*, 1.
2. Bialecki, Haynes, and Robbins, "Anthropology of Christianity," 1140.

think of themselves as secular and thus have trouble imagining that there is any spiritual reality behind Christian or traditional beliefs. Third, anthropologists tend to be repelled by the apparent docility of the Christian congregations they encounter because they think that they recognize the conservative values of some Christians in America and Europe that directs individual Christians away from engagement in social and political issues. Finally, anthropologists tend to prefer established traditions as an explanation for behavior, and not more recent additions to culture and religion.[3]

Fenella Cannell has added an interesting reason for the modernist aversion to studying Christianity.

> In advancing the well-known division between male culture and female domesticity, some of these early ethnographers also made a less widely noticed assignment of Christian practice to the female and therefore implicitly noncultural sphere. A complementary deficit in the consideration of Christian experience can be found even in that feminist scholarship which helped to correct the assumption that women had nothing to say.[4]

The new anthropology of Christianity is refreshing because young anthropologists realize "that it is not sufficient to assume that we know in advance what Christian experience is."[5] Some new ethnographers have reconsidered the relationship between Christianity and modernity with respect to the concept of the person, human agency, and the integration of traditional theology with Christian theology.[6] Others see a kind of culture clash between traditional narratives of power and introduced narratives, in one case, "the result of competition between Methodist Church authorities and traditional chiefs."[7] If disease and death were a problem for traditional religion, they remain a problem for Christianity, especially in the midst of an AIDS epidemic.[8] Finally, studies of the nature of conversion itself,[9] and the place of language

3. Ibid., 1140–41.
4. Cannell, "Introduction," 9–10.
5. Ibid., 29.
6. Keane, *Christian Moderns*.
7. Tomlinson, *In God's Image*, 6.
8. Klaits, *Death in a Church of Life*.
9. Harris, "Eternal Return of Conversion."

in actualizing and verifying conversion,[10] offer fresh insights for missiologists who are concerned about these issues.

Anthropology has changed, and it would be worthwhile for missiologists to discover anew how fresh insights can contribute to their understanding of local cultures, local Christianities, and the missionary situation.

Anthropology, Christianity, and Postmodernity

Premodern Europe, and in some ways the whole premodern world, was concerned about daily life; whether convincing by argument, mandating by force, or discovering by observation what is real. The formal term in the European philosophical tradition is *ontology*, and the question is: What exists, what is really out there? The answer ranges from the religious (forces, spirits, ghosts, devils) to the scientific (quarks, bacteria, Tasmanian devils, plate tectonics). But, for most people, it has been practical. Will this seed variety produce under drought conditions? Will this medicine cure my child? Will the fish return in the spring?

Modern Europe elevated mathematics and the sciences in an attempt to discard what is false and misleading from what is true. The search for what is true, however, requires that we ask how we know what we know. This area in European philosophical tradition is called *epistemology*. Modernity has placed the thinking and reasoning self at the center of knowing, thus decentering tradition and the church.

Postmodernism questions the objectivity of the thinking and knowing self, and thus doubts the narrative about reality that is dependent on an objective observer. The postcolonial critique specifically rejects those European and American narratives that define the "other" while claiming a Eurocentric understanding of reality. Every interpretation suffers as it is deconstructed; the philosophical tradition of hermeneutics reigns. With reality in doubt, and with truth in doubt, the postmodern philosopher has lost his way, and the nihilist branch sees no hope of recovery.

Describing himself, Jesus said, "I am the way, the truth, and the life, no one comes to the Father but by me." Jesus fulfills premodern (the life), modern (the truth), and postmodern (the way) desires; but who is in a position to introduce Jesus in a winsome, attractive, and compelling

10. Engelke, *Problem of Presence.*

manner? Will we have to relearn our lessons in mission, or can we build on the foundations of Scripture, history of mission, and anthropology of mission and move into the postmodern era of missiology?

Here are ten guidelines for reaching postmodern people.

1. **Hospitality.** Be an inviting, welcoming, non-judgmental, and inclusive people. Postmodern people need a place, a people, and the presence of God, because they are alone, without hope, and without meaning.

2. **Relationships.** Find ways to build relationships, to integrate the seeker or novice into small groups and networks of Christians. Postmodern people are fleeing from individualism.

3. **Community.** Tolerate uncertainty, doubt, immaturity, and an exploratory spirit. Work to build community. Postmodern people tend to belong before they believe.

4. **Involvement.** Provide clear paths and easy access to lay ministry in and for the church. Let your motto be: Every member in ministry. Postmodern people do not want to pay for other people to do things; they want to be in ministry.

5. **Diversity.** Be intentional in recruiting and preserving variety among the membership. Let your model be: The Kingdom of God gathered around the throne in Revelation 7:9. Postmodern people have little time for the divisions of the past and already practice what we mean when we say that there is no difference between male and female, slave or free, in Christ.

6. **Dialogue.** Provide a non-threatening atmosphere for honest sharing. Be prepared to listen, learn, and appreciate the story of the other. Let the Holy Spirit guide the transformation. Remember: We are God's witnesses, not God's lawyers.

7. **Narrative.** Tell the story of the church, and situate it within the larger story of God and the Missio Dei. Invite the story of the seeker, and show how they too fit into the story of God and the church. Repeat as necessary. It is not creed but the Bible in all its fullness that engages postmodern people.

8. **Incarnation.** Engage people with the whole gospel on all levels, in sermons, in public celebrations, in confession, and in counseling. Address whole persons in their intellectual, emotional, and ethical dimensions. There is no place for modernist dualisms among postmoderns: body/soul, spiritual/natural, knowing/doing,

9. **Contextualization.** Encourage the work of doing local theology by forming hermeneutical communities to consider Christ and culture in their day and place. Teach the difference between form and meaning. Read the Bible for all its worth.

10. **Integrity.** Be sure that Jesus shines through you. Postmodern people are suspicious and will not tolerate duplicity. Meet suspicion with authentic Christlikeness. With the Holy Spirit, we point to Jesus.

Bibliography

Achebe, Chinua. *Things Fall Apart*. New York: Anchor, 1956.

Adams, David Wallace. *Education for Extinction: American Indians and the Boarding School Experience, 1875–1928*. Lawrence: University Press of Kansas 1995.

Aguirre, Carlos. *Breve Historia de la Esclavitud en el Perú: Una Herida que no Deja de Sangrar*. Lima: Fondo Editorial del Congreso del Perú, 2005.

Allmen, Daniel von. "The Birth of Theology." *International Review of Mission* 64.253 (1975) 37–55.

Al-Roubaie, Amer. *Globalization and the Muslim World*. Selangor Darul Ehsan, Malaysia: Malita Jaya, 2002.

Anderson, Benedict R. *Imagined Communities: Reflections on the Origin and Spread of Nationalism*. Rev. ed. New York: Verso, 2006 [1983].

Anderson, Walter Truett, editor. *The Truth about the Truth: De-Confusing and Re-Constructing the Post-Modern World*. New York: Penguin, 1995.

Appadurai, Arjun. *Modernity at Large: Cultural Dimensions of Globalization*. Public Worlds 1. Minneapolis: University of Minnesota Press, 1996.

Aragon, Lorraine V. *Fields of the Lord: Animism, Christian Minorities, and State Development in Indonesia*. Honolulu: University of Hawai'i Press, 2000.

Arnold, Bill T., and David B. Weisberg. "A Centennial Review of Friedrich Delitzsch's 'Babel und Bibel' Lectures." *Journal of Biblical Literature* 121.3 (2002) 441–57.

Ayoub, Millicent R. "Parallel Cousin Marriage and Endogamy: A Study in Sociometry." *Southwest Journal of Anthropology* 15.3 (1959) 266–75.

———. "The Family Reunion." *Ethnology* 5 (1966) 415–33. Reprinted in *The Nacirema: Readings on American Culture*, edited by James P. Spradley and Michael A. Rynkiewich, 133–148. Boston: Little, Brown, 1975.

Bakke, Ray, with Jim Hart. *The Urban Christian: Effective Ministry in Today's Urban World*. Downers Grove, IL: InterVarsity, 1987.

Barber, Benjamin R. *Jihad vs. McWorld: How the Planet Is both Falling Apart and Coming Together—and What This Means for Democracy*. New York: Times Books, 1995.

Barnes, J. A. "Class and Committees in a Norwegian Island Parish." *Human Relations* 7 (1954) 39–58.

Barrett, David B. *Schism and Renewal in Africa: An Analysis of Six Thousand Contemporary Religious Movements*. Nairobi: Oxford University Press, 1968.

Barth, Fredrik. "Segmentary Opposition and the Theory of Games: A Study of Pathan Organization." *Journal of the Royal Anthropological Institute* 89.1 (1959a) 5–21.

————. *Political Leadership among Swat Pathans*. Monographs on Social Anthropology 19. London: Athlone, 1959b.

————, editor. *Ethnic Groups and Boundaries: The Social Organization of Culture Difference*. Oslo: Universitetsforlaget (Scandinavian University Press), 1969.

Bateli Vavaluna. Port Moresby, PNG: Bible Society of Papua New Guinea, 1997.

Bede, Venerable. *Ecclesiastical History of the English People*. Translated by B. Colgrave and R. A. B. Mynors. Oxford: Oxford University Press, 1969.

Benedict, Ruth Fulton. "Anthropology and the Abnormal." *Journal of General Psychology* 10 (1934) 59–80.

————. *Patterns of Culture*. Boston: Houghton Mifflin, 2006 [1934].

Benedict, Ruth Fulton. *The Chrysanthemum and the Sword*. Boston, MA: Houghton Mifflin, 1942.

Berger, Peter L., and Thomas Luckmann. *The Social Construction of Reality: A Treatise in the Sociology of Knowledge*. Garden City, NY: Doubleday, 1967.

Berlin, Brent, and Paul Kay. *Basic Color Terms: Their Universality and Evolution*. Berkeley: University of California Press, 1969.

Bible Society of Papua New Guinea. *Nupela Testamen*. Port Moresby, PNG: Bible Society of Papua New Guinea, 1987.

Bialecki, Jon, Naomi Haynes, and Joel Robbins. "The Anthropology of Christianity." *Religion Compass* 2.6 (2008) 1139–58.

Bishop, Ryan, John Phillips, and Wei-Wei Yeo, editors. *Postcolonial Urbanism: Southeast Asian Cities and Global Processes*. New York: Routledge, 2003.

Boas, Franz.. *Social Organization and Secret Societies of the Kwakiutl Indians*. Annual Report, Smithsonian Institution, 1895. Washington, DC: United States National Museum. 1897

Bodley, John. *Victims of Progress*. 5th ed. Lanham, MD: AltaMira, 2008 [1975].

Bourdieu, Pierre. *Outline of a Theory of Practice*. Cambridge Studies in Social and Cultural Anthropology 16. Cambridge: Cambridge University Press, 2002 [1972].

Bott, Elizabeth. *Family and Social Network: Roles, Norms, and External Relationships of Ordinary Urban Families*. 2nd ed. New York: Free Press, 1971 [1957].

Brueggemann, Walter. *The Land: Place as Gift, Promise, and Challenge in Biblical Faith*. 2nd ed. Overtures to Biblical Theology. Minneapolis: Fortress, 2002.

Bulmer, Ralph. "Why Is the Cassowary Not a Bird? A Problem of Zoological Taxonomy among the Karam of the New Guinea Highlands." *Man* 2.1 (1967) 5–25.

Bunnell, Tim, Lisa B. W. Drummond, and K. C. Ho. "Critical Reflections on Cities in Southeast Asia." In *Critical Reflections on Cities in Southeast Asia*, edited by Bunnell, Drummond, and Ho, 1–27. Asian Social Science Series 3. Leiden: Brill, 2002.

Burridge, Kennelm. *Someone, No One: An Essay on Individuality*. Princeton, NJ: Princeton University Press, 1979.

"Buying Farmland Abroad: Outsourcing's Third Wave." *The Economist*, May 23, 2009, 61–63.

Campbell, Lyle. *Historical Linguistics: An Introduction*. 2nd ed. Cambridge, MA: MIT Press, 2004.

Cannell, Fenella. "Introduction." In *The Anthropology of Christianity*, edited by Cannell, 1–50. Durham, NC: Duke University Press, 2006.

Carson, D. A. *Christ and Culture Revisited*. Grand Rapids, MI: Eerdmans, 2008.

Cauthen, Kenneth. "H. Richard Niebuhr Revisited and Revised." *Encounter* (Summer 1996) 267–79.

Central Intelligence Agency. *The World Factbook*. Washington, DC: CIA, 2011.Online: https://www.cia.gov/library/publications/the-world-factbook/index.html.

Césaire, Aimé. *Discourse on Colonialism*. New York: Monthly Review Press, 2001 [1955].

Chance, Norman A. *China's Urban Villagers: Changing Life in a Beijing Suburb*. 2nd ed. Case Studies in Cultural Anthropology. Fort Worth, TX: Holt, Rinehart and Winston, 1991.

Clarke, Peter. *Encyclopedia of New Religious Movements*. London: Routledge, 2005.

Clifford, James. *Routes: Travel and Translation in the Late Twentieth Century*. Cambridge, MA: Harvard University Press, 1997.

Cohen, Abner. *Custom and Politics in Urban Africa: A Study of Hausa Migrants in Yoruba Towns*. London: Routledge and Kegan Paul, 1969.

———. "Introduction: The Lesson of Ethnicity." In *Urban Ethnicity*, edited by Abner Cohen, ix–xxiv. Association of Social Anthropologists Monographs 12. London: Tavistock, 1974.

Comaroff, Jean, and John L. Commaroff. *Of Revelation and Revolution*. Vols. 1 and 2. Chicago: University of Chicago Press, 1991–1997.

Conn, Harvey M. "Genesis as Urban Prologue." In *Discipling the City: A Comprehensive Approach to Urban Ministry*, edited by Roger S. Greenway, 13–33. 2nd ed. Grand Rapids: Baker, 1992. Reprint: Eugene, OR: Wipf and Stock, 1997.

———, editor. *Planting and Growing Urban Churches: From Dream to Reality*. Grand Rapids: Baker, 1997.

Damazio, Antonio. *The Feeling of What Happens: Body and Emotion in the Making of Consciousness*. Boston: Harcourt, 2000.

Demissie, Fassil, editor. *Postcolonial African Cities: Imperial Legacies and Postcolonial Predicament*. New York: Routledge, 2008.

Diamond, Jared. *Guns, Germs, and Steel: The Fates of Human Societies*. New York: Norton, 1999.

Dirlik, Arif. "Modernity in Question? Culture and Religion in an Age of Global Modernity." *Diaspora* 12.2 (2003) 147–68.

Donovan, Vincent J. *Christianity Rediscovered*. Maryknoll, NY: Orbis, 2003 [1978].

Douglas, Mary. "Cultural Bias." *Occasional Paper No. 35 of the Royal Anthropological Institute of Great Britain and Ireland*. 1978.

Downie, Mark. "Conservation Refugees." *Cultural Survival* 34.1 (2010) 28–35.

Drucker, Philip. "Rank, Wealth, and Kinship in Northwest Coast Society." *American Anthropologist* 41 (1939) 55–65.

Dufoix, Stéphane. *Diasporas*. Translated by William Rodarmor. Berkeley: University of California Press, 2008.

Dumont, Louis. *Homo Hierarchicus: The Caste System and Its Implications*. Rev. ed. Chicago: University of Chicago Press, 1980 [1966].

Dundes, Alan, editor. *Every Man His Way: Readings in Cultural Anthropology*. Englewood Cliffs, NJ: Prentice-Hall, 1968.

———. "Seeing Is Believing." In *The Nacirema: Readings in American Culture*, edited by James P. Spradley and Michael A. Rynkiewich, 14–19. Boston: Little, Brown, 1974. Reprinted from *Natural History Magazine*, May 1972.

Durkheim, Emile. *The Elementary Forms of Religious Life*. Mineola, NY: Dover, 2008 [1915].

Eberhard, David M. *Mamaindě Grammar: A Northern Nambikwara Language and Its Cultural Context.* Vol. 1. Utrecht: Landelijke Onderzoekschool Taalwetenschap, 2009.

Elphick, Richard. "Missions and Afrikaner Nationalism: Soundings in the Prehistory of Apartheid." In *Missions, Nationalism, and the End of Empire,* edited by Brian Stanley. Studies in the History of Christian Missions. Grand Rapids: Eerdmans, 2003.

Engelke, Matthew Eric. *A Problem of Presence: Beyond Scripture in an African Church.* Anthropology of Christianity 2. Berkeley: University of California Press, 2007.

Eriksen, Thomas Hylland. *Ethnicity and Nationalism.* 2nd ed. Anthropology, Culture, and Society. Sterling, VA: Pluto, 2002.

Erikson, Erik H. *Childhood and Society.* New York: Norton, 1993 [1950].

Evans-Pritchard, Edward Everett. *The Nuer: A Description of the Modes of Livelihood and Political Institutions of a Nilotic People.* New York: Oxford University Press, 1940.

Fanon, Frantz. *The Wretched of the Earth: The Handbook for the Black Revolution That Is Changing the Shape of the World.* New York: Grove, 1963.

Fitzgerald, F. Scott. *The Great Gatsby.* New York: Scribner, 1925.

Flanders, Christopher L. *About Face: Reorienting Thai Face for Soteriology and Mission.* American Society of Missiology Monograph Series 9. Eugene, OR: Pickwick, 2011.

Flemming, Dean E. *Contextualization in the New Testament: Patterns for Theology and Mission.* Downers Grove, IL: InterVarsity, 2005.

Frank, Andre Gunder. *Latin America: Underdevelopment or Revolution: Essays on the Development of Underdevelopment and the Immediate Enemy.* New York: Monthly Review Press, 1969.

Frazier, James G. *The Golden Bough: A Study in Magic and Religion.* 12 vols. London: Macmillan, 1911–15 [1890].

Freeman, Derek. *Margaret Mead and Samoa: The Making and Unmaking of an Anthropological Myth.* Cambridge, MA: Harvard University Press, 1983.

———. *The Fateful Hoaxing of Margaret Mead: A Historical Analysis of Her Samoan Research.* Boulder, CO: Westview, 1999.

Fried, Morton H. *The Evolution of Political Society: An Essay in Political Anthropology.* Random House studies in anthropology, AS 7. New York: Random House, 1967.

Friedman, Thomas L. *The Lexus and the Olive Tree: Understanding Globalization.* New York: Anchor/Random House, 2000 [1999].

———. *The World Is Flat: A Brief History of the Twenty-First Century.* Updated and expanded ed. New York: Picador, 2007.

Galbraith, John Kenneth. *The Affluent Society.* New York: Penguin, 1963 [1958].

Galaty, John G. "Maasai Expansion and the New East African Pastoralism." In *Being Maasai: Ethnicity and Identity in East Africa,* edited by Thomas Spear and Richard Waller, 61–86. Eastern African Studies. Oxford: J. Currey, 1993.

Garofalo, Leo J. "The Quinto Suyo: New African Diaspora History from Peru." *Ethnohistory* 56.2 (2009) 303–7.

Geertz, Clifford. "Deep Play: Notes on the Balinese Cockfight." In *The Interpretation of Cultures: Selected Essays,* by Geertz, 412–53. New York: Basic Books, 1973.

Gennep, Arnold van. *Rites of Passage.* Translated from *Les Rites de Passage* by Monika B. Vizedom and Gabrielle L. Caffee. Chicago: University of Chicago Press, 1960 [1909].

Gilbert, Paul. "What Is Shame? Some Core Issues and Controversies." In *Shame: Interpersonal Behavior, Psychopathology, and Culture*, edited by Paul Gilbert and Bernice Andrews, 3–38. New York: Oxford University Press, 1998.

Giridharadas, Anand. *India Calling: An Intimate Portrait of a Nation's Remaking.* New York: Times, 2011.

Glazer, Nathan, and Daniel A. Moynihan. *Beyond the Melting Pot: The Negroes, Puerto Ricans, Jews, Italians, and Irish of New York City.* Cambridge, MA: MIT Press and Harvard University Press, 1963.

Gleason, Henry A., Jr. *An Introduction to Descriptive Linguistics.* Rev. ed. New York: Holt, Rinehart and Winston, 1961.

Gluckman, Max. *Custom and Conflict in Africa.* London: Oxford University Press, 1955.

Goddard, Michael. *The Unseen City: Anthropological Perspectives on Port Moresby, Papua New Guinea.* Canberra: Pandanus; Research School of Pacific and Asia Studies; Australian National University, 2005.

Goffman, Erving. "On Face-Work: An Analysis of Ritual Elements in Social Interaction." *Psychiatry* 18.3 (1955) 213–31.

———. *The Presentation of Self in Everyday Life.* UESSRC Monograph 2. Edinburgh: University of Edinburgh Social Sciences Research Centre, 1956.

———. *Stigma: Notes on the Management of a Spoiled Identity.* New York: Prentice-Hall, 1967.

Goh, Robbie B. H. "Deus ex Machina: Evangelical Sites, Urbanism, and the Construction of Social Identities." In *Postcolonial Urbanism: Southeast Asian Cities and Global Processes*, edited by Ryan Bishop, John Phillips, and Wei-Wei Yeo, 305–21. New York: Routledge, 2003.

Goldschmidt, Walter Rochs, editor. *Exploring the Ways of Mankind.* 3rd ed. New York: Holt, Rinehart and Winston, 1977.

Goode, Judith. "How Urban Ethnography Counters Myths about the Poor." In *Urban Life: Readings in the Anthropology of the City*, edited by George Gmelch, Robert V. Kemper, and Walter P. Zenner, 185–201. 5th ed. Long Grove, IL: Waveland, 2010.

Goodenough, Ward Hunt. *Under Heaven's Brow: Pre-Christian Religious Tradition in Chuuk.* Philadelphia: American Philosophical Society, 2002.

Graham, Billy. *Just as I Am: The Autobiography of Billy Graham.* San Francisco: HarperSanFrancisco, 1997.

Grant, Madison. *The Passing of the Great Race, or, The Racial Basis of European History.* New York: Scribner, 1916.

Green, Joel B. *The Gospel of Luke.* New International Commentary on the New Testament. Grand Rapids: Eerdmans, 1997.

Grigg, Viv. *The Spirit of Christ and the Postmodern City: Transforming Revival among Auckland's Evangelicals and Pentecostals.* Asbury Theological Seminary Series. Lexington, KY: Emeth, 2009.

Gudorf, Christine E. "A Matter of Veils." In *Ethics and World Religions: Cross-Cultural Case Studies*, by Regina Wentzel Wolfe and Christine E. Gudorf, 148–71. Ethics & World Religions. Maryknoll, NY: Orbis, 1999.

Gulick, John. *The Humanity of Cities: An Introduction to Urban Societies.* New York: Bergin and Garvey, 1989.

Gulliver, Philip H. *Social Control in an African Society: A Study of the Arusha; Agricultural Masai of Northern Tanganyika.* Boston University African Research Studies 3. Boston: Boston University Press, 1963.

Habel, Norman C. *The Land Is Mine: Six Old Testament Ideologies of Land.* Overtures to Biblical Theology. Minneapolis: Fortress, 1995.

Handy, E. S. Craighill, and Mary Kawena Pukui. *The Polynesian Family System in Ka-'U, Hawai'i.* Rutland, VT: C. E. Tuttle, 1972 [1958].

Hannerz, Ulf. *Soulside: Inquiries into Ghetto Culture and Community.* New York: Columbia University Press, 1969.

Hansen, Thomas Blom. *The Saffron Wave: Democracy and Hindu Nationalism in Modern India.* Princeton, NJ: Princeton University Press, 1999.

Hanson, K. C., and Douglas E. Oakman. *Palestine in the Time of Jesus: Social Structures and Social Conflicts.* Minneapolis: Fortress, 1998.

Harris, Olivia. "The Eternal Return of Conversion: Christianity as a Contested Domain in Highland Bolivia." In *The Anthropology of Christianity*, edited by Fenella Cannell. Durham, NC: Duke University Press, 2006.

Harvey, Graham. *Animism: Respecting the Living World.* New York: Columbia University Press, 2005.

Hawkins, Simon. "Cosmopolitan Hagglers or Haggling Locals?: Salesmen, Tourists, and Cosmopolitan Discourses in Tunis." *City and Society* 22.1 (2010) 1–24.

Hays, Richard B. "Reading the Bible with Eyes of Faith: The Practice of Theological Exegesis." *Journal of Theological Interpretation* 1.1 (2007) 5–22.

Hayward, Douglas James. *Vernacular Christianity among the Mulia Dani: An Ethnography of Religious Belief among the Western Dani of Irian Jaya, Indonesia.* Lanham, MD: University Press of America, 1995.

Heider, Karl G. *Grand Valley Dani: Peaceful Warriors.* Case Studies in Cultural Anthropology. New York: Holt, Rinehart and Winston, 1979.

Henderson, James E., and Anne Henderson. "Yele (Milne Bay Province)." In *Reports of Vernacular Literacy Programs conducted by the Summer Institute of Linguistics in Papua New Guinea*, edited by Neville Southwell, Mary Stringer, and Joice Franklin, 13–14. Workpapers in Papua New Guinea Languages 28. Ukarumpa, PNG: Summer Institute of Linguistics, 1980.

———. *Rossel Language, Milne Bay Province: Rossel to English, English to Rossel.* Dictionaries of Papua New Guinea 9. Ukarumpa, PNG: Summer Institute of Linguistics, 1987.

Hendry, Joy. *Other People's Worlds: An Introduction to Cultural and Social Anthropology.* 2nd ed. Washington Square, NY: New York University Press, 1999.

Heslam, Peter, editor. *Globalization and the Good.* Grand Rapids: Eerdmans, 2004.

Hessler, Peter. *River Town: Two Years on the Yangtze.* New York: HarperCollins, 2001.

Hiebert, Paul G.. *Konduru: Structure and Integration in a Hindu Village.* Minneapolis: University of Minnesota Press, 1971

———. *Cultural Anthropology.* 2nd ed. Grand Rapids: Baker, 1983 [1976].

———. "The Flaw of the Excluded Middle." *Missiology* 10.1(1982) 35–47. Reprinted in *Anthropological Reflections on Missiological Issues*, by Hiebert, 189–201. Grand Rapids: Baker, 1994.

Hoebel, E. Adamson. *The Cheyennes: Indians of the Great Plains.* Case Studies in Cultural Anthropology. New York: Holt, Rinehart and Winston, 1960.

Hohfeld, Wesley Newcomb. *Fundamental Legal Conceptions as Applied in Judicial Reasoning, and Other Legal Essays.* New Haven, CT: Yale University Press, 1919.

Hoijer, Harry. "The Sapir-Whorf Hypothesis." In *Language in Culture*, edited by Harry Hoijer, 92–105. Comparative Studies in Cultures and Civilizations. Chicago: University of Chicago Press, 1954.

Holmes, Lowell D. *Samoan Village*. Case Studies in Cultural Anthropology. New York: Holt, Rinehart and Winston, 1974.

———. *Quest for the Real Samoa: The Mead/Freeman Controversy and Beyond*. South Hadley, MA: Bergin and Garvey, 1987.

Hostetler, John Andrew. *Amish Society*. 4th ed. Baltimore: Johns Hopkins University Press, 1993.

Hubert, Henri, and Marcel Mauss. *Sacrifice: Its Nature and Function*. Originally titled *An Essay on the Nature and Function of Sacrifice*. Chicago: University of Chicago Press, 1981 [1898].

Hunter, George G. *The Celtic Way of Evangelism: How Christianity Can Reach the West—Again*. Nashville: Abingdon, 2000.

Hymes, Dell H., editor. *Language in Culture and Society: A Reader in Linguistics and Anthropology*. New York: Harper & Row, 1964.

———. *Foundations in Sociolinguistics: An Ethnographic Approach*. University of Pennsylvania Publications in Conduct and Communication. Philadelphia: University of Pennsylvania Press, 1974.

———. *Ethnography, Linguistics, Narrative Inequality: Toward an Understanding of Voice*. Critical Perspectives on Literacy and Education. Bristol, PA: Taylor and Francis, 1996.

Hymes, Dell, and John Joseph Gumperz, editors. *Directions in Sociolinguistics: The Ethnography of Communication*. New York: Holt, Rinehart and Winston, 1972.

Ibn Faḍlān, Ahmed. "Scandinavians on the Volga in 922." In *Every Man His Way: Readings in Cultural Anthropology*, edited by Alan Dundes, 14–22. Englewood Cliffs, NJ: Prentice-Hall, 1968.

Iteanu, Andre. "The Concept of the Person and the Ritual System: An Orokaiva View." *Man* 25 (1991) 35–53.

Jacobson, David. *Itinerant Townsmen: Friendship and Social Order in Urban Uganda*. The Kiste and Ogan Social Change Series in Anthropology. Menlo Park, CA: Cummings, 1973.

Jakobson, Roman. "Remarks on the Phonological Evolution of Russian Compared to That of the Other Slavic Languages." In *Selected Writings* 1:7–116. The Hague: Mouton, 1962 [1929].Originally published as "Remarques sur l'evolution phonoligique du russe compare à celle des autres langues slaves," in *Travaux du Cercle Linguistique de Prague*, 2:1–118.

Jones, William, Sir. *The Sanscrit Language*. N.p., 1786.

Jones, Lindsay, editor. *Encyclopedia of Religion*. 15 vols. 2nd ed. New York: Macmillan, 2005.

Keane, Webb. *Christian Moderns: Freedom and Fetish in the Mission Encounter*. Anthropology of Christianity 1. Berkeley: University of California Press, 2007.

Keesing, Roger. "Statistical Models and Decision Models of Social Structure: A Kwaio Case." *Ethnology* 6 (1967) 1–16.

———. "Shrines, Ancestors, and Cognatic Descent: The Kwaio and Tallensi." *American Anthropologist* 72 (1970) 755–75.

Keysser, Christian. *A People Reborn*. Translated from *Eine Papuagemeinde* by Alfred Allin and John Kuder. Pasedena, CA: W. Carey Library, 1980 [1929].

King, Russell, Richard Black, Michael Collyer, Anthony Fielding, and Ronald Skeldon. *People on the Move: An Atlas of Migration.* Berkeley: University of California Press, 2010.

Klaits, Frederick. *Death in a Church of Life: Moral Passion during Botswana's Time of AIDS.* Anthropology of Christianity 8. Berkeley: University of California Press, 2010.

Klat, Myriam, and Adele Khudr. "Cousin Marriage in Beruit, Lebanon: Is the Pattern Changing?" *Journal of Biosocial Science* 16 (1984) 369–75.

Kluckhohn, Clyde. "The Influence of Psychiatry on Anthropology in America during the Past One Hundred Years." In *One Hundred Years of American Psychiatry,* edited by J. K. Hall, G. I. Zilboorg, and H. A. Bunker. New York: Columbia University Press, 1944.

Knauft, Bruce M. *Genealogies for the Present in Cultural Anthropology.* New York: Routledge, 1996.

Krader, Lawrence. *The Formation of the State.* Foundations of Modern Anthropology. Englewood Cliffs, NJ: Prentice-Hall, 1968.

Kraft, Charles. *Christianity in Culture: A Study in Dynamic Bible Theologizing in Cross-cultural Perspective.* Maryknoll, NY: Orbis Books, 1979.

Kroeber, Alfred L., and Clyde Kluckhohn. *Culture: A Critical Review of Concepts and Definitions.* Anthropological Papers, Peabody Museum, 47. Cambridge, MA: Peabody Museum, 1952.

Kuah-Pearce, Khun Eng, and Andrew P. Davidson, editors. *At Home in the Chinese Diaspora: Memories, Identities, and Belongings.* New York: Palgrave Macmillan, 2008.

Kuhl, Patricia K., Barbara T. Conboy, Sharon Coffey-Corina, Denise Padden, Maritza Rivera-Gaxiola, and Tobey Nelson. "Phonetic Learning as a Pathway to Language: New Data and Native Language Magnet Theory Expanded (NLM-e)." *Philosophical Transactions of the Royal Society* 363 (2008) 979–1000.

Kuhn, Thomas S. *The Structure of Scientific Revolutions.* Chicago: University of Chicago Press, 1962.

Kwa, Kiem-Kiok. "Towards a Model of Engagement in the Public Realm for the Methodist Church in Singapore." PhD diss., Asbury Theological Seminary, 2007.

Lakoff, George. *Women, Fire, and Dangerous Things: What Categories Reveal about the Mind.* Chicago: University of Chicago Press, 1987.

Lakoff, George, and Mark Johnson. *Metaphors We Live By.* Chicago: University of Chicago Press, 2003 [1980].

Lasswell, Harold D. *Politics: Who Gets What, When, and How.* Glouester, MA: Peter Smith, 1990 [1936].

Lanternari, Vittorio. *The Religions of the Oppressed: A Study of Modern Messianic Cults.* Translated by Lisa Sergio. New York: A. Knopf, 1963.

Lawrence, Peter. *Road Belong Cargo: A Study of the Cargo Movement in the Southern Madang District, New Guinea.* Manchester, UK: Manchester University Press, 1964.

Leach, Edmund Ronald. *Political Systems of Highland Burma: A Study of Kachin Social Structure.* Cambridge, MA: Harvard University Press, 1954.

Leacock, Eleanor Burke, editor. *The Culture of Poverty: A Critique.* New York: Simon & Schuster, 1971.

LeDoux, Joseph E. *The Emotional Brain: The Mysterious Underpinnings of Emotional Life.* New York: Simon & Schuster, 1996.

Lee, Dorothy. "Codifications of Reality: Lineal and Nonlineal." *Psychosomatic Medicine* 12 (1950) 89–97.

Lesser, Jeffrey. *A Discontented Diaspora: Japanese Brazilians and the Meanings of Ethnic Militancy, 1960–1980.* Durham, NC: Duke University Press, 2007.

Lévi-Strauss, Claude. *The Elementary Structures of Kinship.* Translated by James H. Bell, John R. von Sturmer, and Rodney Needham. Rev. ed. Boston: Beacon, 1969 [1949].

Lewellen, Ted C. *The Anthropology of Globalization: Cultural Anthropology Enters the 21st Century.* Westport, CT: Bergin and Garvey, 2002.

Lewis, Oscar. *Life in a Mexican Village: Tepostlán Restudied.* Urbana: University of Illinois Press, 1951.

———. "The Culture of Poverty." *Scientific American*, October 1966, 19–25.

———. *La Vida: A Puerto Rican Family in the Culture of Poverty.* New York: Random House, 1966.

Liebow, Elliot. *Tally's Corner: A Study of Negro Streetcorner Men.* Boston: Little, Brown, 1967.

Lindenbaum, Shirley. *Kuru Sorcery: Disease and Danger in the New Guinea Highlands.* Explorations in World Ethnology. Palo Alto, CA: Mayfield, 1979.

———. "Kuru, Prions, and Human Affairs: Thinking about Epidemics." *Annual Review of Anthropology*, 2001, 363–85.

Lindenbaum, Shirley, and Margaret Lock, editors. *Knowledge, Power, and Practice: The Anthropology of Medicine and Everyday Life.* Comparative Studies of Health Systems and Medical Care 36. Berkeley: University of California Press, 1993.

Lingenfelter, Judith. "Getting to Know Your New City." In *Disciplining the City: A Comprehensive Approach to Urban Ministry*, edited by Roger S. Greenway, 187–92. 2nd ed. Grand Rapids: Baker, 1992. Reprint: Eugene, OR: Wipf and Stock, 1997.

Linton, Ralph. "Nativistic Movements." *American Anthropologist* 45 (1943) 230–40.

Littrell, Mary Ann, and Marsha Ann Dickson. *Social Responsibility in the Global Market: Fair Trade of Cultural Products.* Thousand Oaks, CA: Sage, 1999.

Little, Kenneth Lindsay. *West African Urbanization: A Study of Voluntary Associations in Social Change.* Cambridge: Cambridge University Press, 1965.

———. *Urbanization as a Social Process: An Essay on Movement and Change in Contemporary Africa.* New York: Taylor and Francis, 1974.

Lolwerikoi, Michael. "Orality and Land: The Impact of Colonialism on Lmaa Narrative in Kenya." PhD diss., Asbury Theological Seminary, 2010.

———. "My People." *Cultural Survival* 34.1 (2010) 20.

Longgar, William. "Sorcery and Christianity in the Gazelle Peninsula." In *Sanguma in Paradise: Sorcery, Witchcraft and Christianity in Papua New Guinea*, edited by Franco Zocca, 305–59. Point 33. Goroka, PNG: Melanesian Institute, 2009.

Luomala , Katharine, and Michael A. Rynkiewich. "Micronesian Religions: Mythic Themes." In *The Encyclopedia of Religion*, edited by Lindsay Jones, 6009–13. 2nd ed. New York: Macmillan, 2005.

Lyotard, Jean-François. *The Postmodern Condition: A Report on Knowledge.* Minneapolis, MN: The University of Minnesota Press, 1979.

Malinowski, Bronislaw K. *Argonauts of the Western Pacific: An Account of Native Enterprise and Adventure in the Archipelagoes of Melanesian New Guinea.* Studies in Economics and Political Science 65. New York: E. P. Dutton, 1922.

———. *Magic, Science, and Religion.* New York: Free Press, 1948.

Mallory, J. P. *In Search of the Indo-Europeans: Language, Archaeology, and Myth.* New York: Thames and Hudson, 1989.

Mandelbaum, David Goodman. *Society in India.* Vol. 1: *Continuity and Change.* Berkeley: University of California Press, 1970.

Mannoni, Octave. *Prospero and Caliban: The Psychology of Colonization.* Translated by Pamela Powesland. Ann Arbor: University of Michigan Press, 1991 [1956].

Mauss, Marcel. *The Gift: The Form and Reason for Exchange in Archaic Societies.* Translated from *Essai sur le don* by W. D. Halls. New York: Norton, 2000.

Mayer, Phillip. *Townsmen or Tribesman: Conservatism and the Process of Urbanization in a South African City.* 2nd ed. Oxford Paperbacks from South Africa. Capetown: Oxford University Press, 1971.

Mead, George Herbert. *Mind, Self, and Society: From the Standpoint of a Social Behaviorist.* Edited by Charles W. Morris. Chicago: University of Chicago Press, 1934.

Mead, Margaret. *Coming of Age in Samoa: A Psychological Study of Primitive Youth for Western Civilisation.* New York: W. Morrow, 1928.

Meeks, Wayne A. *The First Urban Christians: The Social World of the Apostle Paul.* New Haven, CT: Yale University Press, 1983.

Memmi, Albert. *The Colonizer and the Colonized.* Translated from *Portrait du colonisé, précédé du portrait du colonisateur* by Howard Greenfeld. New York: Orion, 1965 [1957].

Menuge, Angus J. L. "Niebuhr's Christ and Culture Reexamined." In *Christ and Culture in Dialogue,* edited by Angus J. L. Menuge et al., 31–55. St. Louis, MO: Concordia, 1999.

Mills, C. Wright. *The Power Elite.* New ed. New York: Oxford University Press, 2000 [1956].

Mintz, Sidney W. "The Localization of Anthropological Practice: From Area Studies to Transnationalism." *Critique of Anthropology* 18.2 (1998) 117–33.

Mitchell, J. Clyde, editor. *Social Networks in Urban Situations: Analyses of Personal Relationships in Central African Towns.* Manchester, UK: Manchester University Press, 1969.

Moe-Lobeda, Cynthia. "Offering Resistance to Globalization: Insights from Luther." In *Globalization and the Good,* edited by Peter Heslam, 95–104. Grand Rapids: Eerdmans, 2004.

Moffett, Samuel Hugh. *The History of Christianity in Asia,* vol. 2: *Beginnings to 1500.* American Society of Missiology Series 36. Maryknoll, NY: Orbis, 1998.

"More Police Killed in Land Rights Dispute." *Evansville Courier and Press,* 7 June 2009, A8.

Morel, E. D. *The Black Man's Burden: The White Man in Africa from the Fifteenth Century to the World War I.* London: National Labour Press, 1920. Republished: New York: Monthly Review Press, 1969.

Morgan, Lewis Henry. *The League of the Ho-dé-no-sau-nee or Iroquois.* New York: Kensington, 1984 [1851].

Morton, Helen. "Creating Their Own Culture: Diasporic Tongans." *The Contemporary Pacific* 10.1 (1998) 1–30.

Moynihan, Daniel. *The Negro Family: The Case for National Action.* Report for the US Department of Labor, Office of Policy Planning and Research. Washington, DC: US Government Printing Office, 1965.

Mujahid, Abdul Malik. *Conversion to Islam: Untouchables' Strategy for Protest in India.* Chambersburg, PA: Anima, 1989.

Needham, Joseph, editor. *Science, Religion and Reality.* London: Sheldon; New York: Macmillan, 1925.

Neill, Stephen, and Owen Chadwick. *A History of Christian Missions.* 2nd ed. New York: Penguin, 1986 [1964].

Nida, Eugene A. *Customs and Cultures: Anthropology for Christian Mission.* New York: Harper & Row, 1954.

Nida, Eugene A., and William A. Smalley. *Introducing Animism.* New York: Friendship Press, 1959.

Nkrumah, Kwame. *Neo-Colonialism: The Last Stage of Imperialism.* New York: International Publishers, 1965.

Nordstrom, Carolyn. *Global Outlaws: Crime, Money, and Power in the Contemporary World.* California Series in Public Anthropology 16. Berkeley: University of California Press, 2007.

Oberg, Kalvero. "Culture Shock: Adjustments to New Cultural Environments." *Practical Anthropology* 7 (1960) 177–82.

Oliver, Douglas. *A Solomon Island Society: Kinship and Leadership among the Siuai of Bougainville.* Cambridge, MA: Harvard University Press, 1955.

Palmer, Paula. "When the Police are the Perpetrators." *Cultural Survival* 34.1 (2010) 14–26.

Pantoja Luis L., Jr., Sadiri Joy Tira, and Enoch Wan, editors. *Scattered: The Filipino Global Presence.* Manila: LifeChange, 2004.

Park, Robert E., Ernest Burgess, and Roderick D. McKenzie. *The City: Suggestions for Investigation of Human Behavior in the Urban Environment.* Heritage of Sociology Series. Chicago: University of Chicago Press, 1984 [1925].

Parsons, James. *The Remains of Japhet: Being Historical Enquiries into the Affinity and Origins of the European Languages.* London. 1767.

Parsons, Talcott. *The Social System.* Glencoe, IL: Free Press, 1951.

Pastner, Carroll McC. "The Negotiation of Bilateral Endogamy in the Middle Eastern Context: The Zikri Baluch Example." *Journal of Anthropological Research* 37.4 (1981) 305–18.

Perkins, John. *The Confessions of an Economic Hit Man.* San Francisco: Berrett-Koehler, 2004.

Petersen, Glenn. *Lost in the Weeds: Theme and Variation in Pohnpei Political Mythology.* Occasional Paper 35. Honolulu: University of Hawai'i Press, 1990.

Raheja, Gloria Goodwin. *The Poison in the Gift: Ritual, Protestation, and the Dominant Caste in a North Indian Village.* Chicago: University of Chicago Press, 1988.

Read, Kenneth E. *The High Valley.* New York: Scribner, 1965.

Redfield, Robert. *Tepoztlán: A Mexican Village: A Study of Folk Life.* University of Chicago Publications in Anthropology, Ethnological Series. Chicago: University of Chicago Press, 1930.

———. *The Little Community: Viewpoints for the Study of a Human Whole.* Comparative Studies of Cultures and Civilizations. Chicago: University of Chicago Press, 1955.

Reyna, Stephen P. *Connections: Brain, Mind, and Culture in a Social Anthropology.* New York: Routledge, 2002.

Robbins, Joel. *Becoming Sinners: Christianity and Moral Torment in a Papua New Guinea Society.* Ethnographic Studies in Subjectivity 4. Berkeley: University of California Press, 2004.

Robson, Robert Williams. *Queen Emma: The Samoan-American Girl Who Founded an Empire in 19th Century New Guinea.* Sydney: Pacific, 1965.

Rodney, Walter. *How Europe Underdeveloped Africa.* Washington, DC: Howard University Press, 1972.

Rogers, Everett M. *Diffusion of Innovations.* 5th ed. New York: Free Press, 2003.

Romano, Daniel M. "The Divider Line: Presence as a Left and Right Mental Process." 2003. http://www.dcs.shef.ac.uk/~daniela/2003_Dual_Brain.html.

Rundle, Steven, and Tom Steffen. *Great Commission Companies: The Emerging Role of Business in Missions.* Downers Grove, IL: InterVarsity, 2003.

Rynkiewich, Michael A. "Big-Man Politics: Strong Leadership in a Weak State." In *Politics in Papua New Guinea: Continuities, Changes and Challenges,* edited by Michael A. Rynkiewich and Roland Seib, editors, 17–43. Point 24. Goroka, PNG: Melanesian Institute, 2000.

———. "Chippewa Powwows." In *Anishinabe: 6 Studies of Modern Chippewa,* edited by J. Anthony Paredes, 31–100. Tallahassee: University Presses of Florida, 1980.

———. "Corporate Metaphors and Strategic Thinking: 'The 10/40 Window' in the American Evangelical Worldview." *Missiology* 35.2 (2007) 217–41.

———. "Do We Need a Postmodern Anthropology for Mission in a Postcolonial World?" *Mission Studies* 28 (2011) 1–19.

———, editor. *Land and Churches in Melanesia: Cases and Procedures.* Point 27. Goroka, PNG: Melanesian Institute, 2004.

———, editor. *Land and Churches in Melanesia: Issues and Contexts.* Point 25. Goroka, PNG: Melanesian Institute, 2001.

———. "Person in Mission: Social Theory and Sociality in Melanesia." *Missiology* 31.2 (2003) 155–68.

———. "Revitalization." *Newsletter for the Center for the Study of World Christian Revitalization Movements* 13.1 (2006) 1.

———. "The Ossification of Local Politics: The Impact of Colonialism on a Marshall Islands Atoll." In *Political Development in Micronesia,* edited by Daniel T. Hughes and Sherwood G. Lingenfelter, 143–65. Columbus: Ohio State University Press, 1974.

———. "The Underdevelopment of Anthropological Ethics." In *Ethics and Anthropology: Dilemmas in Fieldwork,* edited by Michael A. Rynkiewich and James P. Spradley, 47–60. New York: Wiley, 1976.

———. "The World in My Parish: Rethinking the Standard Missiological Model." *Missiology* 30.3 (2002) 301–21.

Rynkiewich, Michael A., and James P. Spradley, editors. *Ethics and Anthropology: Dilemmas in Fieldwork.* New York: Wiley, 1976.

Sahlins, Marshall. "Rich Man, Poor Man, Big Man, Chief: Political Types in Melanesia and Polynesia." *Comparative Studies in Society and History* 5 (1963) 285–303.

Samovar, Larry A., and Richard E. Porter, editors. *Intercultural Communication: A Reader.* Belmont, CA: Wadsworth, 1972.

Samuel, Vinay, and Christopher Sugden, editors. *The Church in Response to Human Need.* Grand Rapids: Eerdmans, 1987.

Sapir, Edward. "The Status of Linguistics as a Science." *Language* 5 (1929) 207–14. Reprinted in Sapir, *Culture, Language, and Personality: Selected Essays*, edited by David G. Mandelbaum. Berkeley: University of California Press, 1964.

———. "Why Cultural Anthropology Needs the Psychiatrist." *Journal of the Biology and Pathology of Interpersonal Relations* 1 (1938) 7–12.

———. *Culture, Language, and Personality: Selected Essays*, edited by David G. Mandelbaum. Berkeley: University of California Press, 1966 [1949].

Schluter, Michael. "Risk, Reward and Responsibility: A Biblical Critique of Global Capital Markets." In *Globalization and the Good*, edited by Peter Heslam, 66–78. Grand Rapids: Eerdmans, 2004.

Schneider, David Murray. *American Kinship: A Cultural Account.* Anthropology of Modern Societies. Englewood Cliffs, NJ: Prentice-Hall, 1968.

Service, Elman R. *Origins of the State and Civilization: The Process of Cultural Evolution.* New York: Norton, 1975.

Shankman, Paul. "The History of Samoan Sexual Conduct and the Mead-Freeman Controversy." *American Anthropologist* 98.3 (1996) 555–67.

Shibutani, Tamotsu, and Kian M. Kwan. *Ethnic Stratification: A Comparative Approach.* New York: Macmillan, 1965.

Shweder, Richard. "Santa Claus on the Cross." In *The Truth about the Truth: De-Confusing and Re-Constructing the Postmodern World*, edited by Walter Truett Anderson, 72–81. New York: Penguin, 1995.

Sikkand, Yōgīndar Singh. *Muslims in India since 1947: Islamic Perspectives on Inter-Faith Relations.* Royal Asiatic Society Books. New York: RutledgeCurzon, 2004.

Sine, Thomas. *Mustard Seed vs. McWorld: Reinventing Life and Faith for the Future.* Grand Rapids: Baker, 1999.

Smalley, William Allen. *Manual of Articulatory Phonetics.* Ann Arbor, MI: Cushing-Malloy, 1963.

Smith, William Robertson. *Lectures on the Religion of the Semites.* 1st series. New York: Appleton, 2010 [1889].

Snyder, Howard A. *EarthCurrents: The Struggle for the World's Soul.* Nashville: Abingdon, 1995.

Spradley, James P. *You Owe Yourself a Drunk: An Ethnography of Urban Nomads.* Little, Brown Series in Anthropology. Boston: Little, Brown, 1970.

———. *The Ethnographic Interview.* New York: Holt, Rinehart and Winston, 1979.

———. *Participant Observation.* New York: Holt, Rinehart and Winston, 1980.

Spradley, James P., and Brenda J. Mann. *The Cocktail Waitress: Woman's Work in a Man's World.* New York: Wiley, 1975.

Spradley, James P., and David W. McCurdy, editors. *The Cultural Experience: Ethnography in Complex Society.* Chicago: Science Research Associates, 1972.

Stack, Carol. *All Our Kin: Strategies for Survivals in a Black Community.* New York: Harper & Row, 1974.

Stanley, Brian. *The Bible and the Flag: Protestant Missions and British Imperialism in the Nineteenth and Twentieth Centuries.* Grand Rapids: Eerdmans, 1990.

———, editor. *Christian Missions and the Enlightenment.* Studies in the History of Christian Missions. Grand Rapids: Eerdmans, 2001.

———, editor. *Missions, Nationalism, and the End of Empire.* Studies in the History of Christian Missions. Grand Rapids: Eerdmans, 2003.

Steffen, Tom, and Mike Barnett, editors. *Business as Mission: From Impoverished to Empowered.* Evangelical Missiological Society Series 14. Pasadena, CA: William Carey Library, 2006.

Stiglitz, Joseph E. *Globalization and Its Discontents.* New York: Norton, 2002.

Strathern, Marilyn. *The Gender of the Gift: Problems with Women and Problems with Society in Melanesia.* Studies in Melanesian Anthropology 6. Berkeley: University of California Press, 1988.

Sugirtharajah, R. S. *Asian Biblical Hermeneutics and Postcolonialism: Contesting the Interpretations.* The Bible & Liberation Series. Maryknoll, NY: Orbis, 1998.

United Methodist Church (US). *The United Methodist Book of Worship.* Nashville: United Methodist Pub., 1992.

Thiong'o, Ngũgĩ wa. *Decolonizing the Mind: The Politics of Language in African Literature.* Books in African Studies. Portsmouth, NH: Heinemann, 1986.

Tiplady, Richard, editor. *One World or Many?: The Impact of Globalisation on Mission.* Pasadena, CA: William Carey Library, 2003.

Tobin, Jack A. *Stories from the Marshall Islands: Bwebwenato Jān Aelōñ Kein.* PALI Language Texts. Honolulu: University of Hawai'i Press, 2002.

Tomlinson, Matt. *In God's Image: The Metaculture of Fijian Christianity.* Anthropology of Christianity 5. Berkeley: University of California Press, 2009.

Tonkinson, Robert. *The Jigalong Mob: Aboriginal Victors of the Desert Crusade.* Menlo Park, CA: Cummings, 1974.

Turner, Victor Witter. *The Ritual Process: Structure and Anti-Structure.* Lewis Henry Morgan Lectures, 1966. Chicago: Aldine, 1969.

———. *The Forest of Symbols: Aspects of Ndembu Ritual.* Ithaca, NY: Cornell University Press, 1970.

Twiss, Richard. *One Church, Many Tribes.* Ventura, CA: Regal, 2000.

Tylor, Edward Burnett. *The Origins of Culture.* Vol. 1 of *Primitive Culture.* New York: Harper & Row, 1958 [1871].

Uberoi, J. P. Singh. *Politics of the Kula Ring: An Analysis of the Findings of Bronislaw Malinowski.* Manchester, UK: Manchester University Press, 1962.

Uchendu, Victor Chikezie. *The Igbo of Southeast Nigeria.* Case Studies in Cultural Anthropology. New York: Holt, Rinehart and Winston, 1965.

Udotong, William Effiong. "Transnational Migration and the Reverse Mission of Nigerian-Led Pentecostal Churches in the United States of America: A Case Study of Selected Churches in Metro Atlanta." PhD diss., Asbury Theological Seminary, 2010.

United Nations Centre for Human Settlements. *Cities in a Globalizing World.* Global Report on Human Settlements, 2001. London: Earthscan, 2001.

———. *The Challenge of Slums.* Global Report on Human Settlements, 2003. London: Earthscan, 2003.

Vähäkangas, Auli. *Christian Couples Coping with Childlessness: Narratives from Machame, Kilimanjaro.* American Society of Missiology Monograph Series 4. Eugene, OR: Pickwick, 2009.

Valentine, Charles A. *Culture and Poverty: A Critique and Counterproposal.* Chicago: University of Chicago Press, 1968.

Valerio, Ruth. "Globalisation and Economics: A World Gone Bananas." In *One World or Many?: The Impact of Globalisation on Mission*, edited by Richard Tiplady, 13–32. Pasadena, CA: William Carey Library, 2003.

Varma, Rashmi. *The Postcolonial City and Its Subjects: London, Nairobi, Bombay.* Routledge Research in Postcolonial Literatures. New York: Routledge, 2010.

Veblen, Thorstein. *The Theory of the Leisure Class.* New York: Dover, 1994 [1899].

Vertovec, Steven. *The Hindu Diaspora: Comparative Patterns.* Global Diasporas 5. London: Routledge, 2000.

Wallace, Anthony F. C. "Revitalization Movements: Some Theoretical Considerations for their Comparative Study." *American Anthropologist* 58 (1956) 264–81.

―――. "Foreword." In *Reassessing Revitalization Movements: Perspectives from North America and the Pacific Islands,* edited by Michael E. Harkin. Lincoln: University of Nebraska Press, 2004.

Wallerstein, Immanuel Maurice. *The Essential Wallerstein.* New York: New Press, 2000.

Wallis, Jim. *Justice for the Poor: Love God. Serve People. Change the World.* Grand Rapids: Zondervan, 2010.

Walls, Andrew F. "Old Athens and New Jerusalem: Some Signposts for Christian Scholarship in the Early History of Mission Studies." *International Bulletin of Missionary Research* 21 (1997) 136–53.

Warner, W. Lloyd, and Paul S. Lunt. *The Social Life of a Modern Community.* Yankee City Series 1. New Haven, CT: Yale University Press, 1941.

Warrior, Robert Allen. "A Native American Perspective: Canaanites, Cowboys, and Indians." In *Voices from the Margin: Interpreting the Bible in the Third World,* edited by R. S. Sugitharajah, 289, 291–92. Maryknoll, NY: Orbis, 1991.

Washburn, Wilcomb E. *Assault of Indian Tribalism: The General Allotment Law (Dawes Act) of 1887.* New York: Holt, Rinehart and Winston, 1975.

Weber, Max. *The Protestant Ethic and the Spirit of Capitalism: The Talcott Parsons Translation Interpretations.* Edited by Richard Swedberg. Norton Critical Editions in the History of Ideas. New York: Norton, 2009 [1930].

Westermarck, Edward. *The Origin and Development of Moral Ideas.* Reprint of the 2nd ed. London: Macmillan, 2010 [1912–17].

Whiteman, Darrell L. "Anthropology and Christianity: The Incarnational Connection." The Third Annual Louis J. Luzbetak, SVD Lecture on Mission and Culture. Chicago, IL: CCGM Publications, 2003.

―――. "Contextualization: The Theory, the Gap, and the Challenge." *International Bulletin of Mission Research* 21.1 (1997) 2–7.

Williams, F. E. *The Vailala Madness and the Destruction of Native Ceremonies in the Gulf Division.* Papuan Anthropology Report 4. Port Moresby, PNG: E. G. Baker, 1923.

Wilson, Bryan, and Jamie Cresswell, editors. *New Religious Movements: Challenge and Response.* London: Routledge, 1999.

Winter, Gibson. *The Suburban Captivity of the Churches: An Analysis of Protestant Responsibility in the Expanding Metropolis.* New York: Macmillan, 1962.

Wirth, Louis. "Urbanism as a Way of Life." *American Journal of Sociology* 44 (1938) 1–24. Reprinted *Urban Life: Readings in the Anthropology of the City,* edited by George Gmelch, Robert V. Kemper, and Walter P. Zenner, 101–18. Long Grove, IL: Waveland, 2010.

Wolfe, Regina Wentzel, and Christine E. Gudorf, editors. *Ethics and World Religions: Cross-Cultural Case Studies.* Maryknoll, NY: Orbis, 1999.

————. "Marriage Is for Life." In *Ethics and World Religions: Cross-Cultural Case Studies*, edited by Regina Wentzel Wolfe and Christine E. Gudorf, 86–107. Maryknoll, NY: Orbis, 1999.

Worsley, Peter. *The Trumpet Shall Sound: A Study of "Cargo" Cults in Melanesia*. 2nd ed. New York: Schocken, 1968.

Wright, J. H. Christopher. *God's People in God's Land: Family, Land, and Property in the Old Testament*. Grand Rapids: Eerdmans, 1990.

Yamamori, Tetsunao, and Kenneth A. Eldred, editors. *On Kingdom Business: Transforming Missions through Entrepreneurial Strategies*. Wheaton, IL: Crossway, 2003.

Yoder, John Howard. "How H. Richard Niebuhr Reasoned: A Critique of *Christ and Culture*." In *Authentic Transformation: A New Vision of Christ and Culture*, edited by Glen H. Stassen, D. M. Yeager, and John Howard Yoder, 91–126. Nashville: Abingdon, 1996.

Zwemer, Samuel Marinus. *The Influence of Animism on Islam: An Account of Popular Superstitions*. New York: Macmillan, 1920.

Index